D1540243

The Stones Cry Out

THE STONES
CRY OUT

A Cambodian Childhood
1975–1980

MOLYDA SZYMUSIAK

Translated by Linda Coverdale

ⓌⓌ HILL AND WANG · NEW YORK

A division of Farrar, Straus and Giroux

959.6
5

Translation copyright © 1986 by Farrar, Straus and Giroux, Inc.
Originally published in French as *Les pierres crieront*,
copyright © 1984 by Editions La Découverte
All rights reserved
Published simultaneously in Canada by Collins Publishers, Toronto
Printed in the United States of America
Designed by Jack Harrison

First edition, 1986

Library of Congress Cataloging-in-Publication Data
Szymusiak, Molyda.
The stones cry out.
Translation of: Les pierres crieront.
1. Szymusiak, Molyda.
2. Cambodia—Politics and government—1975–   .
3. Refugees, Political—Cambodia—Biography.
I. Title.
DS554.83.S99A3513   1986   959.6′04   86-7628

NEW HANOVER COUNTY PUBLIC LIBRARY

MLib

Contents

If my disciples were silenced,
the stones themselves would cry out.
LUKE 19:40

One

THE EXODUS

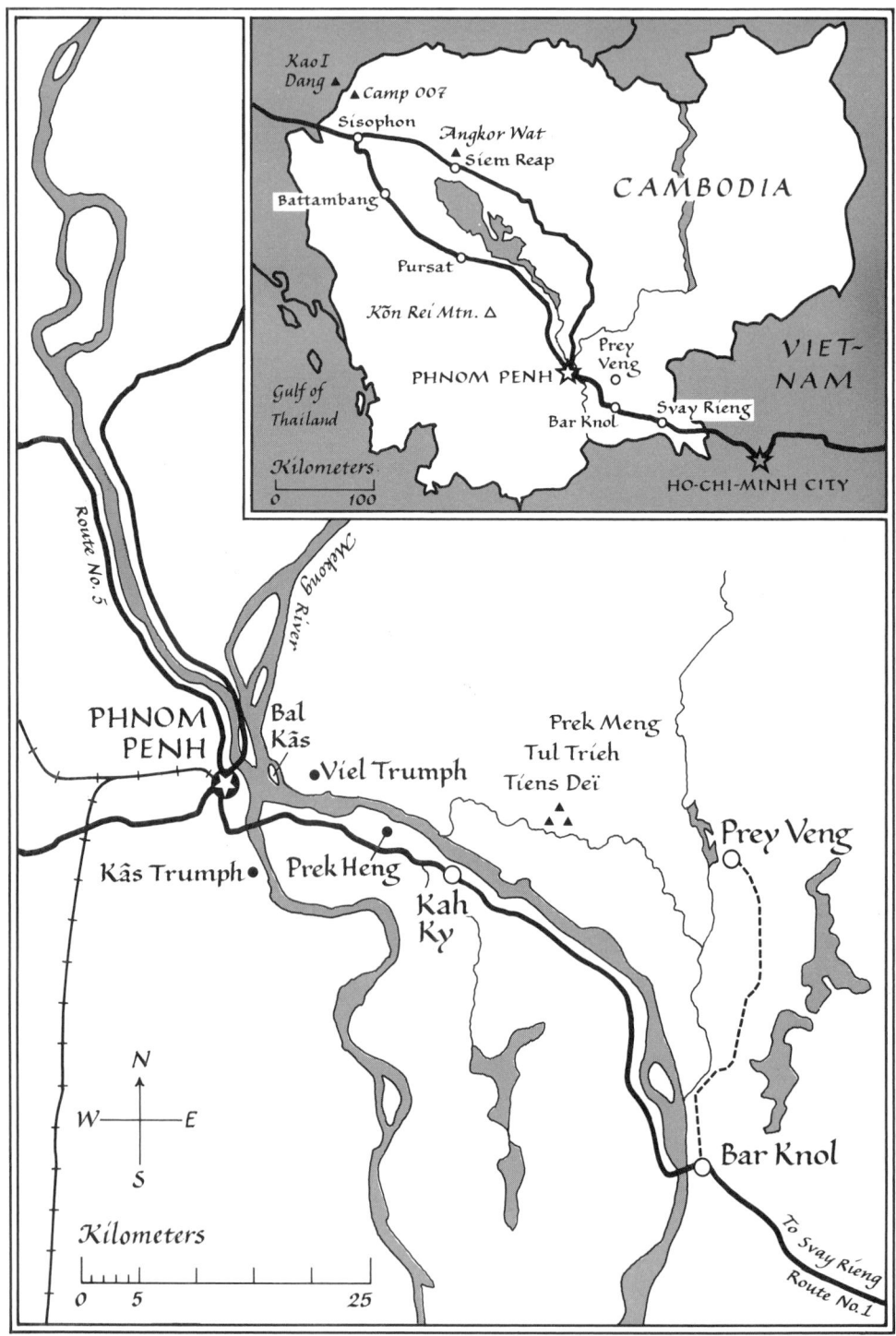

1 THE WAR had been raging out in the countryside for a long time, but during the last two years in particular peasants had been streaming into the city, passing by our neighborhood, Tuol Svay Prey, not far from the sports stadium. My parents had long forbidden me to go walking alone. Rockets often flew over our heads when we went to school, but we hadn't gone to school for several days. One afternoon my Aunt Vathana, a young girl not yet eighteen, came to get me for a motorbike ride. I always enjoyed going off with her; the tree-lined avenues gave us the illusion of being out in the country. We were approaching the Chinese hospital when the motorbike skidded and I heard what sounded like a tire bursting. My aunt stopped short. Sitting behind her sidesaddle on the bike, I clung tightly to her belt, listening to the whistle of the shells. A man on a bicycle went past us, and I was stunned to see that he was still pedaling even though his head had been blown off! His bike crashed into the closed front gate of a high school, the Lycée du 18-Mars. A few people were sprawled on the sidewalk, and we could hear the sirens of several ambulances. We ran home terror-stricken, dragging the motorbike with its flat tire. Vathana went home to her mother while I slipped quietly into my parents' house. My maternal grandmother lived next door to us with her two daughters, Vathana and my Aunt Nang, the mother of my cousin Tôn Ny, who would be so close to me in the months to come.

The next day was April 16, 1975, of evil memory: the heaviest shelling I remember, fires everywhere, the sky full of smoke, and explosions in every part of the city. My family—my parents, four daughters of whom I was the second oldest at twelve, and a little four-year-old brother—had been joined by the family of my Uncle Vong, whom we called Mitia Mir, with his wife, Nang, and their nine children: the oldest, Tôn Ny, was

3

eleven, and the youngest, Sreï Peu, was eighteen months. We spent the day together in a deep trench that had been dug at the far end of the garden. Nearby my father and uncle buried a rifle and a pistol, family souvenirs that had never been used. I later learned that there had been a directive ordering everyone to hand in all weapons in their possession.

The next morning, everything was calm. No one dared to go out; we were waiting for something to happen. Suddenly we heard cheering and triumphant cries: "Kampuchea is free!" Through closed windows we saw the crowd of loiterers and homeless people who straggled around the city all day line up on both sides of the avenue, while down the center of the pavement, in single file, were marching kids in black pants and jackets, their guns on their shoulders, wearing sandals made out of pieces of tires. Without a word or a smile, they stared straight ahead. They were heading toward the center of the city. My sister pointed out to me a jeep at the head of the line, with a white flag flying over it. My father and uncle rushed to tear up a sheet, making a white flag that they hung from the window. To go out into the street, they changed from their overly "bourgeois" trousers into a cloth they wrapped around their hips, Gandhi-fashion. Was that what liberation was all about? Suddenly I heard them run back inside the house and rummage through the bathroom for a large towel—a red one. "The red flag is up; we have to have a red flag or they'll ransack the house!" The kid soldiers didn't look as if they wanted to loot anything; they just kept coming on silently, without looking at anything or anybody. My father waved his red flag. After the young soldiers came men who seemed a little older, dressed in black like the others, but their outfits were dirty, even filthy. One of them called out to us: "We've come to save you" or "to help you," I couldn't hear too clearly. My father opened the door and seemed about to go out, but the man shouted, "Don't come out! We're going to clean up the city first, there are thieves looting the stores." We had heard, in fact, that under cover of the bombardment some people were breaking into grocery and jewelry stores.

Toward noon, we were about to have something to eat when a motorbike stopped in front of the house. My father went to see, and I followed him: it was a Khmer Rouge. "Get your things together," he said. "You have to get moving as soon as possible. You're going two or three kilometers from here, you'll be told where. We have to empty out the city. And whatever you do, don't think you can hide in the house!"

We all packed our bags, then ate a little rice and grilled fish. Our parents got the luggage ready. Father was still able to buy twenty small loaves of bread and some butter. Mother and my aunt brought out small packs wrapped in blankets to hang on both ends of the bamboo poles the adults would carry on their shoulders. Everything was collected by the front steps. Night fell; the surrounding silence was broken only by dogs howling in the neighborhood. We waited, hoping that perhaps we wouldn't have to leave after all. In any case, there wasn't any hurry. Thousands of people passed in front of our door, heading out of the city, and then nothing more. The children stayed in the house, curled up on the rugs and in the armchairs. The two men positioned themselves, with blankets, behind the front gate at the street. I huddled against the garden wall, frightened and shivering in the damp night air.

Suddenly we heard cries and banging on our neighbors' front gates: "Come out! Come out!" No one stirred. The house was apparently empty. I prayed to heaven that they wouldn't see us. They stopped in front of our gate. "Is anyone there?" No answer. Please don't let them break open the gate! No, their footsteps faded away.

We got what sleep we could, but my mother awakened us at daybreak; we had to leave after all. We redid our luggage, tied up in sheets. Everyone got a portion of rice to carry on his or her head.

The sun had just come up, and along came a Khmer Rouge: "Come on, let's go, you have to get out of here!"

"But I don't know where to go," my father said.

"Three kilometers out of town. Hurry up, we have to clean out the city. After that, you can come back, it'll take two or three days."

2 SMALL GROUPS of people began to pass in front of our house. They seemed tired already—only the children ran from one group to another. We began to load up our bundles, but there were way too many, and we had to leave about half of them in the vestibule. If we were going to be coming back in two or three days . . . I ran quickly to see my big doll once more, patiently sitting on a straw mat. We had to leave all our beautiful things: books, paintings, statues, rugs. I did see my mother slip a few saucepans into a bundle, with some small silver articles, ashtrays, I think, and a few pieces of silk. Finally, everyone had a bundle to carry. A Khmer Rouge passed by. "Come on, hurry up! If you're not gone by nine o'clock, I'll blow up your house!"

What could we do? We left. It was already hot. The children lagged behind, the crowd was getting jammed together. We had to hang on to each other. Our dog Bobo, a young Alsatian, tried to follow us.

"No, no, that's not allowed, no dogs!"

"Go back, Bobo, we'll be home in three days."

We left him inside the front gate, but he managed to get out and slip back to us. It was impossible to catch him, so my uncle called him: "Come here, Bobo! Now go home, you have to guard the house." The dog obeyed and turned back, his tail drooping. I tried to get a last glimpse of him, but I had to watch where I was going to keep from getting lost. It was hard to move forward surrounded by people tightly packed together, bumping into each other. It was almost ten o'clock and we hadn't even gone one kilometer. At noon it was impossible to stop and fix something to eat. We would move two steps ahead, put down our baggage, then another step, then another. Hours went by. It was going to be night soon and we were only at the Phnom Boko Cinema, in the middle of the city, normally just a short trip from the house. Two of my mother's brothers joined us from the surging flood of humanity. "Where is Grandmother?" they asked. For three weeks she had been at the bedside of my cousin Sy Neang, in the hospital: he had been hit by a car while riding his bicycle and had a broken leg. In the general uproar no one had worried about them. "We have to go get them." So back my uncles went, struggling against the flow of the crowd. They returned in an hour, saying the Khmer Rouge wouldn't allow anyone to go toward the center of the city. It was beginning to be chilly, and we huddled together on the sidewalk at the edge of the steps leading up to the movie theater. We all ate a sandwich. Under cover of darkness, my two uncles set out again into the city, returning at dawn: the hospital had been evacuated. A Khmer Rouge told them he had seen an old lady pushing a carriage with a little boy. Sy Neang was only nine years old, and his mother didn't want to go any farther until he had been found, so my two uncles went off to look for him once more. That was the last we ever saw of them.

We had to get moving again, so Sy Neang's father tried to encourage his wife, saying that his mother-in-law was an energetic woman and that she'd find a way to join up with us—and his intuition proved correct. Meanwhile, we had to move forward in tiny steps. The west wind began to bring us disquieting odors: many people had been killed over by the airport, where the fuel depot was on fire. Straight ahead we could see a thick cloud of smoke. The outskirts of Phnom Penh were in ruins. We stopped behind a stretch of wall to prepare something to eat. I collected dry leaves and old papers to start a fire and cook a bit of rice. With the heat, the dust, and the smell of decay, there were innumerable flies whirl-ing around our heads and we had to chase them away constantly. A fire engine made its way through the crowd with two Khmer Rouge hanging on at the back, looking the crowd over as if they were searching for something. "Can we help you?" shouted my father, or maybe it was my uncle.

"Are you mechanics?"

"Yes."

"Then come with us!"

We watched them go off together, swallowed up by the crowd. We didn't dare move. After what seemed to us a very long time, a Mercedes made its way through the crowd, followed by a truck, with my uncle at the wheel. He had managed to start the broken-down truck again, and the Khmer Rouge had offered to take his family along.

"But there are two families."

"Get them in the truck!"

Without asking any questions, we tossed our baggage into the truck as it slowly moved along with the crowd. The two women climbed in first, and the children were handed up to them. We weren't really going any faster, but at least we weren't dragging ourselves along and constantly checking to see if all the children were still with us.

And yet, when I looked at all those poor people pressing in on us from all sides, I was sad and ashamed. It was as if the crowd itself were carrying us along. I would almost have welcomed their envy, but they looked at us without expression, doubtless assuming we belonged to a new class of exploiters. In the midst of the ruins, on the edges of what had been a street, I could see corpses lying here and there. Families had stopped nearby to cook their rice—there was no space anywhere else. And the waves of people went slowly by. They moved out of the way just a bit to let the truck pass through their midst. The children were silent, crushed by the heat. Our mothers were in a corner of the truck, and my father was at the back with the two Khmer Rouge.

"Why did you take us with you?" he asked them.

"We're Sihanouk Khmer," said one of them, looking at his companion.

"You're not all the same?"

"Yes, but there are different groups. We're from the East. Here, the North is in command, under Khieu Samphan."

I didn't really understand what they meant. I knew about Prince Si-hanouk; my uncle was distantly related to him and used to go to receptions at the palace. We were familiar with the palace, since Father worked near

it, in the official government buildings. I knew my parents weren't happy
with Sihanouk's policies, but I didn't know why. At home, the adults
spoke French among themselves, a language I didn't understand yet. I
had been about to start school at the Lycée Descartes, where I would
have learned French.

The truck moved slowly out of the city, then suddenly made a right
turn down a broad avenue, leaving the crowd behind. In a huge park,
many soldiers were bustling about under the trees. A vast courtyard with
a building at the far end came into view: the palace of President Lon Nol.
We used to come here on walks, when the Prince still lived there. The
place was called Cham Kamoun. Now I was horrified to see headless
corpses spread out on the ground. No one paid any attention to them.
Soldiers were drilling. Two young Khmer Rouge started toward the truck,
but went instead to talk to the driver of the Mercedes, which had pulled
up alongside. The Mercedes was transporting a shipment of medical supplies, but this wasn't its destination. We set off again.

Back in the middle of the crowd, we inched along, coming to Bar Knol—
I recognized the way: it was the road we used to take every week to our
house in the country. Here again there were bodies on either side of the
road, with entire families weeping over their dead. We stopped for a
moment; the people around us pushed ahead to get onto the bridge.
Wondering if my grandmother and Sy Neang might be here, I looked for
them in the crowd. On the other side of the bridge the road became wider,
and we pulled off onto the shoulder. Hoping to get some rice cooked, we
looked for a little space among the throngs of people. The heat was unbearable, and there wasn't one tree on that swampy terrain. From our
neighbors' conversations we learned that many people had died on the
other side of the river, near the silos of rice just before the bridge. They
were starving and had tried to break into a silo, but the bombardments
had weakened it, and it collapsed on the unfortunate people, crushing
them under tons of rice in a cloud of dust.

It was time to get moving again. There was another bridge over the
Mekong River to cross which put us on Highway 1, heading toward Svay
Rieng. It was still very hot. My father knew this route very well and
offered to take over the driving from my uncle Mitia Mir, who was exhausted and glad to hand over the wheel. He wanted to stop at our country
house and wait there for events to sort themselves out, but the Khmer
Rouge told him that was impossible. "We're going to collect supplies and
ammunition there for the army. The house doesn't belong to you anymore,
it belongs to the Khmer nation."

"Could we stop there for just five minutes?"

"No. Make up your minds. Either you stay there on your own or you come with us."

"But where are you going?"

"To Kah Ky village. It's a reorganization center for our men."

"Okay, we'll go with you."

Two or three hours went by, and the crowd around the truck began to thin out somewhat. At the end of the afternoon we halted at the edge of Kah Ky village, finding a spot for ourselves among the people encamped everywhere. We were all stiff from the long ride, and our whole band of children had a refreshing dip in a big duck pond. My mother and aunt busied themselves fixing a meal for us.

The Khmer Rouge soldier who had been most talkative had gone off for a moment. Accompanied by a small boy, he returned with two or three jute sacks containing about twenty pounds of freshly slaughtered chickens. "Take this, you're going to need it." We couldn't believe our eyes.

The Khmer Rouge had introduced us as his family to our closest "neighbors"; his name was Sakhron. After the meal he produced a guitar from out of nowhere and played music while we danced. After sundown the truck went back to Phnom Penh, but Sakhron stayed with our group. In the cool of the evening, under a clump of trees, he told us that he had been in the forest with Pol Pot's men for ten years. "My heart is not with the Khmer Rouge," he said. "If you like, I'll take you into Prey Veng Province, on the Vietnamese border. In any case, you can't go back to your house in Prek Heng, so close to Phnom Penh."

Neither my parents nor my aunt and uncle wanted to go to the frontier. "You're wrong," Sakhron told us. "If you're related to the royal family, you won't survive here."

The next day he brought us fruit and told us it came from Prey Veng Province. "There are Sihanouk Khmer in Prey Veng, it's your only chance." My parents were doubtful, and wondered if they should still have faith in the Prince. "If you don't believe me, do as you like. In the meantime, take this bag of medicine, you can always trade it for food."

One morning Sakhron announced that he was leaving for Phnom Penh. "I'll try to find out about Sy Neang and his grandmother. I'll also bring you back some sarongs and material. Wait for me here." Six days later he came back—it was impossible to get into Phnom Penh, and the Khmer Rouge guards had fired at him. He had escaped only by throwing himself into the Mekong, where he swam all night, hanging on to a big piece of mangrove root. "I'm going to report this to general headquarters in Prey Veng." He left with the Mercedes and returned that evening bringing sugar, soybeans, and other provisions for us, but he didn't tell us what the authorities had said to him regarding Phnom Penh. He insisted once more that we must make a decision.

"Do you want to come to Prey Veng?"

Our parents told him no.

"Think about it some more. You don't have a chance here. I'm definitely leaving tomorrow."

Just after he left at daybreak, two young Khmer Rouge came up to us.

"You have until eight o'clock to get out of here."

"To go where?"

"Anywhere. Not here. You don't belong to this village."

3   FATHER conferred with my uncle about us all going together to our country house; Mitia Mir thought it would be better to get a bit farther away from Phnom Penh. They decided we should go to Bal Kâs, an island in the middle of the Mekong, far from the main network of roads. Our fathers found two boats to rent in the village in exchange for one sack of rice per trip and some money. We did have money—my aunt had cleaned out their bank account—but nobody wanted paper money anymore. Two kilos of sugar cost 5,000 rials, whereas a month earlier a kilo of bread had been only 5 rials. Luckily, both women had brought along some gold and jewelry.

My older sister and Tôn Ny stayed with the baggage while our fathers helped the two peasants maneuver the overloaded boats, which were taking on water. One peasant told us children, "Whatever you do, don't move!" He seemed frightened; some boats had already capsized in the swirling water, and people had drowned. It was difficult for us to sit still in the boats for half an hour, but we could see that the island was really beautiful, its shores lined with trees, flowers, and bamboo. We hoped we could stay there and grow our own food while waiting to go home. Our fathers went back to get our luggage while we found a shady spot to fix our food. Afterward we looked for a place to spend the night. The weather was so mild, all we needed was a roof of banana leaves. Later on we could build a shelter for protection against the rain. I heard my father and Mitia Mir making plans; living on the island wouldn't be that easy, because other people had thought about settling there, too.

At dawn the next day, two Khmer Rouge came to tell us that no one was allowed to live on the island. "You'll go to Viel Trumph." The trip back through the rushing water was even more difficult the second time, and cost us another hundred kilos of rice and more pieces of material.

The two peasants let us off on the riverbank. We had to proceed on foot, our parents carrying the heavily laden bamboo poles on their shoulders, the children with bundles of rice and personal effects on their heads—except for Sreï Peu, the youngest, whom our parents took turns carrying. We must have stopped for a while around noon, but I no longer remember anything except our arrival in the village. We felt sick to our stomachs, since all along the river we had seen corpses floating downstream and smelled that appalling odor of rotting flesh. We set up camp under some fruit trees and took a bath in cool water, which was somewhat dangerous because the water's edge was quite muddy and you could sink deeply into the mire. You had to get out quickly by grabbing on to lianas.

We had just started to eat when three or four young soldiers dressed in black came up to us.

"What are those girls doing with long hair? You'll have to cut all that off. It's unsanitary."

"Oh, sir, they're only children."

"No more 'sir,' no more 'mister.' We're all addressed as 'Met' [comrade]."

"Oh, Mâ," said my older sister, "I don't want to cut my hair!"

"You, Met Sreï [comrade girl], learn to talk like everyone else."

He meant that no one was supposed to use city language anymore, we all had to talk like peasants: "Meh" instead of "Mâ," "Poh" for "Pâ," when we addressed our parents, and "Pou" for "Uncle," which is how we addressed strangers. Same thing for the everyday words for eating and sleeping . . .

"If you won't cut your hair, I'll cut it myself with clippers," one soldier said. "And the rest of you, get out, this spot is reserved for someone else."

"Where do you want us to go?" asked my uncle.

"The comrade village headman will be here, he'll assign a place to you."

We had lost our appetites, but we had to eat in a hurry before the village headman arrived. He was a short man, very dark-skinned. He was called Met Krom, and he came toward us escorted by two armed soldiers.

"You, comrade, what work did you do?" he asked my uncle.

"I'm a man of the people. I drove taxis."

"What's your name?"

"Vong." (That was the last syllable of his "city" name.)

And that's how my father came to be called Rêth; my mother, Nêm; my aunt, Nang. As for the children, they were called "girl" or "boy," using the various Khmer forms of these words.

"Met Vong, how many houses did you have, how many cars, how many bicycles?"

"I didn't have any of those things. My taxi belonged to my Chinese boss."

That was the only answer I heard. They questioned us individually, away from one another—first the parents, then the children, one by one, even the four- and five-year-olds. Met Sakhron, before leaving, had taught us carefully: "Answer as briefly as possible and always the same thing."

"Did your children go to school?"

"Of course not. We didn't have anything for them to wear."

"And those brightly colored clothes they're wearing?"

"We took those from a house before we left the city."

"It's forbidden to talk about the city. Tonight will be mild, you'll stay here under the trees. Tomorrow I'll find you a house."

The next day our two families were installed on the bare ground under a huge house built on piles, as were all the houses near the river. It was still the dry season. That night a boy who seemed pretty sharp came to our camping spot under the house and spoke to my uncle.

"You, Comrade Vong, I know you. I've seen you at the border. You were the chief customs inspector."

"Comrade son, you're dreaming. I've never been to the border."

That night, the boy came back with two soldiers in black. "Met Vong, come with us, we're going to interrogate you." My uncle returned at dawn, sad and worn out. While we were cooking the morning rice, Met Krom arrived with his two men in black.

"Met Vong, you're going into the forest. There will be work for you. And you need special education: you're going to study the doctrine of Pol Pot. Don't attempt any resistance. This is for your welfare and that of your family."

"Am I supposed to take anything with me?"

"Don't ask any questions, the Angkar is watching over you."

We heard this word for the first time. We thought for a long while that it meant a new king or president, but it was a word from the new language we had to learn and referred to the supreme organization that governed the people's destiny.

My uncle followed Met Krom toward a big pagoda on a hill. We learned the next day that he had left with a group of about sixty men, all former civil servants, doctors, engineers, lawyers, and other professionals.

4   THE THREE DAYS given us by Met Krom when we arrived had now gone by. We had to leave, and in any case, my parents didn't want to stay there. We gathered up our things, and early in the morning our family of seven took their places in a boat rented, at great cost in gold, from a peasant in the village. Met Krom had given us his permission to do this.

"Where are you going?"

"To another village where we can find a house and where we can work."

We crossed the river without mishap, as there was no wind. We were about thirty kilometers from Prek Heng, the village where we had our country house. A peasant on the other side of the river agreed to rent us an oxcart, and we piled on our baggage and my little brother; everyone else had to walk. Night was falling when we arrived at our house. My father was so exhausted he looked like an old man.

The gate was open, and we went in. In front of the steps, a middle-aged man watched us arrive.

"Who are you?"

"I'm the owner of this house," said my father.

"You're lying, this house doesn't belong to you."

My father didn't dare give particulars about who he was, but he called a neighbor over, an old woman who had known him for years. The neighborhood headman was alerted. Trusting the testimony of the neighbor, he decided: "This house is in fact the house of Met Rêth." The current occupant, a major in the army, had with him his eighty-year-old father, who was ill. He asked my father to let him stay, and they came to an agreement.

We were too tired to celebrate being back in our house, which was in terrible shape, probably from the pillaging of all the people passing by. Mother fixed us a bit of rice, and everyone found a spot to curl up in for the night.

The next morning my parents went out behind the house looking for fruit in the orchard. Since the closest trees had already been stripped, they set off for the farthest section, more than a kilometer away. Left alone, I went out into the garden to see to the flowers I had loved so much. I started to put a little order in things, weeding and picking off the faded flowers.

Suddenly a Khmer Rouge appeared—you could always recognize them from their black trousers and close-fitting jacket.

"What are you doing there?"

"I'm weeding the flowers."

"That's enough, Met Sreï. Stop that! This is no time for flowers."

And he trampled the patch of flowers I had just weeded.

"All right. How many people live here?"

"Seven." (I was forgetting the major.)

"Are your parents here? Call them."

"They're not here, but they'll be back soon."

"I'll wait. By the way, do you have any rice?"

"No."

"Go get a napkin or a *krâmar*." (A *krâmar* is a big scarf that the Khmer Rouge and peasants wore around their necks or on their heads to protect them from the sun.)

I went with him to the courtyard of the village headman, where he gave me twenty tin cans of rice. The Nestlé's concentrated-milk can was the common unit of measurement in Democratic Kampuchea. When we got back to the house, my parents were there, having brought back lots of fruit bundled up in a sheet.

"Met Rêth, the Angkar needs this house. You cannot stay here."

"But we've only just arrived, and the children are tired."

The major intervened: his father was dying. Couldn't he stay there one more night?

"All right. But tomorrow morning I want everyone out of the house."

That night I heard the old man's death rattle. My father helped the major bury him under the trees.

5 THE WHOLE FAMILY set out again before daybreak—the Khmer Rouge were deadly serious. The major went off alone in another direction while we retraced our steps of two days ago. Where could we go? My mother wanted to return to Viel Trumph. Her sister needed her: Mother was her only trusted friend, and they used to spend a lot of time with each other. Father didn't want to go back to the place where his brother-in-law had been arrested; surely it would be better if the two families were to separate. But in the end my mother won out.

Toward evening we found the spot where we had disembarked two days earlier, and went to sleep under the trees. The next morning came the palaver over renting a boat. Mother had managed to salvage a few things from our house, and they paid for our river crossing.

We found the Vong family still camping out under the big house: my aunt had obtained permission to stay there while awaiting the return of her husband. We had to work, however; that was the new order of things. My Aunt Nang had to help clear the ground where corn would be planted.

"What are you doing there?" asked Met Krom when he saw us under the house.

"I had a house," replied my father, "and I thought we could live there, but the Angkar needed it, so I gave it up. Now I want to find a place to work. And I'm waiting for my wife's mother to arrive."

"Where is she?"

"She should be here soon. She's with my little nephew; he was injured and is being taken care of in a hospital. She has to be able to find us someplace, after all."

"You should have registered with your neighborhood committee. You would have had an identity card for traveling through villages, and she would have located you more quickly."

"Register us here. We'll work while we wait for her."

"No, you can't stay here. But I'll give you work to do in the meantime."

Our mothers went to work in the fields. Father was sent to help demolish the pagoda, breaking down the walls, and decapitating the Buddhas. My father was a religious man, brought up by monks, and this was for him the most painful of tasks. He set himself to taking apart the roof, leaving the dirty business of profanation to others. It goes without saying that the Khmer Rouge didn't believe in God. Praying in public was forbidden; we used to pray in secret. Some people died for doing this.

As for me, I was too weak to work. I took care of Sreï Peu at home, and when our mothers came back from work, Tôn Ny and I would go to catch shrimps under the lotus leaves in the many little ponds surrounding the village. We were living on our reserves, because they weren't giving us any new supplies—we didn't belong to the village.

We had gotten to know our few companions in misfortune. Some were there because they had found a distant relative, others because they had met up with an old friend. Aunt Vathana had remained with my Uncle Vong's family. She hired a boy from the village to go with her in search of her mother and Sy Neang.

6   THIS IS WHAT my aunt told us after she returned from her journey. She had been able to rent a boat in exchange for a piece of her jewelry, and got as far as our country house near the orchard. Perhaps Grandmother was able to find refuge there? But no . . . the garden was full of soldiers camping out under the trees, and my aunt was afraid to go any farther. She set out again, carrying a bag of food and a canteen of water. She passed through several villages where there were refugees from the city, but no one had seen an old woman and a little boy with an injured leg. She crossed back over another branch of the Mekong, sleeping at night in the houses of peasants or under the trees, in the open air. At Kâs Trumph, about fifty kilometers from our country house, she ran into a large group of refugees from Phnom Penh, but they weren't from our neighborhood. Mustering up all her courage, she asked for information from a Khmer Rouge. It turned out that he had indeed seen a hospital cart, and he offered to help my aunt look for Grandmother and the boy. They were soon found—they were so happy to see each other again! Sy Neang's hair had grown as long as a girl's.

Then Grandmother told us her story. The bombs hadn't touched the hospital. From the window she could see terrified people running in the streets and the Khmer Rouge arriving in perfect marching order. She would have liked to know what was going on, but the hospital personnel had disappeared. At midmorning on April 17, the Khmer Rouge entered the hospital. These were not the kids in black uniforms but officers in fatigue dress. The hospital was to be evacuated. A soldier fired three shots into the air. "Let's go, you have to get out!"

"But I can't, my grandson has a bad leg, he can't walk."

"You have to leave. We're going to clear out the hospital."

"But I'm not strong enough to carry my grandson. Help me, son."

"Pack your things. If you're not gone in ten minutes, I'll shoot."

A second soldier was there, and Grandmother turned to him. "Help me, son." The soldier picked up the boy in his arms and carried him down to the courtyard. "Stay here, grandmother." He left them alone for five minutes, then came back with a hospital cart loaded with ten big loaves of bread, some grilled fish, and some pork. "Here, this should last you a month. Now you have to go. Escape with your grandson. You should go outside of the city, not far. You'll be back in two days. First we have to empty out the hospital and kill off the stubborn ones."

He helped her get Sy Neang onto the cart with the food and told her to get away quickly. "Go two or three kilometers and then see how things are."

The street was full of soldiers, and on the sidewalks lay corpses that had simply been pushed up against the buildings—the stench was appalling. Grandmother walked all day, but she was never allowed to stop anywhere. "Not here," said the soldiers. "Not here," said the village headmen. She wanted to rejoin the family and thought we would be at our country house, but the Khmer Rouge had sealed off the road. There were too many corpses along the wayside, and they had to be burned before the road could be reopened.

She made it as far as Kâs Trumph, where she stayed a month and a half, sleeping in the open air, using up her provisions. The meat she had brought from the hospital started to go bad, so she dried it in the sun, keeping the flies away from it. She would have liked to go to Prek Heng, our country house, because she had dreamed that her daughters were there, but it would have meant crossing the river, and she didn't have a sack of rice to pay for the boat trip. At that time we were between harvests, and the boatmen wanted rice. Grandmother was not entirely without resources—for three months she had been walking around with all her jewelry sewn into a belt that she never took off—but jewelry had not yet become a medium of exchange.

My aunt finally found her mother among those waiting in hopes of eventually obtaining passage across the river. Vathana used all the rice she had left to buy passage for herself, Grandmother, Sy Neang, and the village boy who had accompanied my aunt.

We were all happy to be together again. "But where is Mitia Mir?" My Aunt Nang began to cry and explained that her husband was in a re-education camp. No one knew when he would return. When Sy Neang asked for his father, we told him that he had "gone to study." The boy was accustomed to the periodic absences of his father.

7 EVERYBODY was required to work. Each morning there was one hour of civic instruction. "You must learn to work for everyone and not just for yourselves. You must learn to be sparing with rice, which is becoming scarce. The cornfields must be kept in good shape for the harvest, which won't be long now. There will be enough for everybody. The Angkar is watching over you. If you're not loyal to the Angkar, you cannot live with everyone else." And, in fact, people were beginning to disappear.

The corn was ripening, manioc had been planted, the river would be rising, and it was time to prepare the fields for planting rice. Met Krom chose that moment to tell my mother and father that we could no longer stay in his village, which had been our home for almost three months. In any case, we didn't have a place to live, because the water was going to flood the area under the houses. We were forced to leave.

Our family began to get our things together. My older sister Naroeun, who was fifteen, helped take care of my younger sisters Sitha and Sithân, ten and eight, and our little brother Vannah. Aunt Nang had a more difficult time of it, with three girls: Sreï Peu, the baby; Robona, who was nearly five; and Tôn Ny, the eldest. The boys weren't much help: Sy Neang, almost ten, was an invalid (his leg wasn't healing properly), and the other five were all very little. Grandmother was with them, but she wasn't strong. Luckily my Aunt Vathana was there to help carry the baggage and keep things under control.

We stayed with some neighbors for a few hours while Father went looking for a cart and some water buffalo, which we would need to ford the river upstream from the village. My aunt also found an oxcart. They haggled over the price, and we ended up paying five remnants of silk.

The paths were muddy all along the river, which we crossed in the evening. The water buffalo were up to their muzzles in water, and we had to untie them or they would have drowned. Some peasants helped my father pull the carts across the river. The children were carried piggyback by the men, their little bundles perched on their heads. Father had me wade across. Five hundred meters farther there was another branch of the river to ford. We arrived on the other bank completely exhausted. Father wanted to get going again right away, but the peasants advised against it: there were robbers on the roads, or perhaps they were Khmer Rouge who killed travelers. It was better to travel by day.

We caught a few fish that had been asphyxiated in the mud kicked up by people and buffalo crossing the river, and I found some shrimps under the water lilies. We stretched out under the trees, always so beautiful and welcoming at the river's edge.

That night I needed to relieve myself, and woke up my young aunt, who accompanied me to a tree a short distance from our camp. When I crouched down in the grass, I could see, not two meters away, three men lying on the ground with their heads separated from their bodies! Horrible. We decided not to say anything to the others, but my aunt couldn't help telling my mother, who wanted to get away as soon as dawn arrived. Mother asked the peasants who slept in our camp about the bodies, and they said the men were traveling alone and must have been attacked for their possessions.

Other people had joined our poor caravan, as it was better to travel in large groups. Mother would have liked to stay by the river two or three days to catch a supply of fish, but we had to leave. We couldn't go very fast because of the children and the heavy bundles, and the heat was brutal. Around noon we asked the people of Prek Meng village to let us rest a few hours within their walls. In front of the house where we were relaxing was a little lake, with lots of fish; we needed a net to catch some, but the peasants didn't want to lend us one. So I went looking along the edge of the lake for little round shellfish, which I dipped in salt and dried on pieces of paper in the sun. They cooked in half an hour, and when my parents woke up I offered some to everyone. A man from the family camped next to ours told us there were lotus seeds a bit farther along the lake, so all the children followed him, and within the hour we were back with several big handfuls.

By then the midday heat was over, and we had to be on our way. The paths were getting more and more muddy. Water was seeping out of the earth, and in some places the mud was up to our knees. The baggage became heavier because of the mud sticking to it, and when a warm wind blew the mud hardened into a very tough shell. We were exhausted, and were happy to arrive in sight of a village set on a slope between the river and a forest. If only we could stop there! We rested under the trees while Father went to talk to the village headman, Met Won. He accepted some medicine and a piece of cotton fabric in exchange for permission to stay in Tul Trieh for three days—providing that we give him a "little something" every day.

8 THE NEXT MORNING we were surprised and overjoyed by the arrival of my Uncle Vong, who had been following our trail since the day before. He had been liberated from the re-education camp after three months, one of only three survivors out of the sixty originally comprising their "course": day by day they had simply disappeared. When the three months were up, the "re-educated" ones were told they could rejoin their families. During the journey back from the camp, one of the three, a filmmaker from Phnom Penh, had sighed in a moment of weakness: "My poor wife, will I ever see her again?" Two soldiers from the escort immediately stopped him by the side of the road and hustled him into the forest. It was absolutely forbidden to show any emotion. He was never seen again. This was all my uncle would tell us, and we were forced to draw upon this lesson in the future to survive.

"Don't ask me any questions," he told us straight out. He was a skeleton, as yellow as a lemon, sunburned, and dried up like the old Chinese paper used for lampshades. "We worked, that's all, but my pencil was a broom and my notebook a reed basket." When my mother pressed him, he told her, "Sister, I can't tell you anything. Later, when the country is free again, then I will speak. Tell your children only this: they must be deaf and dumb if they want to survive." Later on, at Vat Thmey, he told me that he ate out of a communal cooking pot with nine others, all of them sharing a single fish. If one of the men was being punished, no fish. The soup they got was a liquid of a violet color, probably from the water lilies cooked in it. My uncle knew only that he didn't want to die in the camp like almost all his companions. He wanted to see his wife and children once more, and if he had to die, then let it be with them.

He found his family in more or less good health, except for Tôn Ny. Barely twelve years old, she had worked hard at her mother's side to lighten her burden as much as she could. In fact, my aunt had just realized that she was expecting a baby. One day Tôn Ny emerged from a pond with a circlet of nine leeches around her leg and foot; they were very difficult to remove and Tôn Ny was now subject to attacks of malaria every day around noon.

After three days, Met Won, tempted no doubt by the gifts he might get out of us, agreed that our two families could live near the village. We had to build our houses ourselves, however, and we absolutely could not all live together. Mother wanted to stay close to her sister, who, while always dignified and serene in front of her children, would often come to Mother's house and weep. "It's wrong to be attached like that to one's family," Met Won said. He gave each household ten square meters of land. Met Vong's area was at the edge of the village, on a hill near the lake, while "Met Rêth and his complaining wife" would go to a hollow at the edge of the forest, about a half hour's walk from the village. There would be only one family farther away than us. And we would have to build the house on very tall pilings, because the hollow was often deeply flooded.

Father had to go out into the countryside to find bamboo tall enough to use as pilings and he also needed tools, at least a pickax and a machete. In exchange for presents, Met Won allowed us to live with him while Father built the house: one month's time was granted for the project. Mother, my older sister, and I had the job of clearing the site—cutting down trees and removing the underbrush. I couldn't manage to cut down trees with a machete, but I could handle the thickets, and we put the brushwood aside on a platform so it wouldn't wash away during the rainy season. Work at the edge of the forest was quite hard: we were bitten by horseflies, afraid of snakes, and fearful that there might be a tiger.

I spoke of my fears to Won's wife, Met Roeun, who told me, "If you're afraid, you cannot live here. You have a lot to learn. Before, you city people learned with paper and words; now you must learn with wood and knives. You don't really know anything about rice—how it is planted, harvested, and husked."

"How do you plant it?"

"You take seed grains and dry them in the sun; while they're drying, the earth is plowed with oxen, and after a month, you plant the rice. Once it has sprouted, you transplant it, gathering the stems into small bundles that must soak for two or three days in a corner of the field. Everyone has to help plant out the seedlings. I'll show you how: you take a bundle in the crook of your arm and stick the seedlings into the mud in alternate rows as you move backward down the line. You have to work very fast so that all the rice is planted more or less at the same time. While it's growing, you have to weed the rice fields all day long—it's hard work. And that's your school now."

Met Won lent us some machetes, and showed us how to sharpen them on a stone. We had exhausted our reserves of food, so Mother traded some valuable items for rice, but it was unhusked. She had to learn how to husk the rice with a pestle in a big basin. I tried to help her, but I made the rice fly all over the place. After that, the rice had to be tossed in a reed winnowing basket to separate it from the husks. I watched my mother laboring away at this, and again I tried to help her, but half the rice would fall on the ground, and it had to be gathered up quickly or the chickens would rush in to devour it.

Met Roeun showed me how to manage the pestle so as not to scatter the rice. "You don't bang hard, you simply let the pestle drop down into the bowl." It took me more than a week to learn.

Met Won had supplies of wood, but his wife didn't give us any, so we had to get our own in the forest. All the dry wood had been collected by the villagers, however, so I had to learn how to dry out green wood by heating it on a grill, like fish, turning it at just the right moment. Met Roeun would say to me, "Learn, or you won't survive." My eyes watered, smarting from the smoke.

Meanwhile, my mother and older sister were cutting rushes by the edge of the lake, bringing back enormous bundles every evening. They were for the village, to be spread on the ground as a bed on which ears of maize were laid out to dry. Mother and Naroeun would come home staggering with fatigue, bent double under their burdens. Met Roeun showed them how to carry the rushes on their heads with their backs ramrod straight.

One day I said to Met Roeun, "I'd like to give my mother some fish to eat when she comes home so tired."

"I'll give you a fish for three cans of rice."

"All right. But how do I kill the fish?"

"You hit its head on the ground very hard."

I cooked the fish, and Mother was very pleased, but she told me, "We must keep the rice for your father, he's working so hard to build our house." He would get back late at night, without having eaten much during the day. I offered to carry him some rice at noon, but it was too far away, and there was a lot of work to be done in our temporary household. My sister and I would go out together to gather wood. We were afraid of tigers and snakes, so Met Roeun told us how to watch out for them. "If you hear birds calling, be careful: there's a snake or a tiger around. Learn to listen to the birds, they warn us of danger." She also taught us how to twist vines together to tie up our bundles of firewood.

The rice had been planted and was beginning to grow. It was time for us to go down into the paddy field. Met Roeun lent us black sarongs like the ones the peasant women wore. "No more brightly colored city dresses!"

We waded into the water to pull up the seedlings. The first day I pulled with one hand, holding my hem up with the other. But I saw how Met

Roeun went about it: she had tied up her sarong and used both hands to pull seedlings in a wide arc around her, tapping the roots against her feet to knock off the earth and tying the bundles with dried rush leaves.

With all the water in the paddy field, fish were within arm's reach, but how did one catch them? "It's quite simple," said Met Roeun, "you take a knife and slice them in two." I tried it, but the fish slipped away. We had to catch some, however, if we wanted to make our own rice supplies last until the next harvest. I settled for gathering shrimps, which were also good to eat.

During all this time, Father was building our house in the forest. He bought twelve bamboo poles five meters long with some cans of gasoline we had, but he had to pay with pieces of material, too, and some medicine. He dipped into our precious store of gold. It took him three days to bring back the bamboo, which he had to cut himself. He hired a peasant to help him, and they built a raft out of the different lengths of bamboo, tied together with ropes of braided rushes. His shoulders were swollen, his feet were all puffy and bleeding. The day he got back, he had an attack of malaria and went to bed trembling with fever, with the children huddled close to him to give him some warmth. He stayed like that for three days. Mother still had three capsules of quinine, which gave him some relief.

"I have to get back to work," he said the next day. "The house is waiting." I wanted to go with him to help. "No, you stay here and weave vines together, then bring them to me."

He went off with bare feet. Met Won went with him the first time to show him how to make the postholes. Mother fixed him some rice and dried fish, but he didn't come back at noon. Met Won came to tell us that Father was at the house site, shaking with fever. Mother decided to go see him, and I went with her. We found Father lying under a tree, with a gunny sack thrown over him. Mother heated some stones to warm his feet, and I sat on his stomach to give him a bit of warmth. We gave him a massage. Eventually he was able to get up, and we took him back to Met Won's house, where he went to bed. I heard him moaning the whole night long. He stayed in bed all the next day. Met Won came to see him.

"If you're better tomorrow, I can help you all day."

"Thank you, I'll be feeling better."

The next day he got up, his head aching, but he went off with Won. Just before noon his teeth began to chatter, but he kept working. Every day was like that. He came home only at night.

In a few days the framework for the house was ready. Won told my father to build it solidly, to last a long time, or else the water would carry it away. So Father used more of our gold to buy stronger materials. He made some changes here and there.

"Now you and your children can get by on your own," Won told us. To make the floor for the house, we had to gather reeds and supple bamboo, which we wove together with more reeds. The reeds had to be dried, and the leaves cut my hands. "Work fast," Won told us, "the water will be rising soon."

After several days' work, we had one hundred and thirty reed braids. Mother went looking for firewood to build up a three-month supply. Every day the water rose higher.

One day Father stepped on a protruding nail; his foot began to bleed, and then his usual attack of fever came on around noon. I tore up a cloth to make him a bandage, then ran to find my mother. We put hot stones up against his feet, and before evening came he was up again: the house had to be finished. The roof was on, but the floor had to be made fast, for which we cut slats of bamboo. We had to strengthen the ladder, which was five meters long—the house was taller than the trees. The pile foundations were already surrounded by water.

9 WE MOVED from Met Won's household into our new house. The floor was ten square meters. In one corner there was a kitchen area with two hearths of packed earth set in a half-section of thick bamboo, which was itself packed around with earth. In another corner was a toilet with a hole through to the outside.

In yet another corner we kept the rolls of matting that would be our beds at night. It didn't take us long to move in. On the platform five meters high, close to the house, where we stored our firewood we soon had five cubic meters of wood, enough to last us until the dry season. Every day the water rose several centimeters. Father tied a weir to the base of one of the pilings, and it was a rare morning when we didn't find one or two fish there to grill for our lunch.

The house of my Uncle Vong—who had never, no more than had my father, touched carpenter's tools before this—was as large as ours, but it was at the edge of the village on the hill, so there had been no need to build it on stilts like ours. A veranda ran all along the façade, where my little cousins would cluster like swallows, dangling their feet. They were called "the little rabbits" because of their bonnets of rose wool with two rabbit ears on top. There were five of them, too small to work, too weak to play, waiting for someone to bring them something to eat.

The day after we moved in, a boat came up to the house: it was a Khmer Rouge leader, accompanied by a woman. There was a meeting in the village to which every household had to send a representative, and obviously Father had to go. He started to climb down our ladder to the boat. "Oh no, Met Rêth, you have to follow us. Anyway, you'll need to build a boat for your family."

"How do I do that?"

"You hollow out a palm tree or a banana tree."

"I can't cut down a tree by myself."

"You buy one in the village."

"And then?"

"You do the best you can."

So we had to buy a tree "in the village" when we lived at the edge of the forest!

That first day Father swam to the village, or rather, floated along, hanging on to a piece of wood. When he returned from the "educational session" he gave us a summary. It was forbidden to eat three times a day, since rice had to be economized until the next harvest. It was forbidden to use perfume, or to keep items that came from the city—these had to be thrown away or given to the village headman. It was forbidden to wear colored skirts.

"But we haven't any others." (Met Roeun had taken back her sarongs.)

"Dye them black. It's not hard: you boil tree leaves, then dip the clothes in the water and roll them in the mud."

We had to do this ten times before the "dye" took. The cloth became stiff and scratchy, and quickly wore out, so that we all looked as if we were in rags. It would take time for us to get used to these sinister outfits.

Father had to get some banana-tree fibers to build a little canoe, because the children were supposed to attend these indoctrination meetings and they couldn't possibly swim that far. The first time we had to go, the two young soldiers who came to fetch us allowed me to go in their boat with two of my sisters, Naroeun and Sitha.

After three days of "education," two hours a day, I was supposed to have understood my obligations toward the community, and the Khmer Rouge told me, "Met Peuw [that was my revolutionary name], tomorrow you'll go with the boys to gather grass for the cows." All the village cows were gathered together on an island about two kilometers away, and every day they had to be brought mountains of grass gathered from the water, or rather cut off at water level.

At dawn the next day, two boys in a boat came to pick me up. Naroeun was to join a different work group. To protect myself from the sun, I wrapped a black turban around my hair, black like everything else we could wear from now on. We set out, and the roofs of the village quickly faded from view. It was cold. The work was somewhat dangerous, since you had to lean out of the boat, and sometimes snakes would be hiding in the dense grass or in the tops of trees rising up out of the water. I felt the boat tip under me each time I stretched out my arm to cut a tuft of grass. The sickle I was using, borrowed from the Mekong (that's what our Khmer Rouge overseers were called), kept slipping from my hands. I was so afraid of losing the sickle or of being bitten by a snake that I wet my pants. I couldn't possibly complain to the boys, whom I didn't know and who were concerned only with filling the boat with grass to finish this chore as fast as possible. I did muster up enough courage to point out to them a snake that was keeping its cold eye on us from the top of a tree we were going around; the boys beat among the branches with their oars, and the snake disappeared.

When we were unloading the grass on the island, the cows rushed at the food as if they hadn't eaten for a week, and almost tipped us over into the water. Getting back into the boat, I automatically looked down at the spot where I was going to put my foot and there was a snake all coiled up, as if asleep. My scream didn't wake him—everyone knows snakes are deaf. The boys chased him away, prodding him with the tips of their oars.

10 AFTER THREE DAYS had gone by, I asked to be allowed to row, thinking that it would be easier than leaning over the edge of the boat to cut the grass sticking out of the water. I quickly realized that the oars were too heavy for me, but I didn't say anything, and that night I went home exhausted.

The next day the Mekong came alone to get me. "Met Peuw, you know how to row, and the boys have to go get seed rice. You'll go out alone to feed the cows." I cried, protested, said I couldn't handle everything by myself, but it was no use. "Get on with it!"

Before leaving, he spoke to my mother: "Met Nêm, I brought you a loom. You'll be weaving rush mats." It was a big wooden frame, one meter by two, with strings and wooden knobs. Mother didn't say a word and set everything up in a corner of the one large room; there she slaved over her rush mats, after which were to follow mosquito netting and who knows what else.

Father was tearing his fingers to shreds braiding ropes from palm branches, which he had to cut and strip himself. Everyone was working for the community.

And so that day I had to set out alone.

"Mommy, do I really have to do this all by myself?"

"Go on, dear. God will look after you. And try to bring back some water-lily stalks."

We used these stalks for food, when we could gather some without being yelled at by the Mekong. When I was with the boys, I couldn't collect any; we had to work for the community and not for the family. Alone in the boat, after the Mekong had gotten out when we passed near the village, I thought about Phnom Penh. Barely four and a half months have gone by, and it seems so long ago! Here there's nothing but silence. Oh, if only I could hear music again! It's been so long since I've heard any music. If I could just have some cake! And see the lights of the city again, the lights of our old house . . . Here we haven't any lights in that place we use as a house, except when the fire is lit for cooking. A piece of bread! My friends at school used to make fun of me when I brought bread instead of the bowl of rice everyone else had. I loved eating bread, in the French manner. And chocolate. Oh, a piece of chocolate! And also a pencil for writing. And a book! I had been about to start seventh grade. I'd like to read a bit, to study. But there's nothing . . .

Out on the water I began by cutting water-lily stalks—there would be something for my family, at least. And lotus flowers. Mommy and Daddy would be pleased. I tucked the flowers away at one end of the boat. I began to cut some grass, and the boat was soon almost half full. The sun was already high in the sky; it even looked as if it was beginning to dip toward the horizon. But where was the treetop we used as a landmark? Nothing on the left or the right—where could it have gone? Well, there was lots of grass around, I would fill up the boat. I kept an eye on the horizon to see if anyone turned up. It was nice to have all that grass, but I still had to take it to the cows, they were waiting for it. The sun was definitely starting to set. Still no one in sight. But what was that over there? A huge dark cloud—that was all I needed! A terrible gust of wind whipped the boat around and trapped me in a vast sheet of water plants, tangled like a mass of unruly hair. The plant tendrils grabbed the sides of the boat, so that I couldn't see the water's surface through their thickness. I was a prisoner, and I started screaming, "Help, I'm trapped!" My throat dried up, my voice started to crack. I said a prayer, fearful of ghosts. Night had fallen, and off to my right the round yellow moon looked down at me. "What's that little girl doing out on the water at this hour?"

My voice was gone when suddenly, sharply etched against the moon, appeared the silhouette of a man standing in a boat, a fisherman, rhythmically bending overboard. Gathering my last strength I screamed, "Come and help me!" The man stood up straight, turned in my direction, and steered his boat over toward me. When he got to within a few meters of me he started to tear out the water plants in bunches, then in great armfuls, making his way to my boat, which moved as soon as he had dislodged the mass of greenery. I grabbed the stern of his boat as soon as I could reach it: he had cleared a path while going backward, pushing aside the plants with his oars. For a moment we floated along side by side, and I told him I had to feed the village cows. He sent me off in the right direction, and I thanked heaven for his help.

At night the cows were less frantic. It was way past their feeding time, but they woke up when I arrived and eagerly devoured the grass I unloaded for them. From here I knew the way home, and the moon illuminated the landmarks. At the foot of the ladder at our house a Mekong girl was waiting in her boat.

"Why are you getting home so late? And what is that bouquet of flowers?"

"It's for my mother."

"You're not supposed to pick flowers, they're to be kept for their seeds. You're wasting them!"

"Yes, but in any case the cows don't like them."

"That's not the point. You wasted time picking them. Tomorrow, educational session."

I told her that I got lost, that I couldn't cut grass and keep track of the landmarks all by myself.

"You're incompetent. From now on the boys will go with you."

That was good news, at least. My mother was pleased with the lotus-flower bouquet. She had been very worried, and after the Mekong girl had come asking questions, she had prayed silently for me. The next day I set out again with the boys, a bit more confident.

11 THINGS WENT ON like that for the next few days. There was hardly anything left in the house to eat, however. They had been giving the seven of us only three cans of rice a day, enough for one daily meal. But for the last three days they hadn't distributed any rice at all, and our reserves were almost gone, even though we had been mixing the rice with water-lily stalks. My parents decided to try to obtain some supplies from the neighboring province. The Mekong had said that everyone was on his or her own; there were still plenty of things to barter, he said, and peasants liked things that came from the city.

Father obtained a three-day pass for himself, Mother, Naroeun, and me. Mother fixed a bit of our small supply of rice for the youngest children, who would be staying at home. We went to the village in our little palm-fiber boat. To cross the lake, we had to rent a sturdier boat, and Met Won found us what we needed—for payment, of course.

Before the morning was over we reached the little village across the lake.

My parents tried to buy some rice with silver pieces, but the peasant answered, "What do you expect me to do with that?"

"How about this silver ashtray?"

"No."

"Some cloth?"

"I've got everything I need."

We walked about four or five kilometers beyond the village. Around noon Father had his usual attack of fever, and we had to stop. Mother went up to the first house we came to; it seemed properly cared for, surrounded by an orchard.

"My husband is ill—would you let us rest for a moment in the courtyard?" she asked the woman who came to the door.

"Come on in. I'll make you some herbal tea."

We sat down on mats on the ground among our bundles, while the woman heated some water to make a decoction of bitter roots. Mother helped her fix rice, grilled fish with *niok mâm* sauce, garlic, and red pepper. It was mouth-watering, absolutely delicious. "I'm so glad to offer this to you," the woman said, "because there may come a day when I won't have anything myself."

We learned that she had had a baby two days ago, and I noticed that there were live coals in a pan under the bed.

"Are you cold?" I asked her. "Or is the baby cold?"

"I have the fire going to make sure I keep warm enough. By the way, I take it none of you smokes?"

I was going to ask more questions, but Mother motioned to me to be quiet. Later I learned that one mustn't smoke in a house where a baby has just been born, because it attracts ghosts. As for the fire under the bed, it drives off witchcraft and the spirits of death.

Father was too feverish to eat anything, so the peasant woman gave me a rice ball wrapped in a banana leaf. I asked her if I might scrape out the cooking pot, and I got enough for another rice ball for later. When I looked longingly at the ripe bananas in the orchard, Mother asked the young woman if she would trade a remnant of cloth for some fruit. "Take six bunches of bananas and all the oranges you can carry."

Mother gave her a silver ashtray and enough cloth to make a layette for the baby. Then the woman offered us ten cans of corn; we would have loved to find some rice. "You ought to go to Prey Veng; people have lots of rice there, but no fish or vegetables." Prey Veng was way out in the countryside, toward the east, in an area of considerable turmoil near the Vietnamese border. "If you can bring me back fifty cans of rice, I'll lend you two bicycles." Her offer was eagerly accepted, and we set out: my sister took Father on her bike, and I had Mother on mine.

We soon came to a marketplace, where we saw eggplants, green mangoes, even cucumbers. Mother bought a bit of everything, plus two enormous pumpkins, and for my sister and me—who hadn't seen any cakes or sweets in months—she purchased eight cookies made from rice flour and coconut, which she wrapped in a banana leaf. She also found some fresh fish. All this made an enormous package tied up in a piece of cloth on Mother's lap as she sat on the bicycle behind my sister, who was stronger than I and better able to handle the extra load. This time I had Father as a passenger; he was unable to carry anything because he was ill. My legs were too short for the big bike, so I pedaled on tiptoe, but riding the bike was easier with Father on the back because he used his feet on the ground as brakes at the right time. A ferry took us across the river, with Mother carrying her big bundle on her head. Then we took the road going east.

We pedaled along for several hours, but night fell before we reached our destination, so we stopped at the entrance to a village. I wish I could show you my poor mother, so stiff and sore, trying to get off the bike. It had been a long time since any one of us had smiled, but at that point

we just couldn't help ourselves, and Mother was the first one to laugh.
We sat down by the side of the road, and I massaged Mother's aching
thighs, which were as stiff and hard as wood.

Father knocked at a house to ask for a night's hospitality, and a peasant
woman kindly allowed us all to sleep out under the trees. Although we
were completely exhausted we couldn't fall asleep because of the hordes
of mosquitoes; we hadn't brought any mosquito netting with us, and the
next day my neck and hands were swollen with bites.

"How many kilometers away is Prey Veng?"

"If you go at a good clip, you can get there by the afternoon."

We set out as soon as it was light, my legs still hurting from the day
before. Father decided that we would stop every twenty minutes so that
Mother wouldn't get so stiff. It became hot very quickly, but the road
was a good one, built just before the war, and we made good time.

Evening was coming on. Father decided that we were far enough into
Prey Veng Province to stop and think about getting our provisions. He
went up to a big house by the side of the road, where a middle-aged man
asked him where he had come from.

"From Tiens Deï. See, here's my pass."

"Don't bother. Pol Pot's people haven't taken over here yet. Stay here
tonight."

"Would you have any rice to sell? Look, we have fish and vegetables."

"Rice? You can have a cartload of it."

"Well, I don't have a cart."

"But you could put a hundred kilos on each bike. If you come back
again, I'll give you more. You and your vegetables are certainly welcome."

"Why don't you have any vegetables here?"

"The dry season lasts too long. The rainy season is just enough for the
rice, which can grow as long as there's mud. Afterward the earth turns
to dust and we haven't any water to spare."

Unfortunately, he couldn't offer us shelter for the night, as he was just
leaving for Phnom Penh to see his daughter and try to bring her back
with him—he hadn't had any news of her since "the events." The family
next door welcomed us under its roof, however, and we stayed the night
with them. Rested, we set out on foot the next day, two fifty-kilo sacks
on each bicycle. As we left, the neighbor told us, "Pol Pot hasn't reached
here yet: that's why we've been able to welcome you as if we were offering
hospitality to Buddha himself. In a few days, perhaps we will be dead."
He saw things clearly: when we returned a few weeks later, there was
nothing to bring back with us.

We walked all day to get back to the house of the young mother who had lent us the bicycles. There we could rent a boat, but no one wanted to take us over at night, so we stayed there until morning, when we picked up the belongings we had entrusted to the young peasant woman. Father gave her sixty cans of rice. We put all our provisions on the boat, and the current carried us in two or three hours right to our house, to the door itself, because the water had risen even more—all we had to do was unload everything. I couldn't take my eyes off the water that had carried us home to a house hemmed in on all sides by flowering water lilies. If it hadn't been for Father's uneasiness, I would have felt very happy: water under the floor is quite entertaining. Just dropping a few grains of rice through the openings in the floor would bring hundreds of colorful fish rushing up. When there wasn't any rice, all you had to do was spit in the water and you'd see all the colors of the rainbow flashing and swirling.

Father was worried, however. What would we do if the water rose any higher? It was already just under the floor; we could hear it lapping under our sleeping mats at night. "There's only one solution," Met Won told him. "Build a second floor over the first one." Met Won was perfectly willing to lend his boat, in return for a small present (nothing was free with that man), and Father went off to look for bamboo. The floor had to be tied together with vines and raised twenty centimeters higher: we could just barely stand up straight under our roof.

12 FOR SEVERAL DAYS the rains poured down, but the water didn't seem to rise more than a centimeter, and then remained at that level. There was a terrific wind, however, and several houses in the vicinity collapsed; ours remained standing, as did that of the Mekong in charge of our group, who arrived to summon us to an educational session as soon as the storm had died down. It was six in the evening when the entire family assembled in the meeting hall. The gist of the proceedings was that we would have to work even more after the water had receded, because the rice had to be planted. In the meantime, my job was to gather grass by moonlight, taking advantage of the calm weather. The grass had been growing throughout the storm, and the new shoots were very tender. Tears ran softly down my face, but I was obliged to set out at night in the boat along with two boys. The night air was very mild; it reminded me of pleasant evenings at Phnom Penh. "Oh, moon, you're so beautiful! You were just the same when I used to lie on

the grass in our orchard at Phnom Penh and look up at you." I talked to
the moon like that, crying quietly. "Why don't you come help our beloved
country now? Why are you still beautiful when we're all in rags? Why
are you still changeless, when everything is in an uproar down below?
Up in the sky you're full of light, like a pretty woman, so fresh, while
the whole country is lost in darkness."

In the distance, while I rowed the boat, I could see the outline of our
house, the house my father had built with his own hands. It was beautiful.
Of course it was quite another thing to have to live in it: the space was
cramped, we had to sleep head to tail to keep from knocking out the walls.
But bathed in the moonlight flooding the sky, how elegant it was! I had
always dreamed about having a simple little house surrounded by water,
ringed with water lilies. My wish had been granted: there was the house,
and I was so unhappy. Fresh tears rolled down my cheeks.

The grass had grown high over the water, and in less than two hours
the boat was full. The boys and I came back at around ten in the evening.
Before going inside the house I washed my feet, and I heard my parents
discussing the children's future. What future? When I went inside Father
was listening to the American station on his tiny transistor radio with
worn-out batteries. My parents were glad that I'd come home safe and
sound (they were afraid of snakes, too). Mealtime was over, but I was so
hungry I'd have really liked to nibble on a nice crusty piece of bread and
drink a glass of milk; and then I'd have loved to put on a pretty night-
gown—but here we had to sleep in the clothes we wore all day, we hadn't
anything else. Back in Phnom Penh, Grandmother had warned us that
the country was going to fall on hard times, and I had laughed at her
predictions. She had told us to be careful with food, not to spill any rice
on the ground. And now I would indeed have carefully picked up a single
grain of rice fallen in the dust, only there wasn't any rice at all.

The days went by. The water hadn't risen any more, but it hadn't yet
started to go down, so we couldn't possibly begin planting the rice. Everyone waited. Father asked for a three-day pass to renew our rice provisions,
since the peasant at Prey Veng had told him he could come back for the
rice he hadn't been able to carry away on our first trip. Father felt well
enough to make the trip alone; it would be quicker that way.

In fact, the trip did take less time. Father bought vegetables on the way
to exchange for rice farther along, then borrowed a bicycle and managed
to find the peasants with whom we had traded before. They fed him,
they accepted his vegetables, but everyone was sad: it wasn't possible to
give him any more rice. The Khmer Rouge had arrived, and from then

on all rice belonged to the organization, the Angkar; the villagers were allowed only one can of rice per person per day. At least that was better than in our village, where we were no longer getting anything. The friendly peasant's big house had been judged to be too grand: it was to be destroyed and replaced by a smaller, one-family house. And he should consider himself lucky not to have been chased off his land!

Father had to come back empty-handed, with nothing to pay for the bicycle he had borrowed, and nothing for his boat crossing. All day long he asked peasants with boats to take him across the lake, but in vain. Finally, an old man steering a palm-fiber boat told him he could come with him if he'd bail out the boat while the old man rowed. The boat was quite leaky and had to be bailed out constantly, but they arrived safely at our house. Father said simply, "I haven't anything with me, I'm tired."

There was nothing to eat at home but water-lily stalks. You had to strip out the tough fibers, cut the stalks into pieces, and cook them. We had no seasonings, not even salt, and they were not very appetizing. Father went to complain to the Mekong.

"The children must eat, after all."

"We're expecting some rice at the end of the week, in five days."

To keep our minds off our empty bellies, Father taught us to swim during our rest hour. He tied lianas between two of the pilings that supported the house; the water had already dropped by a few centimeters, so we had room to hold on to the vines and kick our feet. Mother, lying down to rest her aching back, shouted at us, "You're making the house shake! Stop, it's going to collapse!" I just laughed. Father stuck a sheaf of bamboo into the water near the house and stretched a vine over to the platform where our firewood was stored. He made a float out of a banana-tree trunk, and we each used it in turn. We had a lot of fun, and for one moment hunger was forgotten.

My little brother, Vannah, tired easily, so Father gave him the job of keeping an eye on our fishing line, a string passing through two bamboo sections of our "floor" down into the water and a hook baited with a bit of light plastic, which floated, or sometimes a grain of corn. When the string twitched, Vannah would call, "It's moving!," and Father would dash over and pull up the fish. Several times we had to break one of the bamboo sections to get a big fish up; we plugged the hole by weaving lianas into the gap. Mother didn't have much time to cook because she had to fill her quota of mats, but she put the fish on to boil while she was working. When it was cooked, she would take the meat off the bones and leave them to cook a while longer to make soup. It didn't taste very good without salt or vegetables, but we were always hungry.

13 ONE OF OUR RELATIVES on my mother's side of the family was a hermit. He was over eighty years old, the son of one of my great-grandfathers. My parents decided to visit him, and they took my older sister along with them. He lived somewhere in the forest, clothed in the saffron robe of a Buddhist monk. Pol Pot's men had of course directed him to dress like a peasant, and he had replied, "Why don't you just kill me right away."

"You won't lose anything by waiting."

He had withdrawn into the woods somewhere near Prek Meng. Some peasants had let us know where he was, and my parents decided to ask his advice about the future, as they used to do in Phnom Penh when he was still living among the bonzes.

After the customary greetings, Mother asked him, "Grandfather, do you think we'll stay here much longer?"

"No, my daughter, soon you will set out toward the rising sun."

"Will our family stay together?"

Without answering her, he began to cry; then he slowly shook his head. "Listen to me carefully: Learn to remain deaf and dumb." Mother started to weep.

"Don't be afraid, my daughter. It's the country's destiny. Don't reproach anyone for the evils that befall us."

"And our family?"

"The children who survive will have more freedom than those in our country. But you, nothing can destroy you, you are consecrated."

What he meant, Mother explained to us later, was that something heaven-sent had alighted on us, as if to protect us. When Naroeun related all this to Tôn Ny, her cousin told her, "I want to devote my life to others."

The old monk also reminded my mother that we were not the only ones suffering. "All families of our country will endure great hardship." At that moment a violent thunderstorm broke out, and our poor house began to sway on its bamboo pilings, while black clouds torn by lightning descended on the surface of the water. Frightened, I clutched my little brother in my arms, and my little sisters hung on to me. I thought the house was going to be blown away: pieces of the roof were torn off and water was pouring down inside the walls.

Naroeun told me that the same storm had buffeted the hermit's cabin. He said that he could see me with my little brother and sisters, all huddled together in a corner of our house. "But don't be afraid," he told Mother, "your children are not in any danger." He went out in front of his hut with a white scarf in his hand; he waved the scarf and the storm subsided.

My parents set out immediately for home, taking with them some rice, fish, and lotus seeds. They found us soaked and trembling. The damage to our house was quickly repaired, and in fact it got off lightly—several huts close by were carried off by the high winds, and people were drowned.

From that day on, though, the water began to subside, centimeter by centimeter, and then it became thick with all the mud carried down from the mountains; the fish would soon begin to die from lack of oxygen.

14 ONE MORNING the Mekong came by. "Everyone to the village, assemble in your assigned groups." Our group was Number 10; the center of the village was Group 7. At the entrance to the village, at the water's edge, we found a huge mound of fish, as high as the headman's house, that had been unloaded from a big boat at dawn. Each group was allotted five wagons of fish, but they had to be loaded at some distance from the water, because the bank was very muddy. Everyone was given a rush basket and we began transferring the fish. I filled my basket up to the edge and placed it on my head, determined to make as few trips as possible, but my weakness hampered me. My legs, usually light and agile, plunged into the mud up to the calves. It took quite an effort to pull them out of the muck; the basket tipped, and the fish fell back into the mud. I returned to the pile and took only half a basket, which had to be carried five hundred meters to where the oxcarts were waiting in the village. Old women and children had picked up all the fish that I dropped; when I passed by the spot, they asked me, "Please let a few fish fall from your basket, you can see we're hungry." I tipped my basket to let some fish slide out, but when I looked up I saw a Yotear (an armed Khmer Rouge soldier) coming toward our group. Had he seen me tip the basket? There was only one solution: to slip so I could say that I had tripped the first time.

"What's going on?"

"I slipped, boss."

"No bosses here, comrade. Pick everything up and be more careful!"

When I got to the wagon, the Yotear chief found the basket very light and the fish very dirty. I watched him without saying anything while he ate a grilled fish. "Hurry back and get another basketful!" I motioned to my youngest sister, Sithân, who was playing with the little children. She came along with me, and I told her to stay on the path while I pushed through the mud to the pile of fish, which didn't seem any smaller. I quickly filled the basket halfway and emptied the fish into a sarong tied into a bag held out by Sithân. "Carry this to Papa's boat; hurry, but don't let anyone see you!" Superfluous advice, as we had acquired the reflex of hiding from everything and everyone, sometimes even our parents. I rushed back to the fish to fill my basket. The whole day was spent going back and forth, and by evening the pile wasn't gone yet, because all the adults had been put to cleaning the fish for smoking or cooking: this was to be the village's food supply until the next rice harvest, three months away.

Some people gutted the fish, others prepared the bamboo sticks half a meter long on which the fish were strung by their gills, four to ten fish per stick, according to their size and weight. The fires for drying the fish had to be tended all night long. In the morning, when I went back to where the pile of fish had been, all I could see were a few scales glittering in the mud—nothing else was left. The soldiers had made a mistake by going to bed after filling their bellies with fresh fish. Whom could they punish? It belonged to everyone: they had certainly drummed that into our heads.

The fish-drying went on all morning; our group was running out of wood. "Hey, Met Rêth," said the soldier on guard, "there's a nice pile of wood in front of your house. You have to share." And that was that. A few women were sent by the Yotear to carry off our firewood. "So many days of work," sighed Mother, "and the sweat of our children." Other people lost their woodpiles in the same way. Finally, after ten days, we wound up the operation; what was left of the fish was past drying, it had to be grilled and eaten as fast as possible. The fish were laid out on a huge rack supported by poles held over the fire by several men. It must be said that most of the fish went directly to the families. At one point I crept up behind Father and whispered, "Give me a few fish for the house."

"No, I can't, you'll have to manage on your own."

And I managed.

The day after we finished cooking, the Yotears divided up the dried fish: twenty skewers of bamboo per family.

"You would have had more if there hadn't been so much stealing."

"But we were so hungry!"

"That's tough, there's less to share now."

He didn't mention that the Yotears' house had taken the lion's share. We did have enough fish to last out the rainy season, but now we lacked wood for cooking and heating water. Everything in our area was still flooded, except the island where the cows were quartered. I had been there often enough to know that we could find a great deal of reasonably dry wood there. My older sister and I set out for the island. When we got to the mudflats, which had to be crossed on foot, the stench was awful, we could hardly breathe. We weren't the first to come to the island with the same idea: there was no wood left standing, only the stumps of a few big bamboo, which we chopped up with a machete. Each blow resounded in my head—I wasn't as strong as a woodcutter. I filled up my basket, while Naroeun fashioned a cloth sack for her wood, and we put our loads upon our heads to carry them. As we left the island, the cows began to low. Were they saying goodbye to us? They seemed agitated, and mooed louder, so that I began to think, Maybe there's a snake over there! All of a sudden, a few meters to my left, a huge serpent reared up, hissing—it was as thick as my thigh! The cows were terrified, and so were we. Dropping our firewood, we ran as fast as we could through the sticky mudflats, arriving empty-handed and exhausted at the house. Mother sent word of the snake to the Mekong.

The men were called together, and an expedition set off for the island. The snake must have been digesting a meal; it was caught and killed, and brought back rolled around two big bamboo poles. It was a good seven meters long. The head Mekong hacked it into pieces, about twenty centimeters for each family. I was able to recover the wood and, most importantly, the machete we had left behind on the island. Father brought our allotted piece of snake meat back to the house.

"I won't touch any of that," announced my mother.

"Nor I," said Naroeun.

"Not us," said the little girls.

I didn't say anything. I fetched water for Father, who boiled the snake meat with the last handful of rice we had in the house.

"Just taste that," he said.

"I'm a boy," announced my little brother, Vannah. "I want to have some like Papa."

"Wonderful, my son. You're not afraid, you're like me."

He offered me some, but I refused. He almost begged us to try some. "At least have a taste of it." But none of us wanted any except Vannah, so he and Father shared the snake meat, which lasted several days.

15 THE NEXT DAY I went out looking for lotus seeds with nine other girls. We had to go through the forest to the ponds on the other side, about an hour's walk from the house. It was a dangerous area, because the mud was sometimes several meters deep. I would never have obtained Mother's permission to go on such an expedition—she thought that I was working as usual with my group. We could always arrange something with the Yotear so that we could go off scavenging, since anything we found to eat was welcome, and we weren't yet under the rule of complete terror we would come to know later on.

We had had our eyes on the lotus pond for some time, as it wasn't far from where we were working, and now that the floods had receded somewhat, we could try to harvest lotus seeds. Of course we didn't all wander off on our own but formed a line, each girl about five or six meters away from the next one, and we moved forward carefully through the thigh-deep mud. Each girl had a bamboo stalk to use as a sounding rod as she advanced, and from time to time one or the other of us would raise her arm and call out, "Hey! Hello!" to make sure that we were all still together. The girl on my right didn't answer one of these calls, and when I turned to look, lifting up my bamboo stick, I felt myself sucked under by the mud. I tried to lean on my bamboo rod, but I was up to my neck in slime; only my fingers stuck out of the water. Two girls came over to me and held out their sticks, and with great difficulty managed to pull me free, but the girl next to me never came back to the surface. Despite my fear I managed to save my sack of lotus seeds, but I didn't look for any more. We were all miserable over our companion's death. Down at the river where we went to wash off the mud, I picked a few lotus flowers to bring along with the seeds to my mother. "Good girl, you always bring back something for its beauty alone." I didn't boast about our escapade, but Mother found out about the girl's disappearance and formally forbade me to expose myself to such danger. "It would be better for us all to die of hunger together than to know that you had drowned in mud."

I went back to work the following day. We had to methodically clear out the dense weeds that sprang up between the newly sown rice seedlings. Our Mekong, a young peasant from the north, Met Sân Koung, was furious. "Just what did you think you were doing when you went to the lotus pond?"

"But we have nothing to eat at home."

"That's impossible. I'll go with you at noon and check up on what you're saying."

At twelve she came home with me. From the foot of the ladder I called up to my mother, "Mama, here is Met Sân Koung!" Mother appeared on the threshold.

"I've come to see if it's true that you haven't any rice."

"Oh, Met Sân Koung, you know yourself that we haven't been given any for more than a month."

The Mekong went into the house, looked into all the pots and pans, rummaged through our belongings, and finally found one pot near the hearth with a few lotus seeds in it, left over from the day before.

"All right. The girls can pull up water-lily bulbs from the lake, but they must stay away from the lotus pond. Met Peuw, you needn't come to the rice paddy this afternoon."

"I'd rather stay and weave cloth with my mother," said Naroeun.

"You may, since your mother is behind in her weaving."

"And I need my daughter Peuw to help me strip palm fibers," said Father, "or we'll never have enough rope ready in time."

To our astonishment, the Mekong allowed us everything we asked. She even addressed Father as "Met Pou" (Comrade Uncle) instead of the official "Met Rêth." I hurried over to see my Aunt Vathana, who was still living in Uncle Vong's house. The water-lily lake wasn't far from Grandmother's hut, and I had gone there several times when the water was at its highest level. My grandmother had also tried, without success, to teach me how to swim. There was no one home at Uncle Vong's, however, and one of the little girls, whom I found trying to fish down at the river, said that her mother and aunt had gone off in a boat looking for food.

So I went water-lily hunting that afternoon with my sister Sitha. The water wasn't very deep, and we went in wearing our panties, holding the only basket we had in the house, with our *krâmars* knotted into bags hanging around our necks. When Sitha, famished, started eating raw bulbs, I reminded her that she should think of everyone else in the family.

"No, I'm collecting just for myself. I'm hungry."

"But Mama's hungry, too, and Papa and Vannah. And besides, you're supposed to boil the bulbs first."

"I'll boil them myself at home."

"We won't give you any firewood."

When we got back to our house, Mother peeled the bulbs and stalks I'd brought, while Sitha went somewhere behind the house to prepare her small harvest by herself. Everyone had a handful of bulbs to eat, and I put aside some for Sitha. Mother called her two or three times, but she insisted on staying outside. Finally she managed to cook a good-sized handful of bulbs, and came happily inside to offer them to everyone.

Two

DAUGHTERS OF POL POT

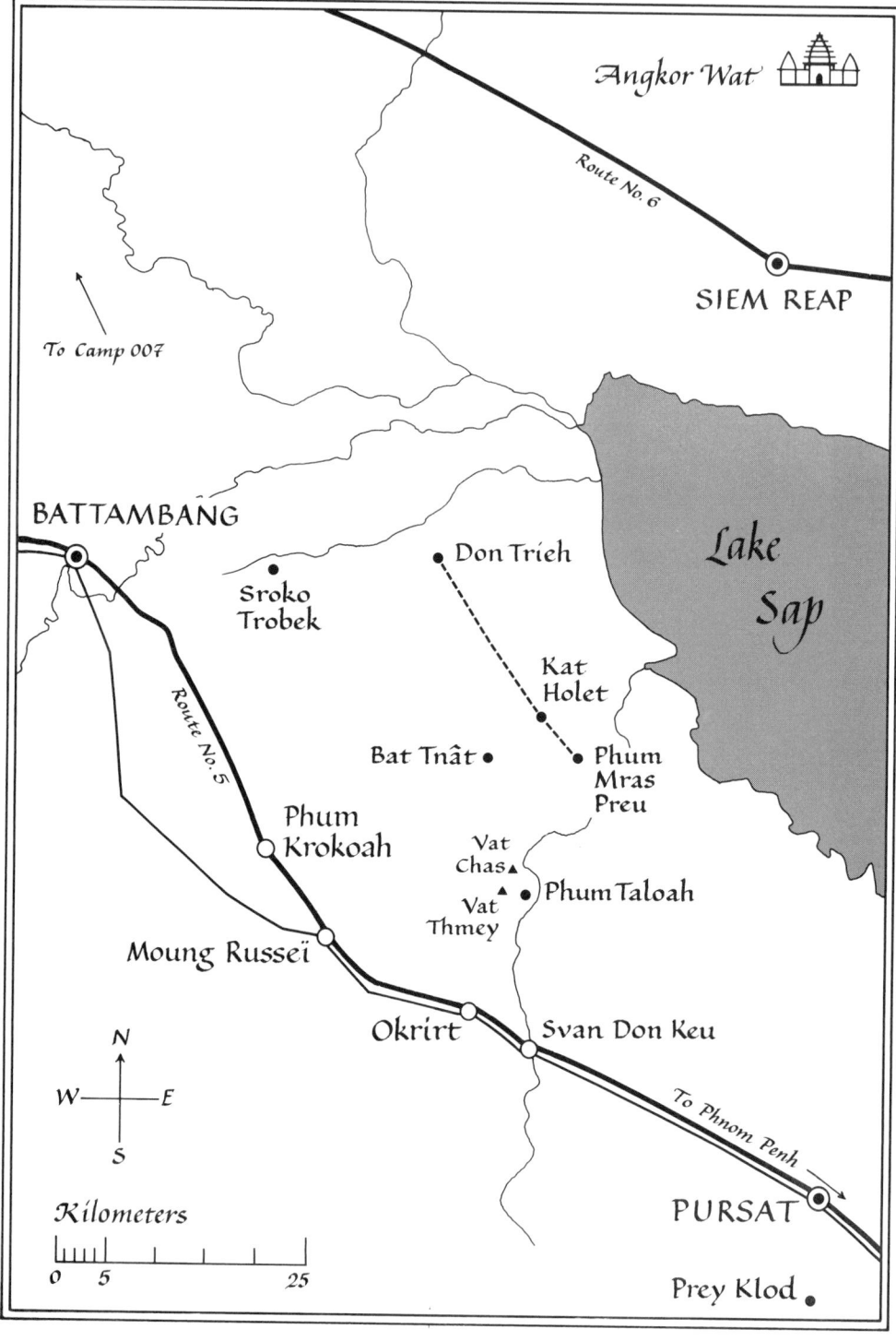

THE WEEKS went by. It had been more than six months since we had been jolted out of our life in Phnom Penh, and everything we had been used to had been turned upside down. We had learned about the hard lives of those who work the land. I hadn't known anything about how rice was grown, and there I was, watching its green stems shoot up out of the water. I had transplanted the seedlings into muddy rice fields along with the other inhabitants of this village where my family had taken refuge. The ears of rice had formed and were swelling "like a young woman expecting a baby," as we say in Khmer. My parents were happy, saying, "Soon we'll be able to feed you properly, and it will be with rice we have all helped to grow." The Khmer Rouge were delighted. "Our rice is growing nicely. Don't worry—it'll be ripe in a month." The whole village showed its joy: everyone was talking, visiting in the evening. Soon it would be the December full moon, when sundown is at exactly six o'clock. The sun was setting in the mauve evening sky when I noticed people from neighboring houses carrying their belongings on their heads or on bamboo shoulder poles going by on the path about twenty meters from our house.

"Papa, come and see, quickly, something's going on!"

"I'll say! Mama, pack our bags, we won't be eating any of this rice. Naroeun, hurry and warn Mitia Mir."

Naroeun ran off. "I'll warn Grandmother, too." A heavy silence weighed on the village. It was dark and we hadn't any light to see by. Naroeun returned with the news that people in the village were talking about a departure by boat. A half hour later, two Yotears arrived.

"Met Rêth, pack your bags. You'll be leaving in ten minutes."

"And where are we going?"

"You have to go to Battambang. The rice there is ripe and there aren't enough people to harvest and eat it; it'll be lost."

"What can we take with us?"

Father was trying to gain some time with his questions so that we might have a moment more to get our things together.

"Nothing at all. Your personal belongings. No hatchets, machetes, no knives. You'll have much better ones where you're going."

Father was at the threshold, the Yotears were at the bottom of the ladder. While he was still speaking to them, he turned toward us and whispered, "Hide the machete among my clothes."

In a sugary voice, one of the Yotears went on: "You can leave the matting you've woven, and the rugs. Why carry all those things? Don't kill yourselves lugging around baggage. You'll find much better things when you get there." I thought he was very nice, so concerned with our comfort. "You'll see, there are new houses just waiting for you. And you'll have as much rice as you want."

Father didn't have any reason not to believe him, since Battambang was a rich province, with more mechanization than other regions. The floods weren't as bad there, the rice ripened earlier. Everything seemed to fit.

My Aunt Vathana came running up, out of breath. "Mâ, where are you going?" she asked my mother.

"As you see, dear, we're leaving."

"I want to go with you."

"Don't worry. We're all going in the same direction."

"No, not together," interrupted the Yotear, "each person stays with his group. Go back to your group."

Vathana went off, and we were ready to go. Father had another knife hidden in his clothes, and I had a knife, too, one with a handle carved by my father and fitted to a blade he found one day in the village. It's the only thing I have left now that once belonged to him.

It was completely dark out. We went up to the village with our heavy bundles, trying to take as much as we could of our poor belongings with us. We all gathered at Met Won's house, where his wife distributed dried fish: five to a person, thirty-five for our family. There were ten families in our group. When the fish were originally handed out, the Mekongs pretended that they had distributed all of it, but in fact they had already put aside this reserve supply. Our departure had been planned for some time.

Mother asked permission to say goodbye to her sister.

"Don't worry," said a Yotear, "you'll see her again. All of you are leaving."

We went by Grandmother's hut, and she waved her hand at us. We hadn't seen anyone from the Vong family.

A Yotear spoke to my father: "Met Rêth, you've got five children. Move up to the edge of the lake."

"What for?"

"To get into the skiff, which will take you to the boat."

We went down to the water's edge, where others were already waiting. They explained to us that there were five small boats going back and forth to Viel Trumph; the round trip took about an hour. Some children from Vong's family came to kiss us goodbye, and my mother's sister arrived. She told us that Tôn Ny was sick, probably with malaria. Mama warned her, "You're going to be leaving, too; the Mekong told us. Be ready, it will be tonight." No one had said anything to them yet, but there was no room for false hope.

My sister Naroeun picked that moment to have an attack of malaria: her teeth chattered, and her whole body was shaking.

"Look, you've got the same illness as Papa!"

A boat arrived. Mother got in with the children and the baggage, but Father had to wait for the next boat. Our feet were soaking wet. It was cold, and the wind had come up, whipping the surface of the water. Mother had put thick socks on Naroeun's feet and was holding her in her arms, fast asleep. The boat passed close to Prek Meng. There were lights in the houses near Grandfather Proung's hermitage, and we thought we could see his silhouette on the shore, so we called out to him. Mama asked the Yotear if we could row closer to shore for a moment, but it was out of the question: all we could do was wave frantically at him. He raised his hand in farewell, and I think he was crying.

We landed at Viel Trumph, but the bottom of the boat became stuck in the mire, and we had to get out and pull it closer to shore to unload the baggage. The mud was halfway up our calves. "Come on, unload your stuff!" None of us had the strength to lift the big bundles out of the boat. Naroeun started to shake again, so Mother stayed with her. When the Yotear called her, she answered, "I can't take care of the baggage, my oldest daughter is sick." The Yotear allowed us to wait for my father to arrive, which he did in the next boat. Father asked Mother to go on ahead with the children—it was about two hundred meters to the edge of the Mekong River, where the big boat was supposed to be. It was a dark night, however, and the embankment was a mound of mud. I wanted to help Father unload the baggage. "Stay here with our belongings," he said, "I'll carry everything."

So I remained at the riverbank with our baggage while Father carried away the first bundles. He came back in a moment and told me that Mama was looking for a place for us to sleep. The boat hadn't arrived there yet, and many families were trying to find a dry spot on which to spend the night. Father went back and forth a few times. The boats had returned to the village, leaving me alone at the water's edge. I was afraid, and I drew my sarong up over my head, but I could still see my father moving slowly across the embankment, stopping after every three or four steps. My tears fell softly. "Oh, Papa, you never abandon us, you never change. You're always the same with us, while the children are becoming different. Their hearts are hardening. They don't really know you at all."

I went with Father on his last trip, carrying a little bundle on my head. Mother met us in tears—the Yotear in charge of assigning camping spaces hadn't arrived yet. Father sat down on the ground and Mother gently massaged his aching shoulders. She still had a little pot of balm that she rubbed onto his bruises.

There were plenty of abandoned houses nearby, but we weren't allowed to move into them. The boat could arrive at any moment, and we had to be ready. We dozed by the path, constantly disturbed by the arrival of new groups of people. It was well past midnight when I suddenly heard Mitia Mir, my Uncle Vong: "Come on, Tôn Ny; cheer up, Sy Neang." We called them over quickly, happy to be together in our common distress. They were also waiting for someone to assign them a place to sleep.

Finally our Mekong arrived, smelling of perfume and all dolled up with lipstick she must have confiscated from someone, because it was forbidden to have any. "Where is Rêth's family?" We spoke up. "From now on you belong to Group 2. Come on, line up with Met Vong's family." She took us a few meters farther under the trees and told us that this would be our billet until the boat arrived.

"When will that be?"

"I don't know. Perhaps tomorrow, or in ten minutes, when you'll be asleep."

In the meantime, we spread out light blankets on the damp grass and slept until morning. Yotears came by at that point to distribute rice: fifty cans per family.

"That's a bad sign," agreed Father and Mitia Mir. "Where are they going to take us?"

"Perhaps to the other side of Lake Sap."

"No, I think we'll be staying on this side. The other side has been settled for a long time, they don't need us to work over there."

"Do you really think they're going to make us work again? Maybe they want to get rid of us once and for all."

"You mean drown us in the middle of the lake?"

"Perhaps we'd better not talk about it."

I was going to ask Mother to explain what I'd heard to me, but just then a new group that included Grandmother arrived, so now we were all together again. The long wait began. We had to find something to cook with; people were beginning to burn the ladders from the abandoned houses. I brought one over to our camp on my head, and Father chopped it up with his machete. The next to go were the walls, then the floors. When a house collapsed, it was a free-for-all to see who could carry off the most pieces.

Two days went by. My sister had an attack of fever regularly around nine in the morning, after which she dozed. Toward noon the Mekong would check to see that the baggage was all ready. Tôn Ny's fever bout was just then ending; she had her attack around eleven o'clock. There was no more quinine. My Aunt Nang had found a few pastilles of quinine that she bought with gold, but they were all gone.

2   AT SIX in the morning on the fourth day, fast asleep, I heard what sounded like a blast from a ship's whistle. In a flash I was up and running to the water's edge. The boat was arriving, blazing with lights—it was five hundred meters away, then three hundred! I raced back and forth from the water to our campsite to tell Mother what was happening. I thought about the boat I was on one time in Phnom Penh . . . I was all excited, and Father had to calm me down. "They'll call us when they're ready, now sit down." When I told him that I'd seen a second boat coming behind the first, he became worried that family groups might be separated. There was a rumor that an over-crowded boat had already sunk. Mother gathered us all together. "Children, we're going to pray before we embark. It's all we can do."

I heard my Aunt Nang waking her children. "Come on, everyone on their feet!" My sister couldn't budge. "Try to wake up, sweetheart, you can sleep on the boat."

The Mekongs began to call out: "Group Number 1, to the boat!" After a quarter of an hour. "Group Number 2!" That was us. We tried our best to stay together with Grandmother and Mitia Mir's family. I was the first one in line, and the gangway jounced under my feet as I hurried up, intent on reserving a spot on the bridge for our families, right under the gently waving red flag. Glancing at the rice fields in the distance, I saw them gilded by the rising sun—they looked like carpets of gold. Soon everyone was there, pressed up against each other, and Mother lighted three sticks of incense. There were no Yotears nearby to forbid it, the crush of people was too great, but we knew there were Yotears camouflaged among the passengers. We had been told to be absolutely quiet, but we had to pray before the crossing—what if we were to sink!

The Mekong River is very wide, and we could hardly see its banks. Where were we going? Battambang was mentioned, to the northwest. But who could say? One thing was certain: we were proceeding up the Mekong River toward Lake Sap. All of a sudden my Aunt Vathana, who had lifted up her head, cried out, "Look, it's Phnom Penh!" We were in the middle of the river, which now divided into four branches; we took the one on the left, closest to the city. Wooden piers thrust out into the water. Groups of Yotears were bathing nearby, while others, impeccably dressed, were strolling on the piers. We passed by not far from the park where the entire family used to go walking in better days—was it six months ago, or ten years? I pointed out to my father the big ministry buildings where we used to wait for him after work. The flower beds had been replaced by banana plantations. Formerly, there were always lots of boats, owned by rich Chinese or Vietnamese, but the Khmer Rouge had sunk them with machine guns.

For several hours we passed by the city and its suburbs. The boat was in no hurry, and we were its prisoners. "If only I had wings and could fly to our house," I overheard Father say to Mitia Mir. "Now we work with long pens," he added, alluding to their ditch-digging tools.

A bit farther along, we could make out a vast heap of automobile carcasses, cars that were new but without wheels, along with crates of television sets and refrigerators, everything piled up and beginning to rust. All these vestiges of rotten Western society!

A group of four Yotears waved at us from the shore, signaling us to land. The boat maneuvered close to the bank, and the gangway was lowered. The Yotears came on board, each carrying a heavy sack, which they proceeded to empty out onto the bridge: canned goods, jars of cosmetics, drums of oil. They argued about the best way of opening the cans; then one of them pulled out a pair of pliers and tore off the tops. The cosmetics didn't seem to have the taste that was expected of them—obviously the Yotears couldn't read the labels on anything. The tins of grease didn't look or taste like lard: overboard they went. Motor oil, yuck! They amused themselves this way for an hour or two; no one dared to look openly in their direction. Then they went up to the only Yotear we had seen on the boat, the one who seemed to be in charge, and after they had exchanged some words the boat turned in toward shore again. Some pretty new bamboo houses had just come into view, lined up for more than a kilometer. Would these be the new houses we were promised? They did appear to be empty. Mother told my sister she was sure they were meant for us.

But no! The Yotears were the only ones who went ashore, and we continued our voyage. Night fell and we passed a kind of little village, with children playing in front of the houses while women rocked themselves in colorful easy chairs out on the verandas. These houses belonged to the country's new masters.

Finally, an hour after sundown, the boat pulled in for good. "Everyone ashore! And take your baggage or I'll throw it all in the water!" Father told us to go ashore, he would take care of our things. Mother was busy with Naroeun, who was half unconscious, while I was in charge of the smaller children.

It was slippery on shore, so dark that you couldn't see where you were going, and there was a nauseating stench. Father got all our bundles together after two or three trips, but he had to set them down in the disgusting muck. I could hear families crying and lamenting: "They threw our things in the water!" When we counted our bundles, Naroeun's satchel and mine were missing. Another relic of the past gone forever.

3 WE ALL STAYED TOGETHER and waited while Father went looking for a place for us. He returned shortly for some of our things, taking Mama and Naroeun with him, while I stayed with the rest of the family and the baggage. Father made another trip with more bundles and everybody else but me. I was supposed to keep an eye on the last bundles, but I didn't want to stay alone in the dark without moving and without knowing where I was, so I decided to put a big package on my head and set out right away. What a mistake! Stinking filth from where the package had been sitting dripped down my neck. Father tried to console me by saying we hadn't far to walk, and in fact we soon arrived in the middle of a village square, a covered market lit from the center by a neon tube. My family was installed in a shadowy corner. The awful smell hovered around me and my hair was all sticky, so Mother tore off a piece of sarong to wipe off my head and hands.

"I want to go wash in the river."

"You'd better stay with us. You'd have to come back by the same path," said Father, "and how would you see where you were going without any light?"

"But she's going to make everybody sick," Mother interrupted, "and Naroeun can't stand the smell. Let her go get water someplace. I need some to fix a meal for us."

I don't know what she was planning on cooking, because we didn't have a thing left, but just then two Yotears passed through the market and announced, "Every family will get two cans of rice, come and get them. Latecomers won't get any!" Always that mania for making people rush, and then having them wait for hours. Father told me he would see about finding some water, I'd better get our ration of rice. I tied a *krâmar* into a bag, took a good look at where we were so that I'd be able to find the spot again, and followed the Yotears to a building near the edge of the square. I was among the first to arrive.

"How many people?"

"Seven."

The end of my *krâmar* slipped, spilling a bit of rice. The Yotear, a decent sort, gave me another half a can without scolding me.

Father had found out where there was a well and set out with a basin, but returned empty-handed. "Come with me, my little girl, you're going to help me." We had to find a bucket, because the well was deep and the cord was just dangling with no bucket at the end of it. Father asked one group of people after another if someone had a bucket. One woman was willing to lend him hers if he'd bring it back to her full of water, which was fine with us as long as we could draw some water for ourselves. The first bucketful, which took a long time to draw from over ten meters deep, went into the basin so I could wash: I had a bit of soap saved for just such emergencies, and my father rinsed me off. Then I carried the basin full of water to Mother while Father returned the canvas bucket to its owner, who was surprised when he actually brought it back full of water—too much suffering was beginning to make people lose their trust in common decency.

Mother started to prepare the rice, but there was still the problem of firewood, for which we had to look outside the marketplace. Father and I went over toward the river, where there seemed to be some sort of construction debris. Every now and then Father struck a light. He warned me to be careful where I put my feet, and I snapped back that I wasn't at all anxious to get filthy again right after having washed. That wasn't what he was worried about, however; we had entered what used to be a bonze monastery, littered with bamboo fragments, splinters of wood, and perhaps some rusty nails as well. We tore off a few sections of wall, which Father chopped into manageable size with his machete. I tied it all into a bundle with my *krâmar*.

That night everyone ate their fill without having to pay close attention to how big each portion was. Then we fell asleep amid our foul-smelling baggage.

At sunrise a Yotear passed among the groups to summon a member of each family to an information meeting. Father returned an hour later with the news: we were supposed to go by train toward Battambang, but we might not go all the way to Battambang, we might stop at Pursat, about halfway there—or perhaps someplace else. Whenever we came upon a group of empty houses, that would be our new settlement. There would be plenty of provisions there, and as much rice as we wanted. When would we be leaving? Soon. But when? Doubtless today, perhaps tomorrow, or tonight. But where was the train station? We'd be taken there; the baggage and the little children would travel by oxcart. The Angkar had thought of everything.

That day passed, and then the next. Naroeun was still feverish and exhausted. The well water was running out, along with our patience. The Yotears weren't unkind, however; they distributed rice, and on the third day they really did bring carts to load up the baggage and little children. The cloth of our bundles had become stiff with filth, but there had been no chance to wash anything because we were always supposed to be ready to leave at any moment. We finally got going, and our procession arrived at a paved road where a line of twenty or more trucks was waiting for us. The first two trucks were for Group Number 1, and we got into the third, followed by the Vong family. After a few minutes of waiting, we started moving slowly, then a little faster, rattled around by the jouncing of the trucks, which had no shock absorbers. All along the road we could see new little houses, some of bamboo, others of wood, painted blue. Yotear families lived in them. For a few moments we skirted a mountain, or at least what seemed like a mountain to us townspeople. One hour on the road, then two—this station was a long way away. We were already in Kompong Speu Province, west of Phnom Penh. And there was a train station. I could just make out the words "Damnag Smak." On one side, upcountry, there were fruit trees all the way to the horizon, orange and lemon trees, guava trees, fig trees. On the other side, rice fields golden with ripening grain. Were we going to stay there? We were disappointed when the column of trucks drove by the station, but then it stopped a few minutes later. "Everyone out!" We were perhaps two kilometers from the station, next to recently harvested rice paddies still strewn with rice straw.

A hundred meters farther on, we saw straw huts and people bustling about. As I gathered up some straw, I moved closer to them to see what was going on. They were from Viel Trumph, and had been there for ten days; the train was supposed to arrive for them any minute now. When I got back with my straw, Father went over to the other side of the tracks to look for posts to make a roof, because it was really quite hot and Naroeun still wasn't well. Mother had found water, and she told me to get more straw for the roof. My sister Sitha fetched a few stones to make a hearth. When I returned from my third trip, Father had already set up the posts, and still more straw was needed: the thicker the roof, the more effective it is against the heat. Father tossed the straw I brought him up onto our pitiful shelter. Now we had to find firewood, so off I went with Father. I'd seen some dead wood at the edge of the rice paddies, at some distance from our camp, and Father even found a fallen tree, which he chopped up with his machete while I bundled up the branches in my *krâmar*.

When we got back, the rice was ready. There was plenty of it—two cans per person!—and it was very good. Mother cautioned us, however: "Children, don't eat too much or too quickly because this is green rice, it's going to swell up in your stomach and give you a stomachache if you're not careful." The Yotears warned us, too: "Prepare your fresh rice with lots of water, in a soupy liquid, or there will be accidents." And in fact that afternoon we heard that someone had died from eating too much new rice. We could hardly believe it. The Yotears came by to check everyone's cooking pots: those who had cooked their rice the usual way instead of as they were told to wouldn't get more than one can per person. Mother saved our extra rice, since we didn't know what was in store for us and we had gone without provisions too often.

We let the fire burn that evening, because Naroeun was cold at night and we liked to be able to see. "Tomorrow a train will go by," announced a Yotear. "Keep away from the tracks! This train isn't for you. You may not go near it." Everybody waited impatiently to find out what all this meant. Around nine o'clock, the train approached slowly, went by us, and stopped. I saw two open boxcars full of rice and . . . bread! The first bread I'd seen since Phnom Penh; long, thin loaves lined up on the platform where a group of soldiers was sitting devouring it along with rice, chicken, and pâté. "Mama, there won't be any left for us." I started to go toward the boxcars— "Stop right there, that's not for you!" But the train remained sitting before our eyes.

That afternoon three people died from eating too much green rice. In the evening, Mother called in vain for me to come and lie down for the night: I was fascinated by the bread on the boxcar. Uncle Vong's family had already gone to bed, the children rolled up in rugs from their house in Phnom Penh; I could make out little Sreï Peu's head in her bonnet with the rabbit ears. Everyone was wearing woolen clothing, because it was cool in the early morning. We were keeping a fire going, and tomorrow we'd have to get more wood. At that moment, however, I was hungry for that bread over there, so close. Mother scolded me a bit, so I came to bed. The moon rose, enormous in the sky over the train.

We had been there for three days, and the Yotears seemed nice to us. They were passing among our groups to check their records. Not everyone would be going to Battambang.

"You and your family, Met Rêth, you're on the list. Met Vong, you'll be going to Battambang. And you over there, you're a doctor, I believe. You'll be useful to us."

"That's true, I am a doctor, and my daughter here was in medical school."

"Fine, you'll be staying here."

Other people were describing themselves as engineers, accountants, architects. The whole day was spent drawing up lists. Finally, on the morning of the fourth day: "Group 1, move over to the train!" We picked up all our belongings. "Group 2!" We moved forward. Over by the cattle car in which we were going to ride, three Yotears were distributing rice and—it was unbelievable!—everyone received a loaf of bread, even my little brother. The doctor's daughter, who had been camped near us, came over to our group. "Would you take me with you?" There was no time for Mother to answer; a Yotear grabbed the girl by the arm. "No, for you we have a special treatment." All those who weren't leaving were gathered on the other side of the tracks under the orchard trees. We never saw them again. The warning given to us by the Khmer Rouge who brought us out of Phnom Penh had been explicit and absolute: "Never say that you are of bourgeois origins or that you have had any trade other than a manual one. All such people will be liquidated."

4 WE HOISTED OURSELVES UP into the railway car, and my uncle's family got in after us, but we were assigned to one end of the car while they went to the other. The sliding door was closed, leaving us in the dark. We had each received a spoonful of powdered sugar, which Mother had collected in a cloth. It would be a long time before I'd see any sugar again. At least they had given us two cans of rice per person, which we would have to cook whenever the train made a stop.

After an hour or so, the locomotive blew three blasts of its whistle and we were underway. Our eyes had become used to the semidarkness, and we tried to see who was in the car with us. There was no way of knowing who had gotten on the train and who had been left standing by the tracks, but at least we knew our two families were together. We didn't dare try to get closer to one another, however, because there were surely Yotears hidden among us, and my uncle, as a "re-educated person," was bound to be watched. He was the one who had told Father we'd have to "keep our distance." The heat was overpowering.

The train rolled along, passing through tunnels, then came to a halt for a rest stop at around eleven o'clock. Those who wished got off the train and looked for a convenient spot. The rolling countryside was covered with trees. At the foot of a mountain I came upon sprigs of cumin, and picked a few; it would flavor our saltless rice. One of the soldiers in our escort asked me, "Why are you picking that? There's plenty of it in the meadows around Battambang." Now there, for once, I knew he was lying: we had taken a family trip to that region, which is very marshy, whereas cumin grows only in dry soil.

I quickly collected a few dead branches to use for firewood at our next stop. Since we weren't allowed to bring wood onto the train, I sneaked over and tied my bundle with a vine to an iron bar between our car and the next. At worst it would simply be lost along the way.

A blast from the locomotive and everyone climbed back on. It was past noon, and we were hungry. The train stopped again, and we saw the Yotears get down and seat themselves on the railway track to eat. We were not allowed to follow their example; anyway, the halt was supposed to be only fifteen minutes, so no one dared linger outside. I could see Kōn Rei Mountain through the open door. The rocks resembled human forms:

there seemed to be a woman pounding rice in a mortar, and farther away was a young girl lying on her side, petrified in that position, according to legend, when she ran after her fiancé as he went away to war.

The train was still standing there. Mother asked Father if we couldn't try to cook a little rice. "Let's try it," said Father. "Go get your wood, dear daughter." The branches were still there, hanging lopsidedly from the end of the car. Father placed three stones together, drew water from a hole he found under the trees, and we lighted our fire quite close to the tracks, almost under the railroad car. The rice was beginning to cook when I signaled Father that the Yotears were returning. We got back into the car immediately with our boiling pot, happy to be able to eat something, especially as there was still a small dried fish left for each of us. My older sister didn't want to eat anything. The Yotears yelled at some people still outside, because others had started cooking after we did and were slow to put out their fires.

The train set off again, and after about two hours, in the middle of the afternoon, it stopped once more so we could relieve ourselves. We would have liked to find a little privacy, but the train could have left at any moment. Wandering around the countryside without a pass was quite simply asking to be shot. Still, I went off a little ways and gathered a few dead twigs for our next cooking fire. It was a beautiful region, with lovely trees and big green meadows. Once again I hung my bundle behind the car; if I took it inside with me, it would be stolen. Besides, we were all crowded together, crouching down on our heels. Only Naroeun could lie down, protected by her brother and sisters.

The sun was about to set, so it must have been six o'clock. We stopped at the station at Kompong Trumph, where our escort went off to have supper without bothering with us. We knew they wouldn't be back within a half hour, so my father and I quickly got out on the wrong side of the train and lighted a small fire to heat up our rice.

Night fell very quickly, and we looked at the lights of the city. "Do you remember, Papa, we had a picnic not far from here." We had stopped near a peasant's house to ask for an orange, and the old people told us, "Go on, children, pick from the trees, take all you want." The happy moments of my childhood!

We had to get back into our prison on wheels, where we ate as best we could, huddled in the darkness. I fell asleep in that position, shaken rather than lulled by the train's movement; one of my sisters leaned her head on my shoulder. From time to time I collapsed on someone's back or thighs, causing a flurry of grunts and grumbling. At around nine o'clock, another pee stop. "You've got five minutes!" I got down from the train so as not to be trampled by those who needed to go, then climbed back in more or less still asleep.

At midnight the train stopped again after a few jolts. "They've uncoupled the engine." This time I did wake up, and joined my father by the side of the tracks. We seemed to be in open country, insofar as we could see anything at all in the darkness. We were surrounded by silence and the twinkling of stars. The Yotears appeared to have abandoned the train.

"No, they said they'd be back in an hour."

"If you believe everything they say."

"Hush!"

An hour went by, then another. At last a locomotive arrived and was attached to the cars, and we set out again. We were now in Pursat Province. It wasn't long before the train stopped at a station in Svan Don Keu. We had traveled two hundred kilometers. In any case, this was the end of our train trip. "Everybody out. Take your baggage with you. Let's go, hurry!"

It was dark, it was cold, there was ground fog everywhere, and dawn wasn't far off. My sister was shaking with fever. I could hear crickets chirping in the stubble field. After everyone had gotten off the train, the Yotears went off in it, telling us, "You'll sleep here, we'll come and get you in the morning." Why didn't they just let us sleep in the train? It only went another few hundred meters before stopping again. We settled ourselves on tag ends of clothing. Mother pulled up a few handfuls of straw and asked Father to light it so that we could warm ourselves a little bit. My teeth were chattering, my head ached, and I couldn't sleep, but I hadn't the strength to help Father take care of the fire. I was too cold.

All of a sudden I felt a tickling sensation on my bare feet: it was crickets, all over the place, getting into everything. On all sides people were talking about this invasion; some caught the crickets and roasted handfuls of them in their cooking pots. When I caught one, I looked at it and said, "Run away, at least you're happy to be alive."

The sun came up, rapidly burning off the mist. We found ourselves on a plain, with mountains behind us. It became hot very quickly, so we stayed beneath the trees. Suddenly, around noon, a small van drove up and several Yotears got out.

"Everybody on your feet! Time to go!"

"Where are we going?"

"Follow the road."

"And our baggage?"

"You're strong enough to carry it."

"There aren't any wagons?"

"There aren't any wagons."

"But where are we going?"

"You're to assemble at Moung Russeï."

"Is it far?"

"Oh no, a few kilometers. You'll be there before us, wait for us there."

They drove off, laughing. We loaded up our bundles, on our shoulders or heads, and set out on the burning asphalt under a blazing sun. Could we have run away? There were no Yotears with us, but the countryside was crawling with Khmer Rouge, who massacred fugitives without pity. Walking with bare feet on the tarred surface of the road as it heated up in the sun was real torture. My head didn't ache anymore; in fact, I couldn't feel a thing except the burning in my feet. I'd have liked to stop, but we had to get there before evening, because we didn't know what trouble we'd have finding something to eat and a place to sleep, and whatever we had to cope with would be a little easier if there was still daylight.

5 WE WALKED twenty-five kilometers on that road, a nightmare. One foot in front of the other . . . I tried walking on the shoulder, but the hot gravel wasn't any softer to my aching feet. The younger children began crying, we had to stop—good. But then how painful it was to pick up the bundles and start walking again. Four hours. Five hours. The sun was about to set. Finally we saw the first straw huts as we approached the village. We tried to beg a little drinking water, but there were too many of us, and the inhabitants stayed out of sight.

It was pitch-dark when we arrived, near a village market I recognized from the time when we had bought an entire bunch of enormous bananas. Only the framework was left; the roof was gone, replaced by a huge piece of canvas. Everything seemed dirty and depressing. We piled our belongings at the base of a pillar, and then I saw a man leave our group, going off toward a building where we could see some lights. He was a Yotear disguised among us. Soon he returned with a bicycle. He took down the names of the heads of families, then told us, "You're to go down this little path over here on the right. It leads to the river. You'll find a bridge, and at the foot of the bridge there will be Mekongs who will take charge of you."

We had to set out again, this time plodding through hot dust up to our ankles, a new punishment for our burned and aching feet. We walked for a long time, an hour or more. Everyone was at the end of his tether. We could hear parents threatening to abandon their children if they wouldn't keep up—there was no need for Yotears to harass us. I watched my parents, bent double under their loads; Mother was supporting Naroeun, who was half asleep. Father never once raised his voice to us, and Mother treated us all with quiet tenderness.

We arrived at the bridge, which loomed up over us—were we going to have to climb all the way up there? "Let's find a place to sleep," said Father. "Mama will fix us a bit of rice, I'll go find some leaves to make a fire."

Just as he picked up a few leaves, a voice called down from the top of the bridge, "Met Rêth, Met Nêm!"

"We're here," answered my father.

"Pick up your baggage. You're to cross the bridge and go to your worksite. At dawn you're going to harvest rice."

"But, Met Kong, can't you tell me why I have to cut rice right away?"

"Not only you, but Met Nêm, too, and your children. The rice is ripe, the ears are losing their grains—we must hurry."

"Listen, Met Kong, we just walked thirty kilometers. None of us has eaten; one of my children is sick with fever. Let us spend the night here."

"Not here. This is Sector 20, you belong to Sector 17. Cross the bridge, you can sleep under the mango trees."

"But what about the house we were promised?"

"You'll get it. You'll build it yourself after the harvest."

There was nothing more to say. Dragging our bundles, we crossed the bridge. Father was still carrying the pot of rice, and the leaves he had gathered were tucked in his jacket. There were a great number of mango trees on the other shore, where we settled down to sleep. At cockcrow, a Yotear came by, inviting us to come get rice and salt: fifty cans of rice per family, real luxury. Father returned with the rice in a bag, followed by a Mekong. "That's fine for today. Rest. But tomorrow you'll have to leave before dawn for the harvest at Phum Taloah."

During the day Father looked for a place to leave Naroeun. A Yotear household agreed to take her in with them for a few days, but under no circumstances would Mother be allowed to stay with her. Everyone had to work. The children would glean the ears of rice fallen behind the harvesters, even my little brother—all were needed.

Father decided that we'd set out as soon as it cooled off a little, rather than leave before dawn and have to start working right away. Carrying our luggage, we crossed through fields of stubble that tore our feet to shreds. Off in the distance, we passed by a little town called Don Trieh, but that wasn't our destination. We had to walk along huge rice paddies, kilometer after kilometer, until we came to a place called Vat Thmey. There was grass on the footpaths, but no trees, except for a palm tree here and there. The sun was already setting by the time we were shown the place where we could set up our camp, between two rice paddies. There was nothing but rice as far as the eye could see. Father went to cut a few palm branches to build a shelter, and we found a bit of straw left by the people who had been here before us.

The Mekong came by to speak to my father: "You'll have to build something sturdier than that."

"I would need some bamboo."

"You'll get some tomorrow. Every family is allotted nine bamboo poles."

"But where do we find them?"

"Tomorrow you'll go to Vat Thmey, near the 'new pagoda,' that's what it's called."

Father went to fetch the bamboo the next day, and he also intended to bring Naroeun back with him, since he would be able to borrow a wagon and a water buffalo. Mother had to cut rice, but her right leg was paralyzed and the entire right side of her body was numb. "All right, someone will be sent to take care of you tomorrow, but today you must winnow rice. Here we don't feed sick people who do nothing: everyone works. No one stays in the huts during the day!"

6

AS SOON AS MORNING CAME I went off to the fields carrying a sickle, a little rice, and some dried fish in my *krâmar*. When I returned in the evening, Mother told me that her arms ached from having shaken a winnowing basket all day long. The next day Father brought Naroeun back in a wagon and set right to work building a shelter sturdier than our low hut, which we entered crawling on our hands and knees, along with various wee beasties who came to visit us amid the dust that was so irritating to our eyes and skin.

Father used the bamboo he had brought back with him to best effect, setting up a roof of straw reinforced with bamboo, and our palace was ready, open to all the winds. In a hollow not too far away, within about five hundred meters, there was a pond that furnished water for cooking. I used to go there also to pick up fish. I say "pick up" because during rest hour, at noon, I would leave the rice paddy and run to the pond. All I had to do was build a little mud dike in the middle of the pool, then make all the water go over to one side. The fish were there for the taking. I'd pick the ones I wanted, then let all the water back in quickly so that the fish supply wouldn't be needlessly exhausted. I'd hide the few fish I collected in my bowl until they could be taken to our hut that evening, but unfortunately they'd begin to smell bad in the heat before I could get them home.

When I first started working, I found my cousin Tôn Ny out in the rice field; we'd try to work together whenever possible, but we didn't belong to the same group. Father accompanied me during the first few days after our hut was built, but soon he was assigned to other work, where he found his brother-in-law, my Uncle Vong, treading out rice by driving oxen around in a small space. The rice was then winnowed, which was work for old women, and that was where my mother, in her weakness, had been relegated.

Tôn Ny had attacks of fever from time to time, or else one of her little brothers was sick, and then I would find myself alone among strangers. There were a hundred people working on one hectare. Each worker was to harvest a strip two meters wide with a sickle, and when you reached the end of the field, you could go home. In actual fact, I never finished before nightfall: I was one of the youngest workers and couldn't advance as quickly as my neighbors, who would then cut their swaths progressively narrower so that I would end up with a strip three meters across to harvest. It made me weep with rage and fatigue. One evening, when I was the only one left in the field, the Yotear told me to hurry up. When I pointed out to him the excessive width of the strip I had to harvest, he told me, "It's your own fault; all you have to do is go faster than they do and then you can leave them some of your strip to harvest." He did help me finish the field, though. The next day I kept up the rhythm and didn't let the others get the better of me. From then on I worked faster and faster, so that I could go back to the hut at three o'clock and help my mother—but it took me a good month to reach this stage. Then I was able to "pick up" some fresh fish and bring back water and firewood, too.

Very proud of my skill in the fields, I must have had a moment of carelessness: there I was, so happy over knowing how to cut rice like a peasant, and then I sliced my wrist open to the bone. The Yotear on guard applied a dressing of tobacco moistened with his saliva, which he tied on with a piece torn from his red *krâmar*. The dressing stung like alcohol. He took my place on the line, but after a few moments I asked to go back to work. I couldn't make much progress, however, and I almost fainted, so the guard sent me home, telling me to come back the next day. I would have liked to take a bath, but there was only that tiny pond and two or three other pools in the area, and we had to use that water for all our domestic needs. The only well in the neighborhood was reserved for the Mekongs.

The next day, Naroeun went with me to the rice paddy. A Mekong had passed by our hut and told her, "Don't pretend to be sick. If you can work at home, you can work in the rice field." Someone had seen her the day before, in fact, going to get water for the family. I asked that she be allowed to work near me; that way we had a strip four meters wide for the two of us, and I helped her as much as I could. She had never cut rice before. "Sister," I told her, "just pretend, I'll do your work—I'm a peasant now."

Poor Naroeun tried to keep up, but after half an hour her malaria attack overwhelmed her. They laid her out in the middle of the field, behind the harvesters, with the sun beating down on her. I put my *krâmar* over her and went back to cutting rice. The Mekong told her, "When you stop shaking, go back to work."

After a little while my sister came staggering up to where I was, already far behind the others. The Mekong came and told her to go home. "Come back in two days." I worked until after sunset that day.

When I got home, Father wasn't there: he had been forced to follow a new schedule. Since the water level would soon be rising again, the treading out and winnowing of the rice had to be finished quickly. So Father and Uncle Vong had to work from six in the morning until midnight, with a break at noon and at dusk. After separating grain from the stalks, they would detach the husks in a primitive winnowing machine, then roughly hull the grain in some kind of stone arrangement, I'm not too sure what it was. At around midnight they were given a ladleful of sweetened rice and some rice flakes they could prepare themselves, to make a kind of porridge.

The next day, since I was given my usual work allotment, I finished rather early and ran off to the pond to get some fish. There was more water there than there had been in previous days; it was seeping up out of the earth, no one knew how. If I had had rubber boots or waders it would have been child's play, but the mud was deep, so I laid a few small branches across it to keep myself from sinking in. I had to stick my arm into the mud to grab the escaping fish, and my arm came out encircled with leeches. If they aren't shaken off immediately they're almost impossible to dislodge—five or six of them were starting to rasp open my skin. I had no desire to continue fishing and quickly left the pond. Instead, I went to get some wood from a palm-tree grove about a kilometer away. After piling up a few branches I'd collected, I went behind a big palm tree, and to my horror I saw three men hanging by the arms from a nearby tree—dead! Bunches of bananas were tied around their necks, and there was a banana crammed into each man's mouth. Without the strength to scream, I stood there petrified, my legs quivering. Taking tiny steps, I began to move backward . . . if I turned around, they'd jump on me! The firewood could stay right where it was. Once out of the grove I took to my heels, and within three minutes I was at Naroeun's side, where she lay shivering on her mat. An invalid old woman, a neighbor, dragged herself over to our hut. "What's happening, Met Peuw?" I told her about the horrible thing I'd seen. People were beginning to get back from work; our whole camp quickly heard the news. Then the Mekong arrived. "Assembly at eight o'clock. Educational session."

That evening everyone gathered out in the fields of stubble. "Dead men have been found in the grove. This is a lesson for you: these people stole bananas. You see what happened to them. From now on you will receive two cans of rice per person. There is no reason to steal what belongs to the community." It was easy for him to talk—they were the community, the Mekongs and their men. In any case, I didn't want to go fishing anymore and I wouldn't be going back to the grove.

From then on, during the siesta I gleaned the rice that the children had overlooked, grinding the grains myself in my *krâmar* with my feet, or in my hands when it was just a small amount. This was also forbidden, however, as a rule. At the sound of a whistle, everyone ran back into the field, while the Mekong struck up a revolutionary song he had taught us and waved a red flag—it was like a prayer before work. (Praying with the family was forbidden, and we no longer lighted the little sticks of incense Mother kept carefully hidden, but we prayed together every night before going to sleep.)

Then we usually had five minutes of "education" out in the field. "Don't anyone run off," the Mekong said one day. "I've got some interesting things to say to you." I stayed, which I didn't ordinarily do.

"You have all learned how to harvest rice, I congratulate you on your skill. I'm pleased that you're able to finish your work at four o'clock, which leaves you time to stroll around under the trees and to have a good time.

The Angkar needs your work, however, and since you're excellent work-ers, you'll each be able to handle a section three meters wide in the rice paddy. I hope you're pleased?"

"Oh yes, yes. We have to finish before the rains come."

Everyone agreed. Nobody wanted to disappear one night or be invited to collect their belongings to "go build a house up on the mountain." Such people were never heard from again.

So I cut my three meters and went home in the dark. Many people protested, but without making themselves conspicuous. I went home as fast as I could, because a new terror had me in its grip. That day in the rice field they had talked about a child of three or four who, left alone asleep in a hut, had wanted to rejoin his mother during the morning. It seems he had been attacked by a pack of wolves—only some hair and a few bones were found. I saw the poor mother in the throes of despair, and people started telling all sorts of horrible stories about wolves. I was terrified of being confronted by a starving wolf pack.

7   THE HARVEST was almost over. What would they do with us? The Yotears had promised we'd be allowed to build houses for the rainy season. All sorts of rumors were circulating that we were going to be moved to a new place, and then one night a Mekong made the rounds of the huts. "Assembly for all girls!" Now what did they want us to do—learn a new revolutionary song? No, it seemed some girls would be going to the mountain, which had a sinister ring to it. But why would they kill girls? We weren't in China, after all.

I decided to hide. "Poor child," said my mother, "you'd better go see what they want. They'll find you in any case." So I went to the meeting place, where everyone was squatting on her heels in the middle of a stubble field. My Aunt Vathana was there, and also Tôn Ny. I tried to look very small. Three Yotear women greeted us; then one of them passed among us to ask a few questions in a confidential manner.

"What was your name in Phnom Penh?" she asked me.

"My name is Peuw."

"Really?"

"Yes."

"Do you know how to write?"

"No."

"Did you go to school?"

"No."

I could see she didn't believe me. My aunt, sitting next to me—why did she interrupt?—added, "She doesn't know A from B."

"How much land does your father have?"

"He doesn't have any. He rented the land he worked on."

"How many houses?"

"Just a hut, which didn't belong to us either."

"But you ate well at your house."

"Oh, just a bit more than we have here."

"Did you have bicycles? You know how to ride a bike."

"My father had one, but it belonged to my uncle."

"But you really did go to school."

"No, not at all."

The Mekong wrote something down in her notebook and went directly to my aunt, who was sitting close to me in the next line, even though it wasn't her turn. The Mekong spoke to her very quietly; I couldn't hear what my aunt replied. Finally, the Mekong said, in a voice just loud enough for me to hear, "Met Sreï, go get your things and return here."

"What can I take?"

"Just your clothes and a bowl. Oh yes, and a blanket."

"I haven't eaten yet."

"You'll eat on the way. Don't bring along anything to eat."

Vathana got up and ran to the hut where she lived with her mother. I made as if to follow her.

"You stay here, Met Peuw."

"But I need to pee."

"Hurry up, and come right back."

I ran as fast as I could to Grandmother Ou Yêm's, where my aunt was crying in her mother's arms: although my aunt was eighteen years old, in many ways she was still a child. We all cried together. Vathana decided to argue with the Mekong.

"I don't want to die, I'm going to talk to her."

"Don't do anything," her mother told her. "If they tell you to bring along a bowl and a blanket, that means they're not going to kill you. But if you try to get out of it, you'll get yourself in trouble."

I dashed back to the meeting, and Vathana arrived a minute later.

She went to talk to the Mekong. "Can I stay with my mother? She's old; she'll need me if she gets very sick." And she burst into tears.

"Why are you crying, Met Sreï? I'm not going to kill your mother."

"But if I'm not here, she's going to become ill."

"Stop your sniveling. You'll be back soon. You're going to work."

There were already five girls there with their bundles, but five more were needed. "You, go get your things; you, too."

I tried to make myself as small as possible, not looking at the Mekong, but I felt her eyes light on me like an evil moonbeam in a nightmare. "Met Peuw, go get your things!" What was there to say? I got up and ran to my mother. My grandmother was there, too, and we all wept. Father was still at work. I collected my things and returned to the meeting. It was now dark, and a few straw fires had been lit for illumination, but also to keep wolves away from our camp. All the huts kept fires going throughout the night.

We set out in pitch darkness for Vat Thmey village. I was the last girl, the smallest and the youngest. We all had straw torches, and the Mekong led us. After an hour or two we arrived at the foot of a bridge I already knew, just before Moung Russeï. We all gathered in the house of a high-ranking Mekong. A young Yotear gave each one of us a lump of sugar, and we settled down for the night on the floor. It was impossible to sleep. Where were we going? The Yotear had told us we'd be leaving on a tractor-trailer, trundled along like so many bales of hay. My family was far away. I was frightened. Perhaps I was going to die.

The next morning two girls were awakened before the others and told to prepare rice for everyone. At five o'clock: "Everybody into the court-yard!" Each of us received two ladlefuls of rice in her bowl and a lump of sugar, but we weren't permitted to eat it; it was for later, on the road. There was some rice sticking to the bottom of the cooking pot, and I'd have liked to scrape it clean, but no, the girls who prepared the rice were the ones who got to share it. I told myself that next time I'd volunteer to cook the rice.

It took us an hour to cross the bridge and arrive at Moung Russeï, where we sat down under the trees by the entrance to the city. We were allowed to eat our rice, but quickly, as the tractor could arrive at any time. We knew that meant an hour or two of waiting, but perhaps this time they were telling the truth, so we stayed on the alert. I'd hardly digested my rice before I was hungry again, and sleepy. My aunt, sitting drowsily next to me, began to shake with fever. Just then the tractor arrived. Supporting Vathana, I couldn't manage to climb up, but someone pushed, someone else pulled, and both of us ended up on the trailer, with Vathana's head on my shoulder. Her temperature was rising, and as the sun climbed higher, it beat down on us cruelly.

At noon the tractor was still rolling along through villages, but then it left the road, turning onto a little path leading to the forest. After two or three kilometers, the path disappeared. We were in the forest, on the slopes of a mountain supposedly called Tébédé.

"Okay, get down, stretch your legs." We climbed down from the trailer and went off, each one looking for a little space to herself. A few meters away, under the trees, my aunt and I came upon several dead women: their stomachs were cut open, the entrails spilled out, and tufts of dry grass had been thrust into all their orifices. I wanted to get away from them immediately, but other girls had come over to see. "Look at all those jewels!" The bodies were covered with necklaces, bracelets, rings. It was a great temptation to take one or two pieces of jewelry . . . "Don't touch any of it," one of the girls said in a low voice. "The Yotears have put them there to see what we'll do." I think we might have met the same fate if we had let ourselves be tempted.

We returned rather quickly to the tractor, where the Yotears were laughing up their sleeves. As we rolled along behind the tractor, tree branches caught at our shawls and scarves, forcing us to keep our heads down, but that didn't stop us from picking the little wild almonds that brushed us softly as we went by. From time to time we crossed a clearing, where we saw more corpses, heads and limbs scattered about. Each time the Yotears burst out laughing. "You see what happens to people who don't listen to us!"

After seeing those horrors, I felt stronger. "They won't get me!" I think that was when I stopped being afraid of ghosts.

The tractor stopped in a clearing somewhat bigger than the others, where the ground was uneven. "Everybody out!" Without a word, without a wave of farewell, they unloaded us like a little herd of goats; the tractor turned around and disappeared. A middle-aged man with a rifle slung over his shoulder was leaning against a tree. We all stood around, somewhat at a loss, our bundles lying on the ground. The man, who might have been about thirty-five years old, came forward. "Sit down in a circle. I have some instructions for you." We all obeyed him. The man sat outside the circle and began to go through the instructions and warnings one by one.

"You're in the forest. There are tigers, wolves, and rhinos here. It's strictly forbidden to leave the group. At night a fire must be kept burning at each corner of our camp, which is right here. We're going to collect wood for the fires. Tomorrow we'll look for materials to build huts. Be on the lookout for snakes, too. All right, let's collect some wood. Stay in groups."

It was nighttime. We had all eaten the rice we had been given that morning, and we settled down as best we could under the trees. A whistle blew at dawn. It was as if the man hadn't slept; the fires were lit, the smoke probably announcing our presence to other Yotears in the forest.

"Come with me." He took us to the foot of a tree larger than the others and standing apart from them. At the very top we could see a red flag. "There is your landmark. If you become lost in the forest, always look for this reference point." We had all been given machetes. First we were to prepare bundles of firewood, which we tied up with lianas. "Don't wander off, and no fruit-picking, it slows down the work." He lighted a cigarette, walking back and forth under the tree; every once in a while he yelled, "Hoo! Hoo!" He clapped his hands or beat on a tree trunk with a stick to make noise, supposedly to scare off elephants.

The next thing we had to do was find something with which to cut the stakes for our huts. We all lined up, Indian file, carrying our bundles of wood on our heads. "Don't wander off. I haven't got eyes in the back of my head to watch over you like a shepherd. If one of you strays away, her mother will find her in a plastic bag floating down the stream!" We knew that this was one way of killing troublemakers: they were put in a plastic bag and beaten until they stopped thrashing around.

One of the girls was told to cook the rice the man now produced from a bag, and another had to fetch water from one of the many nearby ponds, while the rest of us set up our huts. The girls who went off to fetch water brought back several fish. We wanted to go to bed as soon as possible, but we had hardly finished the meal when our guardian began to lecture us.

"You can't go to bed now. Educational session. Tonight, you'll listen to my story. I was a robber in this forest before you were born, and I know it very well, its dangers and its hiding places. Don't try to escape, the animals would quickly devour you. I have a wife and two children. They're not with me, but they are being well provided for. I used to feed and take care of them with what I stole from people in the cities. Now the Angkar watches over them. No one ever saw my face when I was a thief: I was masked, and if I had to kill someone, it was always with a knife thrust in the back. And I wasn't alone, I had comrades. People called our band 'the thousand brigands.' If the door wasn't opened to us when we arrived at a house, a machete blow split it in two, and then no one got away. We took jewelry, gold and silver plate, and everything else! All the women in the territory were mine for the taking."

I didn't see what he was driving at, but then his story changed into a practical lesson.

"Now things are different. You don't have the right to go with boys. If one or the other of you loves a boy, you must come and tell me. Because if you get married without saying anything, the plastic bag is ready for both of you. And just one bag will be enough."

No one interrupted the lecture. I listened with one ear, since the problem didn't concern me, and kept nibbling on some bitter almonds.

"Tomorrow I'll show you a few couples sleeping together under the trees. And don't go near them, even if you see that they're still wearing jewelry. And if you find gold lying around the forest, you'd be well-advised to leave it alone. You're here to work. All right, you can go to bed."

My aunt and I lay down in the hut we had built for the two of us at the foot of a tree. Our guardian kept watch over the fires, making the rounds, and I saw the tip of his cigarette glowing between two trees. When he drew near, he reminded us: "Watch out for snakes! If you have any green lemon skins, put some under your head and feet."

The two of us slept with our arms wrapped around each other. I was scared of snakes, and I thought I heard tigers roaring or elephants crashing through the forest. My parents were in my thoughts: perhaps they thought we were both dead.

The next day we were awakened abruptly. "Roll up your mats and get to work!" It was still dark. I had traded my flashlight for three cans of rice in Tul Trieh, but my aunt had one that still worked and was looking for something in her bag. Suddenly she screamed in terror: the head of a snake reared up, hissing, out of her bag. Our guardian ran over with a stout stick, and with one blow at the back of its head he snapped the serpent in two. He pulled it out of the bag, a beautiful black snake, as big as my leg. I was paralyzed with fear, but the Yotear just tossed the snake over by the fire. "Hey you, cook, we'll eat this today, you won't have to go fishing. It'll save us some time, and we have lots to do. Line up, let's go!" We walked through the tall grass; every few meters our guardian tied a knot in the tops of grasses as tall as he was. "These will help us to find our way back." I protected my face from the grass with my *krâmar*.

The grass to be cut was very tough, and the earth was soft; the trick was not to pull up the roots. You cut several armfuls of grass and tied them in a bundle with a last handful. It wasn't easy: the grass was razor-edged and had to be grasped in a certain way close to the ground to avoid cutting the hands. We were skilled workers, veterans of the rice harvest, but even so, the palm of my left hand was torn, whereas my right hand was as hard as leather from holding the sickle. Shining through the scattered trees, the sun began to beat down on us. Despite all this, before the morning was over we had all finished the ten bundles our guardian had told each one of us to cut. "You're good workers, we've still got time to tie up five more bundles each before going back to eat." Another five bundles! And I had thought I would be able to gather some fruit—we hadn't eaten anything since yesterday.

It was long past midday when the last one of us announced that she had finished her fifteenth bundle. We all loaded our bundles on top of our heads and returned to camp, by which time it was about one-thirty. From the cooks we each received an iron plate with a green leaf on it, and on the leaf a ladleful of rice, rust-colored from the cooking water obtained at the pond. On a big iron platter, again on leaves so as to keep the dish as clean as possible and economize on water, were laid out eleven pieces of boiled snake. Its flesh was also rust-colored, but we were so hungry . . . and yet I just couldn't eat the snake. When I offered my piece to Vathana, she told me it made her want to vomit, so back it went to the cook. Our drinking water was kept in gasoline cans and was boiled beforehand, because the stagnant pool it came from was quite filthy. There were ponds two or three kilometers from our camp, but no one had permission to go there. Only the cook was allowed access to water, and our bodies were sticky with sweat after two days without washing, while from our dry throats came the rasping noises of people still half asleep.

"Today is your first day of work here, you may rest for one hour. But don't wander off!"

My aunt had spotted a jujube tree. "Come on, we'll treat ourselves to a few plums." We were allowed to go off behind a bush for a little privacy, so no one paid any attention when we left the camp. My aunt began to tie knots in the grass as she had seen the Yotear do in the morning, but as soon as the noises from the camp died away I became frightened and asked her to turn back. Besides, the guard had told us not to wander off.

"Don't be silly, come with me," my aunt said. "You see, I've marked our path." Perhaps I should have had confidence in her—she was eighteen years old, and courageous, but she was going too far from camp, and ran the risk of being killed. The guard had told us explicitly that he had colleagues in the forest. I didn't want to die with her, so I let her go off alone, while I went back to camp near our hut.

Time passed quickly and the whistle blew. We were all together. "Time to go to work!" Two girls would stay in the camp, to cook and see to the water supply. There should have been eight of us, but one was missing.

"Where is Met Sreï?"

"She went off alone."

"Fine, we'll wait for her."

Fifteen minutes went by. "Sit down in a circle around me, educational session." The guard explained at length to us that we must not do as Met Sreï had done. We had to be careful to be on time for work. People who didn't do things in an orderly fashion ended up in a plastic bag. The plastic bag was definitely his favorite bogeyman.

Obviously my Aunt Vathana had gotten lost. She had told me she wasn't afraid of tigers. "If I die, so what! Right now I'm going looking for fruit." It was true that for our parents death meant deliverance. It was the life we were leading now that was really hell.

"All right, back to work!" The seven of us left. Each one had to cut and tie her fifteen bundles of grass. I worked alone, off by myself, praying silently: "Divine Buddha, and all those whom I don't know and can't see, come help me." Then I remembered what Lota Proung, our hermit grand-uncle, had said to me one day: "Remember all your life, beloved little girl, when you're in trouble, call my name. I'll come help you." He had explained to me that heaven was the same the whole world over, and that although people gave him different names in different countries, there was only one Divine Being. "You mustn't say the Buddha is the only one. Each country has its protective spirits, and heaven is for everyone." So I was praying when suddenly, behind me, I felt the touch of a hand: it was Vathana.

"Where were you? The Yotear is furious with you."

"You know, I was frightened. I lost my knots. But I looked at the forest and the mountain up above, and I thought about our picnics. It was wonderful. Then I found the Yotear's knots."

"Fine, but now you should apologize to him. We wasted an hour because of you, and we still have to cut fifteen bundles."

I was all the more angry because I'd been so scared. But what would the guard say?

Vathana went off to find him, coming back in a few minutes. "You know, he's not really bad. He gave me a big lecture on the proper attitude toward work and the dangers of the forest. He'll overlook my escapade if I do my fifteen bundles."

I helped her as best I could to gather the required amount of grass; then the guard gave the signal to go back. We dropped off the bundles a certain distance from the camp, taking care to spread out the grass; the next day, when the sun had dried it, we would gather it into a big square haystack.

That evening I was happier than ever that Vathana was with me. The snake in her bag obsessed me: what if we had that same terrible visitor again!

The educational session distracted my thoughts somewhat: work, don't think, don't steal, forget the past, trust the Angkar, and our country will become rich. No more need to grow sugar cane or manioc, just rice, which will serve as barter for sugar and vegetables. And so on.

In the meantime, we were there to cut grass to make roofs for straw huts for people like us, who used to live in brick houses with tile roofs.

Ten days went by. We were going farther and farther away from our camp, which meant wasting time. The next day we were going to be doing the same work off to the south. "But be careful," our guard told us, "that side is much more dangerous than the northern side. Stay close together."

We always left before sunrise so as to arrive where we'd be working in daylight. The next morning we had hardly arrived when the Yotear ordered us to begin working, while he climbed a tall tree to attach a tuft of grass at the top to serve as our landmark. We could see the bundle twirling slowly around like a little weathervane. Suddenly our guard shouted: "Clap your hands, scream, make noise!" We did a few dance steps while shouting—but why? He climbed down the tree and motioned for us to follow him. Then we saw, lying down in the grass a few steps away from us, an old tiger with yellow and brown stripes, as big as an ox. "Don't go near him! He just got here and he lay down on his side when you started making noise. I saw him from up above." We could see that he was clearly in bad shape, with his ribs visible under his dirty fur and one of his hind paws swollen as big as a bag of rice. He breathed deeply two or three times, then panted softly. "You can go closer to him, he won't last long." The Yotear didn't finish him off, and we went up quite close to get a good look at him. "And now back to work!"

We'd become quite skilled, so the bundles of grass piled up, but then, as if in unspoken agreement, we moderated our pace: fifteen bundles were quite enough. If we worked too fast, he'd make us do twenty. We returned to camp at noon, but via a different path. When we came to a small clearing where the grass had been trampled, we were horrified to see, lying under the trees, five or six naked couples holding hands, their throats cut. Our guard, who walked at the head of our group, tossed back over his shoulder, "They got married without permission." How did he know, and why did he take us by this place? The bodies were still quite fresh, without the slightest trace of decomposition, which begins so quickly in our climate. He knew where he was leading us. "Rules must be obeyed."

We hadn't any appetite after seeing that sight, and after handing over our dishes to the cook, we were on our feet at our guard's signal—three blasts of the whistle. No rest period that day. We took the same path as we had in the morning.

Ten days like this went swiftly by. "Tomorrow you'll leave your sickles behind," he told us at our educational session on the tenth evening. "We'll be stacking the sheaves we left on the northern side."

We were back where we had first started working. The grass had begun to grow again, and was already halfway up our calves. We were supposed to gather the pile of bundles into one big haystack, checking to make sure the grass wasn't too moist and rotting on the inside of the sheaves. When all the sheaves were piled up, our guard gave the signal to leave while he lighted a cigarette. It was noon when we went back to camp, still guided by the knots made by our guard the first time we had come, because vegetation had already covered all trace of our previous passage.

We were getting ready to eat when suddenly one of us shouted, "Look, the woods are on fire!" The wind bore down on us, filled with smoke from the north. "Collect your things. We're going south."

Each of us got her poor bundle packed up, and in less than five minutes we were ready to go, but then it began to rain. This wasn't the first rain of the wet season; from time to time, since the end of the rice harvest in May, a fine rain had fallen, although nothing like the torrents of water in the rainy season, in October–November. We were at the end of June, at the beginning of what is called the little dry season, which is very hot. For the moment, that rain saved us: the wind changed, and the Yotear allowed us to take shelter in our huts. The cooks reheated the rice, and then we went to see what was left of our morning's work. It was a pile of ashes; the grass had been nice and dry. But was the fire an accident, or did the Yotear start it on purpose? Everyone wondered, but no one said anything. Under the ashes, the fire was still smoldering; the morning dew would put it out. We went back to camp.

Now we had to keep an eye on the grass gathered in the southern sector, which hadn't yet been piled into a haystack. After collecting our usual fifteen bundles for the afternoon, without much heart in our work, we returned to camp. Our guard announced at the evening meeting that he would be gone the next day, asking the authorities for a tractor to come get our harvest from the southern sector, even if the grass wasn't completely dry.

Next morning, assembly: "You will stay near the camp. I'll be back tomorrow morning at the latest." He seemed to hesitate a moment, then added, "I can't leave you alone with tigers and elephants around—I'll be back this evening."

The day was spent gathering wood and fruit close to camp, and tidying up the huts. At suppertime the Yotear returned with a tractor driven by another Yotear. "You're not going to eat now, we have to load the tractor first." So off we went to our piles of grass, and the trailer was soon loaded. We heard the guard tell the driver to come back in three days, which seemed to herald more work. For the moment, we returned to our cold supper.

After our meal, a meeting: "Starting tomorrow, we'll be working to the east of camp." But that side was more or less bare. Instead, the Yotear took us over to the western sector, where we had time to cut five or six bundles apiece before sunset. The next day it was back to the usual fifteen bundles in the morning, the same again for the afternoon. Later I understood why he hadn't had us begin our work in that region in the western sector: there was a Yotear camp nearby. One day we heard a woman screaming. Our guard just looked at us—we were petrified with fear. "Come on, back to work, don't waste time when it's none of your business."

Two days later, as we were going to an area of grassland that we hadn't yet harvested, we caught sight of a body under some bushes: it was a naked woman covered with jewelry. Close by was another woman, with two children about ten years old. No one said a word, and we pretended not to have seen anything: our leaders valued discretion. But our confidence in the guard was severely shaken. When would it be our turn to die?

We didn't go back to camp to eat; the Yotear told us to stay where we were while he went to get the cooks, who turned up shortly, carrying the cooking pots on their heads. Our meal of rice and dried fish was quickly finished. "You can go pick fruit, but don't wander off!"

So there we were, my aunt and I, picking everything within reach: wild lemons, almonds, jujubes, plums, mangoes. There were eggplants beneath the bushes. There was enough for everyone; if only they'd have let us have the run of the forest, we wouldn't have been dying of hunger. My aunt was in a good humor, humming and whistling while she collected her harvest.

Back to work. After cutting our fifteen bundles, we returned to the huts, where everyone spread out their fruit to dry. I was hoping to take back a good supply for my mother.

The days went by, and the month we were supposed to spend in that region was over. One evening, at our educational session, our guard told us, "We've finished here. Tomorrow I'm going to look at another place where there should be grass and not too much forest. Have your things ready and wait for me."

He went off the next day with his bicycle. We were very sad that he hadn't said anything about going back to Moung Russeï. Vathana and I prayed to heaven that the Yotear wouldn't find a new place for us to work. It had been forever since we'd left our families. What had happened to them, and what news had they had about us?

8   OUR GUARDIAN RETURNED with his bike toward noon, with the information that all the grasslands had been harvested by other groups, or else the grass had burned (it was very important to him that grass had burned in other areas, too, as it had in ours!). There was nothing for us to do but go home.

Home! I was already talking as if our lives were destined to be spent vegetating in the rice paddies. We were given a can of rice and a lump of sugar to eat on the way. We'd be leaving at dawn the next day.

Our route took us toward the plain, where the forest ended, after which we'd pick up the main road. Vathana had a plastic bag full of the fruit she had collected and to which she insisted on adding mine, to help me out. The bag hung from the end of a pole she carried on her shoulder, swaying as she walked. "You've got too much baggage," the Yotear told her. "There's no reason for you to be richer than the others. Throw some of it away." But since he didn't go over to her to make her obey his order, she shrugged it off and whispered in my ear, "Let him kill me, tell my mother if I die." She didn't seem to care, as if she knew that one day she would die because of the Yotears. It gave me the shivers.

"No, Auntie, you'll see your mother again."

"It's all the same to me if I die, but I'm tired of obeying their every wish. It's worse than slavery."

"Then let me carry my own fruit, it won't be so heavy."

"No, don't stop, I've got trouble enough trying to keep up."

There was no path, we just walked through the grass. "Don't fall behind," said our guard. "If we come to a place where we can cut grass on the way, you'll build some huts."

A wave of despair washed over me. I had thought we were going to see our families again! At the foot of the mountain, we came to a little road, well traveled, where we could walk more easily. Most of the girls had abandoned their sandals cut from pieces of automobile tire, which the sharp grasses had torn to pieces. The sandals had been requisitioned at the time of our departure from Moung Russeï, and their original owners were out of luck.

When we emerged from the forest, we found all that was left of a deserted house, just a roof swaying in the breeze on its twisted supports. Fifteen minutes to rest. The sun was already high in the sky. We went to quench our thirst at a nearby pool, and my aunt returned, dragging her feet, just as our guard gave the order to leave.

We hadn't traveled very far when the Yotear decided to go ahead on his bicycle. "If you follow this road you'll reach Highway 5. Try to be there by noon, a truck will come pick you up." We walked another kilometer or two, but we were all very tired. We noticed another empty house, with a mango tree growing in front of it. In unspoken agreement we stopped under the tree to wait for Vathana. Two or three girls climbed up to the house on its raised platform, hoping to find something to eat or drink. Suddenly there was a scream of terror: "A ghost!" They all hurtled pell-mell back down the ladder. In the house lay a skeleton, picked perfectly clean by the ants that lived in the anthills we could see under the house. Nobody wanted to linger there any longer, and we set out again.

Soon we began to hear the sound of automobile horns from time to time: the highway couldn't be far away. The sun was hot, however, and we were thirsty. Off to our left glimmered a small pond, and a few of the girls decided to get a drink of water. I saw another pond on the right; as soon as Vathana caught up with me we could get water, too. She arrived, shuffling slowly along. I was so thirsty my throat was on fire, and my temples were pounding. We decided to drink at the pond I had seen on the right.

My aunt put her plastic bag down by the roadside, and we made our way through the grass toward the water we had glimpsed from the road above. As we got closer to the water, however, we saw hands sticking up from the surface, and swollen corpses floating a bit farther on; severed heads and hands were piled up on the bank. The water was iridescent with oily stains. "Let's get away from here," said my aunt. "We can go see how things are on the other side of the road."

Not any better: there were dozens of corpses strewn every which way at the water's edge, and a stomach-turning stench. We all gathered on the road. "The Yotear did tell us we'd find water to drink on the way." Our thirst was too strong. We went back to the first pond, where the odor wasn't quite as bad. I gently pushed away the floating oily patches with my hand and scooped up a little water, which I drank while holding my nose.

Back on the road I tried to help my aunt carry her bag, but the ground was too uneven and she preferred to carry it alone. The closer we got to the highway, the more corpses there were: under every bush lay a body, and the air was pestilential. "When we get to Moung Russeï," my aunt said, "we'll have to drink only boiled water or we'll get cholera."

The road ended, and there again were a dozen fresh corpses, lying in grotesque positions of combat and resistance, their faces swollen by the sun. Several paths led up to the highway above us, and after passing a few more scattered bodies, we reached the edge of the road.

Our guard rejoined us with his bike. "There's no new place to work, you're to go straight back to your families."

No one dared remind him that he'd said something about a truck.

"Did you find water along the way?"

"Yes."

No comment. The first one to complain might have joined the unfortunate ones whose remains we'd seen.

We set out once more, the Yotear going ahead on his bike. He rode for about a kilometer, then stopped to wait for us. Our aching feet were burned by the hot tar surface, but our guard wouldn't let us stop. I stayed close to my aunt; we had slipped the bag of fruit onto the middle of a bamboo pole carried between the two of us, but since I was smaller than she was, most of the weight was on my shoulder.

How many kilometers did we walk that way? I couldn't say. At nightfall we arrived near the hospital at Moung Russeï, where we stopped for a moment, long enough to see a few nurses go by without paying attention to us. Dressed in white! With white caps! Why weren't they in black like everyone else? When we listened to them talk, we realized that they were Chinese.

Back on our feet again. Luckily the night sky was clear, and another half hour brought us to the bridge, where we found our Yotear waiting for us on the other side. "Boil your rice, you'll be sleeping in the house of the head comrade. Tomorrow we'll see how things go."

It was close to midnight, and I collapsed with fatigue near a staircase. In my dreams I was going to carry some fruit to my mother, but when they awakened us at dawn the next day it was only to tell us that we'd be staying put for a day of rest. Going to see our families was out of the question.

I went down to the river—I was finally going to take a bath! There were fifteen steps to descend, cut into the riverbank, and waiting for me at the bottom of the steps was my father.

"How did you get here, Pâ?"

"Last night I heard about a group of girls passing through, and I thought that perhaps our little girl might be among them. You've lost so much weight! And you're as dark as a peasant."

His worksite was not far from there, and he was not allowed to go out to the rice paddies where my mother worked. This prohibition was really superfluous, since he rarely finished his work threshing rice before midnight and the gong rang at six-thirty in the morning to return to work. It was about to ring any minute, as we talked.

"How is Mama? And Naroeun?"

"I think everything is all right now."

"I brought some dried fruits, I can leave you some."

"No, I don't eat much. Keep them for Mama and the kids."

"But I'm not supposed to see them."

"Then leave them with me this evening. There's a man who goes out to the rice fields now and then, he'll take them to Mama. You'd better hurry up and take your bath now; I have to go cut bamboo."

Coming back from my bath I found a man near the Mekong's house where we were staying who was boiling palm milk to get sugar syrup. After making sure we didn't have to do anything in particular that day, I told my aunt to call me if there was any need, and I returned to the sugar refiner. I offered to help him, which I did until noon, when he gave me a bowlful of palm sugar. "Put it aside," I told him. "My father will be back from work, perhaps he has cans to put it in." Three times during the noon hour I went to see if he was back. "You're looking for Rêth? You're Rêth's daughter? Oh, he'll be back."

And he did come back. Quickly I explained to him, "There's some palm syrup for you—do you have any cans?" He had three, but two had holes in them. He rolled them up in his *krâmar*, but there were still dribbles of sugar all down the steps to the river. I told him to put it all on the rice he was going to cook. He wasn't eating enough.

To us, the girls who came back from the mountain, they gave two ladlefuls of rice each day. At night I carried off a handful rolled up in a banana leaf and made the fifteen-minute walk from the Mekong's house to my father's camp.

9 DURING THE DAY we were kept busy husking rice in large earthenware jars; luckily I had learned how to handle a pestle from Won's wife in Tul Trieh. I took care not to finish before the others, but I always managed to filch a few meager handfuls, which I hid in a fold of my skirt.

On the third day I asked a Yotear woman who was in charge of us if I might visit my mother. "Oh, it's not worth going five kilometers, it would be a waste of time. After all, in two or three days they'll have finished working in the rice paddies and everyone will come back here."

Three days passed; no one came from the rice fields. During the ten days we had been there, however, a few girls had begun to have bouts of fever. Sometimes I, too, felt weak and shivery, but I didn't want to get sick because my mother was coming and I wanted to see her.

Soon, however, I was at the infirmary with the others. An old Yotear chief, about fifty years old, came to see us.

"What's going on here?" he asked the Mekong in charge. "These girls need to be looked after. You can let old women die, that's not important, but these girls have been promoted. I've come to tell you that they are now Daughters of Pol Pot, because of the exemplary work they accomplished up on the mountain. You must take good care of them for me. Do you have a resident medical orderly?"

"No."

"Send for one. And give these girls fruit every day."

That was very kind of him, but none of us had any desire to eat anything at all, we were too sick. We were becoming dehydrated, and there was blood in our stool. They gave us injections. My pulse was very weak. After four days, the first girl died, with huge boils on her back. My father was allowed to come see me for two minutes. "No longer than that, she has nurses to look after her. She doesn't need you. And anyhow, she doesn't belong to you anymore, she's a Daughter of Pol Pot." Father told me that everyone had come up from the rice fields, which were beginning to flood. He had to build a hut for the family.

After eight days, the important official from Battambang returned. From then on we sick girls wouldn't be left unattended at night. My fever worsened, and I saw the ceiling of the hospital going around and around over my head, rushing down to crush me.

A nurse named Sim was assigned to me around the clock. She slept on a mat next to me and gave me all the care possible, but didn't dare touch me with her hands—we must have been contagious. So she washed and dressed me with her feet.

When I regained consciousness, they told me I had to go back to my family. Weren't we Daughters of Pol Pot anymore? It was the fault of the girl who had died: since there were only nine of us now, they couldn't let us stay together. I was the last girl to go. The official came by one day shouting, "Since we can't keep all ten of them together, they must go home to their parents as soon as they can walk on their own."

It seems I wanted to leave right away but was unable to stand up, so I demanded to be taken to my mother. Orders had been given, however: "They'll leave when they can walk by themselves." After twenty-four hours I was able to go. Sim told me, "I'll never forget you." She gave me one more shot of vitamins and some extra medicine for my family. "If you're sick again, come see me; I'll swipe some medicine for you. But don't breathe a word!"

I dragged myself weakly along on wobbly legs, my head throbbing. All my companions had gone home to die with their relatives, but I didn't even know where my parents lived. A Mekong woman showed me the way. "You walk a little bit along Highway 5, then you come to a road on the right that will lead you to Vat Thmey. That's where they are."

I must have walked the whole day to cover the four or five kilometers to Vat Thmey. The first hut I came to wasn't finished yet, and there I saw my Uncle Vong. It was the "house" reserved for his family.

"Where are my parents?"

"It's the second straw hut after this one. I heard that you'd been sick, little girl, and I see you have changed a lot. Go on, you'll find your father working on a house for all of you."

I dragged myself along another few dozen meters, and there was Father, busy thatching what had to be our house. He ran to meet me, overjoyed at seeing me again.

"So, a Daughter of Pol Pot can still come and see us?"

"That's over, I'm not a Daughter of Pol Pot anymore. Where's Mama?"

"She's cutting rice near Vat Thmey."

"What? That's not finished yet?"

"No. Here on the high ground the harvest lasts until the first rains. And you, what're you doing?'

"Well, I'm back. I'm too sick to get well at the hospital."

"Sick? But they told me it was nothing, just a little bump."

"Oh, Pâ! All the Daughters of Pol Pot were sick, some of them died, and then they didn't want to keep us in the infirmary anymore. Daughters of Pol Pot aren't allowed to become sick, or they have to get well right away."

"If you don't have to work, my little girl, we'll take care of you here."

"But where are the new houses they promised us?"

"Well, that's just it. We're building them ourselves, as best we can. You know as well as I do that they're liars. The bamboo is too green here. Look, it's all eaten by insects. But come inside and rest."

This new straw hut was much smaller than the one at Tul Trieh, where we had had to sleep head to foot as it was. I went inside, put down my little bundle, and took out the medicines that I had hidden in a fold of my sarong around my waist. My clothes had become much too big for me, and had to be secured with a liana. Father looked at the handful of multicolored lozenges I spread out on a cloth.

"They're for you, Pâ, for your fever. It's Chinese medicine."

"We'll all use them," my father said. "Mama will take care of them, she'll be back at noon."

I poked my head out of the hut. "Here she is!" I didn't have the strength to run to meet her. My little brother and my three sisters arrived, too, from out of nowhere. It was a joyful reunion. "My little girl! I haven't seen you in so long!" Mother quickly busied herself about the hearth. Then, from underneath the house, the floor of which was raised about a meter from the ground, she brought out a plastic bag—the dried fruits I had sent to her two weeks before.

"And we kept these for you."

"Oh no, Mâ, they're for everyone, and first of all for you. And besides," I added, looking away so as not to reveal that I was lying, "I've eaten very well today."

It was true that since my departure I'd eaten much better than all of them, but on that particular day I was quite hungry. My brother and sisters gobbled up the handful of fruits Mother gave them, and I was pleased when Father, and then Mother, each gave me a piece of fruit from their share.

Then it was time for news about everyone, Mother first of all. She wasn't doing too well. Her right leg still hurt, and the entire right side of her body was stiff; she worked at husking the freshly cut rice. Naroeun was having fewer attacks of fever, and was drinking an infusion of tree flowers, quite bitter, but it was doing her good. My grandmother came every evening to massage my mother, without which help she wouldn't have been able to get around. Father worked in the hills above the village cutting bamboo, which was so badly needed that the Mekongs were distributing it to families while it was still green. In his free time he worked on the hut, and was now putting on the roof, which was made of little rollers braided from the grass we had cut in the mountains. My little brother, Vannah, and my sister Sithân chased the birds out of the rice fields, throwing little balls of earth attached to the point of a bamboo stalk. But Sitha, who was ten years old, went along with Naroeun to work on the construction of a dirt road between Vat Thmey and Vat Chas, a distance of two kilometers. They dredged mud from the canals in rush baskets and hoisted it up onto an embankment, which would form the road. My cousin Tôn Ny worked with them, but she was very busy at home because her mother was in the hospital at Vat Chas, having been sick for more than a month. At first her feet and legs were swollen, and then she got a carbuncle on her lower back. They found an ampoule of penicillin they could buy with some gold, but it wasn't enough; the carbuncle had to be lanced. Finally, two weeks before, she had given birth to a little girl. No one had noticed she was pregnant; she had kept it a secret from the Mekongs, but she couldn't hide it forever. She gave birth in the unfinished straw hut, helped by some neighbor women, and was then taken to the hospital without being able to bring her child with her. The little girl, called Nabella, was very pretty. Tôn Ny had looked after her, having been given permission to take three days off from work. She had fed the infant with rice water and a bit of sugar, which they had had to buy with gold. Since Tôn Ny had gone back to work, my cousin Sy Neang was looking after the baby during the day. He would put just a little bit of sugar in the end of the cloth the baby sucked on. After work, in the evening, Tôn Ny would run to the hospital to give her mother news about the baby and to comfort her a little. My other cousins were working like my brother and sisters, except for Sy Neang, who was still having trouble with his injured leg.

But rest hour was over . . . First my mother, then my father and the others went back to work.

Three

THE AGONY

1 AFTER MORE THAN six weeks of separation, I was back with my family, but we didn't get to see one another very much. The first afternoon of my return I spent resting. The next morning, everyone went off to their various occupations while I stayed at home. Toward the end of the morning a Mekong woman came by.

"Who are you? I haven't seen you here before."

"My name is Peuw. I'm the daughter of Met Rêth."

"Where's your father?"

"At work, as usual."

"And you, you're not working?"

"I've just come down from the mountain."

"Fine, you'll go to work tomorrow. You'll join the group under my supervision."

"It's just that I've been sick, and I'm not well yet."

"You must work, comrade daughter, you can't lie around at home. The others are building the road, you go with them. You can't always be sick. You're to go ask for a shovel and a basket."

"But I haven't had anything to eat today."

"Tomorrow you'll be working, you'll get your rice ration with your family."

"A can of rice?"

"Oh no, there's not much rice around here anymore. Each family gets its one can every day."

When my mother arrived, around noon, I told her that I'd been ordered to report to work the next day.

"Where will you be going?"

"To the road they're building."

"Me, I winnowed rice today. They're driving us crazy, changing our work around every day. Your father won't be coming home to eat; he's been sent to cut rushes for weaving baskets."

The next day I left for work. A fifteen-year-old girl assembled all the other girls and divided them into groups of ten. I was assigned to the same group as my two sisters. My cousin Tôn Ny belonged to another group, while my little brother and sister were under the command of a thirteen-year-old Mekong girl. I'd never seen so many "leaders." I heard the new names that had been given to Vannah and Sithân: Met Proh and Met Hân.

One section of workers went down into the canals with shovels to dredge up the mud. I was stationed near the pagoda, picking up the dry dirt with my hands and passing it in handfuls to the girl next to me, and on down the line from hand to hand until it reached the embankment, where it was used to thicken the mud. The pagoda was closed and empty. The statues of Buddha had been taken out and thrown into the four stagnant pools surrounding the pagoda. A few lotus leaves still floated in them, but not one flower or fruit. It was sad.

I reflected once more about what my father had told us at the beginning of our stay near Moung Russeï, when he was working in the rice fields with Uncle Vong. A neighbor had told my uncle about a dream he'd had, in which he heard a Buddha moaning in the mud of a pond: "Help me out of here, my friend!" The dreamer was very frightened, but during the day he went to find the place he had seen in the dream. My uncle agreed to go back there with him. I must mention that at that time, as well as later, it was dangerous to show any interest in religious matters, but many people were vaguely aware that my uncle was related to the royal family, and people of that class were considered to be guardians of national traditions, hence of religion. That was the reason this man had spoken to my uncle Mitia Mir.

They arrived at the spot in question, which was in fact a bend in the river that formed a big pond in the dry season. Searching, they found a large bronze Buddha lying on the bottom in the silt. Most of the Buddhas found that way in the water had been decapitated, but this one was intact. "Let's get it out of there," my uncle said, but the other man was too afraid and the bronze statue might well have weighed more than a hundred kilos.

My uncle went home and told the whole story to his wife. The undertaking was quite dangerous. If one was caught by a Khmer Rouge, the penalty was death—though if one had to die, one might as well risk it for something worthwhile.

My uncle set out alone during the Mekong's evening meal. A passerby whom he asked to help treated him as if he were crazy. So he prayed, "Lord Buddha, I'm alone and you're too heavy. But if you wish it, you can become light." He stretched his muscles, his feet sank into the slime, but the statue moved. He pushed it closer to the edge of the pond, and with a last effort hoisted it up onto the grassy bank. How did he do it? He told my father he felt as if he were carrying something like a big rock, no heavier than one or two bricks. Night had fallen. The next day, each of my uncle's children went, one after the other, to see the Buddha saved from drowning and set up at the water's edge, where it was invisible from the road. Shortly afterward we all left that area, and I don't know what happened to the statue, but my uncle always said to his children, "Only bodies may be killed. Take care to keep peace in your heart."

It was very hot working near the pagoda, but we weren't allowed to leave the line to draw a bit of water from one of the nearby ponds. The river nearby was the source of the water in the canals where we were working, but drink from it? Never. It was too dirty, and every morning there were corpses floating in it. People died for no reason. To reminisce about Phnom Penh, sing a song from before the revolution, speak of a good meal—that was enough to merit death. People were summoned to "work on the mountain" and no one ever saw them again.

2 ONE EVENING, after work, the Mekong couple in charge of our group of ten families arrived at our house. I had never had any contact with the man, whose name was Met Mao. Her I knew well, she was the one who sent me back to work: Met Rôn, a stout woman about thirty years old. They had come to inspect our kitchen utensils.

"You have how many pots? How many spoons? Knives? Rice? Everything must be given to the community."

"May I keep one pot to boil water when one of the children is sick?"

"All right. But donate all your rice. Families are forbidden to cook any in the straw huts. From now on we're all going to eat together."

She was obviously speaking about the workers' families, because the Mekongs, in their houses, had everything in common but lacked for nothing. Mother had hidden a pot with a small bag of rice among my clothes. If the Mekong woman looked through everything, we'd see what would happen. Perhaps she wouldn't look. Meanwhile, my little brother, Vannah, had been sent to my uncle's family to warn them about the search.

At our house, the woman started looking through our things while the man collected the pots. She wanted to take away our machete, but my father explained, "I use that in my work, cutting bamboo for the community."

"That's right, you may keep it for now."

They went to the thatch hut next door. We stayed quiet so as not to attract attention, but Met Rôn returned. "I haven't checked everything." She emptied out a bag of clean clothes into the dirt. Opening another bag, she found silver cups, the use of which escaped her, so she left them. In my bag she found the rice and the pot. When Mother tried to take back this pitiful treasure, the Mekong raised her hand against her; Naroeun grabbed her arm and received a stunning blow that sent her rolling on the ground. Father helped his daughter to get up but said nothing.

"I'll be back tomorrow. You've doubtless hidden other things. The Vong family is also hiding things."

In fact, there was a crowd in front of my uncle's hut. I heard people saying, "There will have to be an investigation of the Vong and Rêth families." Why us? I knew Mother had buried things in the earth under the hut. What would happen to us?

Educational session. From now on it was forbidden to light a fire within the houses. If anyone cooked any rice, they had to let the Mekong on duty know about it. Someone would come to take it away to give to the community. Starting the next day, meals would be taken in the big covered market in the center of the village, announced by a stroke of the gong— after work, of course.

So there was no meal planned for midday. When the gong sounded the following evening, everyone ran up empty-handed. Keep out! Children first! Those younger than five years old, that is. The very little ones could go in with their mothers. Vannah had to eat alone. It took a long time. The Mekong woman told us, "Tomorrow the mothers with very small children will come a half hour earlier."

Then came the stampede of adults and older children. Everyone rushed to find a place. The pots were sitting on the ground, each one surrounded by five flat plates. There were places for a hundred people, but everyone grabbed a plate and tried to fill it. Dust flew everywhere, people were trampled. My mother couldn't find a place, and she didn't dare get too close to the pushing and shoving because she could hardly stand up on her one good leg. When all the places had been claimed, she asked a Mekong woman if she could have a small pot to cook her rice outside.

She was given a little rice from the bottom of a can. We got to eat two or three spoonfuls of rather watery, badly cooked rice. The Yotears shouted to try to calm us all down, but it was useless. When the pots were empty, we couldn't leave: educational session. A few timid voices were raised: "Could we get some fresh air?"

The Mekong woman in charge decided, "You may go outside for fifteen minutes, but after that there'll be a meeting here, and one person per family must attend."

My father went to the meeting and reported back to us on what had been said: "You have eaten the last of the rice supply. Starting tomorrow, you'll be given corn. Don't forget, however, that all the pots belong to the community, and the plates, too. They are made of iron so that they can't be broken. Tomorrow there will be people on duty to keep order. Those who are disorderly will be put outside. Today we had planned for two ladlefuls of rice per person, but some didn't get any. You'll receive one ladleful per person tomorrow, so that there will be enough for everyone. You'll line up single file to come up to the main cooking pot, and you'll wait for the sound of the gong to start eating."

We had nothing but bitter, poorly cooked corn for a week. It wasn't very good, but we could carry away the leftovers. I scraped the bottom of a pot and took the remaining corn with me to dry in the sun during the day, something for us to nibble on.

The corn was very hard for us to digest, and the children had stomachaches. Mother decided to find some rice. She knew a family where the son was a Yotear, and Yotears could get rice whenever they wanted it. We could try offering them diamonds.

"What do you have to give me?" said the Yotear's mother.

"Diamonds."

"Diamonds? Fine, we'll say the same as at the Moung Russeï market: one can of rice for one diamond."

She thought they were cut glass. Mother explained the value of a diamond to no avail, the woman wasn't interested. "Now if you had some gold . . ."

Mother came back to the house to get a chain necklace with big links and returned once more with twelve cans of unhusked rice. We spent the evening husking it by hand. Above all, we had to avoid attracting attention. The next day, at the communal kitchen, Mother asked to borrow two pots. "My son is ill, I must make him an infusion, and I'll reheat his corn in the other pot." My mother always managed to persuade people with her sweetness.

In the evening there was no chance of having a fire, it would have been noticed right away. We waited for early morning. I kept watch on one side of the house, Naroeun on the other, while Father took care of the fire. Mother started cooking the rice as soon as the water began to boil—we had to work fast. We each had a ladleful of firm, clean rice to eat. Suddenly we were on the alert: the Mekong woman arrived to call people to work, as she did every morning, and there was still some rice in the pot. Vannah was lying in bed, so Mother stuck the pot under his coverlet and held it over his tummy. We hadn't had such a feast in a long time.

We couldn't take the same risk every day, but we did have a small reserve of rice buried under the house in a plastic bag.

That day the gong sounded before mealtime, which was most unusual—someone had to see what was happening. Mother, who always got home before the rest of us, hurried as best she could to the central marketplace, where she found the Mekong woman busy at a strange task: there was a big zinc cauldron on the ground, a few dozen bottles of orange juice, and a few of Coca-Cola. How did you divide that among five hundred people? Met Rôn had come up with a solution: she had a block of ice that she put in the bottom of the cauldron, followed by the contents of all the bottles, which she then mixed together.

"Sit down," she said, "while I fix this juice. How many people in your house, Met Nêm?"

"Seven."

"Seven? Let's look at the list. That's correct."

And she put seven spoonfuls of juice onto a flat plate. "Here's your family's share. Next!" Mother returned to the house with the plate.

An hour later the gong sounded again. This time I went. "There is also some milk tonight. It arrived too late for me to give it to you with the juice."

Would she have mixed it in with the juice and Coke? In any case, her milk wasn't any more appetizing: one can of concentrated milk mixed with a pail of unboiled water for ten families! We were allowed another seven spoonfuls of this drink. No other meal for that night, Mother told us. The swallow of orange juice and Coca-Cola went down without protest. As for the "milk," Mother diluted it a bit more before boiling it. And since the fire was already lit, she took advantage of the opportunity to cook a bit of rice: one good rice ball per person, eaten with dispatch. That was the end of our supplies.

3 WE HAD A NEW TASK the following day: fetching seed rice for the next planting. There were ten girls in our group on the Moung Russeï road, including my cousin Tôn Ny and, to my great surprise, someone I'd heard on the radio long ago, in a faraway life, the singer Honir Mir, who had been very popular in Phnom Penh. Our rule of conduct was quite strict: Never recognize anyone, never allude to the past. Someone must have recognized the singer later on, because she was tortured and died impaled on a bamboo.

We girls were each bringing back a basket of rice for the coming seed time. Several times during the journey I was seized with an irresistible need to go off alone behind a bush, and each time a few grains of rice slipped from my hand into the belt of my sarong. In three or four trips I was able to "harvest" four or five handfuls of rice.

The Mekong woman made an announcement: "We're waiting for a delivery of rice on the train. There will be no meal tomorrow. You must all make do with what you have."

The lack of food didn't excuse us from work. We had to take advantage of our rest periods to collect herbs, sweet water algae, and other edible leaves. Trade in gold flourished nicely, but I told my mother not to sacrifice our chain necklaces just yet. "I'll go see the Mekong in the infirmary where they took care of me." So I set off in the direction of the river, to the infirmary, and there I presented myself as a Daughter of Pol Pot. The Mekong couldn't shut the door in my face; she gave me a can from her own supplies of fine, sweet-smelling white rice, but she asked me not to tell anyone about it, so I hid the rice in my sarong. My mother fixed half the can for us and saved the other half for the following day, since we had to wait for the train to arrive.

The train didn't arrive—it was the fourth day of communal fasting, and many people didn't go to work. Met Rôn went through the houses to flush out the shirkers, then announced that we were all allowed to sow vegetables and corn around our huts. Many people would have time to starve to death before their gardens came to life.

The gong sounded three times in the evening, and everyone ran to the central marketplace. A handful of corn kernels was distributed. "Plant these near your houses. In two weeks you'll have shoots you can eat in a salad." It was true, our soil was quite fertile, and the sun made everything grow if it was given a little water. Father attacked the compact earth on one side of our hut with a pick. My sisters and I went looking for a marsh grass called *ptih*: the fleshy leaves shrank in cooking and they were somewhat bitter, but one had the impression for a few moments of having eaten something.

On the fifth day we all stayed in bed. The first Mekong woman to arrive was mine, the one who kept track of the girls. "What's going on? Why haven't you gone to work?" She was full of energy, that one. She had enough to eat.

"We haven't the strength to get up; we haven't eaten in five days."

"Work doesn't stop, you have to go."

She didn't insist, however, and continued her rounds. She wasn't the one who made the important decisions. Many people prayed for death. An atomic bomb over the entire country! Some died by swallowing the pits of a certain fruit, I don't know which one. You had to swallow seven pits. Several families "escaped" in this way. My mother also talked about us dying all together, but not by suicide: "The atomic bomb!"

Mekong Met Rôn arrived. "You have to go to work!"

"We're hungry," answered my mother. "We can't go to work."

"I'm going to sound assembly."

She went off and we heard the gong. Everyone dashed over hoping that the rice had arrived, but it turned out to be gasoline, which was also useful. We could dip cotton wicks in it to make little lights. The single measure of volume was still the condensed-milk can: one can of gas for ten families, which meant one spoonful per family. My father was the one who went to get it. To store the gas, he had a flask that had once contained penicillin. Since we had no shelves or cupboards, he hung it on the wall with a length of vine, out of Vannah's reach, but the gas must have corroded the rubber stopper, because one day the liquid flew out all over the roof. To keep the few drops that hadn't been lost, Father rolled a new stopper from paper.

After this distribution of gasoline, Mother decided to sacrifice another gold chain for a little rice. The first time it had been Naroeun's necklace, this time it was mine. One of the Mekongs from another group agreed to trade three cans of rice for the necklace. Father decided not to save any for later: three cans of rice for seven, when we used to have two cans per person! It wasn't luxury after all those days without eating. "Let's live one day at a time." We really didn't overeat at that meal.

While fetching water from the pond, I heard people say that an old couple had been found dead of hunger. They spoke of a child. One girl said that her mother had died. At my Uncle Vong's they were eating kapok sprouts they had grown near the house. Little Nabella, Aunt Nang's baby, was dead. Her tiny body had dried up, becoming as hard as wood. They buried her behind the pagoda at Vat Thmey. A few days later her mother came back from the hospital: the patients weren't being fed anymore, and they might as well go home to die with their families.

My mother tried again to find rice in exchange for a gold chain, but this time they offered her half a can, and it was really not enough. We set ourselves to hunting the little frogs that leaped around on the dung heaps. We skewered them on fine slivers of bamboo to broil them. According to legend, girls who eat frogs become witches; I was ready to eat even snakes. One day Mother caught a little lizard on the edge of our roof. We went fishing for tadpoles. In the trees we found tiny green locusts. Everything was fine for roasting.

A baby was dying over at our neighbor's; she was a very close neighbor, because we all shared the same roof, separated by a blanket hanging from the ceiling. The child's mother suggested to my mother that they eat the baby when it died. "If you don't denounce me, I'll give you half."

Fearing her vengeance, Mother promised not to say anything to anyone, but she didn't want to share. All day long we could hear the child's death rattle behind the blanket partition. During the afternoon I heard screams outside: "I'm hungry! Why don't they give us something to eat?" It was a woman, her hands tied behind her back, between two armed Yotears. "That's why I dug up a corpse."

Two other Mekongs followed behind her to keep a crowd from forming. I heard them talking.

"The dead were disappearing. At first we thought it was famished wolves who came to dig them up, but now we know it was you."

"I'm not the only one," said the woman.

"We know that. Who was with you?"

"Go find out yourselves."

The group stopped in front of the central market of our miserable collection of huts, and a Mekong woman left them to check our houses. She looked in all the pots, on the fire, and off in the corner. Intrigued and curious, I followed her . . . I wanted to see what human meat looked like. The Mekong seized the cooking pot of the arrested woman and showed the contents to everyone: it was red, neither more nor less red than beef. The fat looked like pork fat, but the smell was different. The Mekong didn't confiscate anyone else's cooking pot. The woman was led away, never to be seen again in the village.

Every morning Met Rôn visited the huts. "Has anyone died in your house?" Our neighbor's child had stopped breathing. No one was dead in our household, but we heard our neighbor answer, "No, my child is sick; I've covered him because he has a fever." The Mekong was satisfied with this. My mother went to see the neighbor.

"Did you see what they did to that woman yesterday?"

"I don't care, I'm too hungry. But if you denounce me, I'll say that you shared with me. You can always say that it's not true. In any case, you know about it, and that's the same thing."

She kept the little corpse for three days. The odor was beginning to upset us, so Mother informed the Mekong. Met Rôn scolded the mother for having kept her dead child, then carried off the tiny body for burial. The mother followed her and returned in an hour; she had become our enemy. I have never heard so many vulgar insults and threats in my whole life. "I'll sharpen bamboo slivers and stick them in your mouth and eyes!" My mother remained silent. The woman went behind the house and began to tear up the few pumpkin and cucumber vines I had planted, which were beginning to climb up the outside wall. The flowers had fallen, and the fruit had begun to form.

4 THE WEEKS WENT BY, and still no food was distributed. We continued to scour the countryside, looking for anything edible. Work had stopped, but the rains were coming: no communication would be possible between Vat Thmey and Vat Chas, except by boat. The hospital was at Vat Chas, however, and it was important to finish the road we had started building. The Mekongs insisted that we work. Those who went to work would get a ladleful of soup at the worksite. It had been more than two months since we'd been given any provisions. I went off to work with my older sister, leaving at six in the morning. At noon they gave us a serving of soup in which a few grains of rice floated. We went home to the family at five. The little ones were in a pitiful state. I went to the Mekong to beg for half a can of rice.

"All right, but you and your sister have to come back to work."

"Right away?"

"Of course, right away."

I went back to work. The girls formed a separate group: some dug with pickaxes, others gathered the dirt by hand into rush baskets and carried it to the top of the dike. I took a pickax, because it was less dangerous to wield one oneself than to risk getting hit by someone else's clumsy blow. There were many accidents, in fact, and those who swung their pickaxes unskillfully risked gashing their own shinbones and breaking their shoulder blades. Blood flowed, and the Yotears carried off the injured in cloth hammocks suspended from bamboo poles. There wasn't any moon that night, and although the Mekong had installed gasoline lamps every thirty meters, they provided only faint light, just enough to see where the dike was and to avoid digging it up. By the time we got home again, it was after eleven o'clock. Mother was waiting for us. "Are you hungry, my little ones?" "No, Mâ." It wasn't true. She had saved us a spoonful of rice, doubtless taken from her share. We ate it anyway, while she brushed away the mosquitoes and flies that glued themselves to our hair.

The three kilometers of road were finished in a month. Each one of us had to pile up a cubic meter of earth every day, or else we didn't get anything to eat.

The Mekong woman gathered us together. "The road is finished, but the work must go on: there's another road to build. You'll stay at the worksite so as not to lose any time. You'll be fed, you'll take turns sleeping, and work will go on day and night."

They did give us something to eat, but it was corn, which smelled bad and left a bitter taste in the mouth. Naroeun was no longer with me; she had been assigned to another group, along with Tôn Ny. Toward midnight I no longer had the strength to lift the pickax. It was very dark, there was just a crescent moon, and the Mekong with her lamp was far away. I huddled up next to the embankment, clutching my pickax to my chest, and fell asleep. In fact, we arranged things among ourselves: there were ten girls in the group, and five were always working while the others were sleeping. The Mekong had ten groups to keep an eye on; in the time it took her to make a complete tour, we had a chance to rest a little. Since it was quite dark, the Mekong blew her whistle three times when she arrived to get the group together. I woke up with a start, running and tripping over clods of earth or stones, getting up again with scraped knees. When I arrived, Met Rôn counted up. One girl was missing, the one who worked next to me. I had seen her get up at the sound of the whistle, but while we were running to join the other girls I had had enough to do to keep from breaking my leg on the uneven terrain. "We'll see what happened to her when daylight comes."

At sunrise the mother of the missing girl arrived, demanding to know where her daughter was. Who knows how she found out . . . The Mekong gathered us together.

"Did anyone sleep last night instead of working?"

"Of course not!"

"You? You? You?"

We all denied it vehemently, but a girl from the neighboring group told her that we all took turns sleeping. After that there was no point in denying it anymore, so we all admitted it. "Be careful, girls, that's how you end up in a plastic bag in the water. You mustn't lie. Don't do it again."

A week later, the day before a holiday (the anniversary of the first Khmer Rouge victories in September 1969), one of the Mekongs from Vat Thmey brought back the lost girl. She told us that she hadn't heard the whistle, but upon awakening had thought she saw a lamp burning faintly in the dark. She walked toward the light and found herself way out in the countryside at daybreak. Too tired to walk anymore, she went to sleep under a bush. Awakened by the noonday sun, she called for her mother and began walking again in the same direction as before, arriving at the village of Phnom Don Tri. She was taken to the head Mekong of the district, who arranged for her to be fed. She told her story, and the Mekong at Vat Thmey was told to come and get her. Because it was a holiday, she wasn't punished.

On that day we didn't have to work. In addition to the rice soup, each person was given a ladleful of dessert: a mixture of rice, palm sugar, and crushed coconut. Beforehand, however, we had to undergo a long educational session. For at least three hours the highest-ranking official of the city of Battambang told us how the Khmer Rouge came into Cambodia with the Viet Cong, going from victory to victory until they reached Phnom Penh.

I didn't listen to very much of it. The adults had to sit still without moving, but the children slipped in and out of line, and I found all sorts of good reasons for being elsewhere. The important thing was to be there at noon for the distribution of the rice with palm sugar.

After the holiday was over, we were all assembled to sow the rice. The next day the pots were retrieved from the huts; they had been given out to people during the long period when there were no provisions to distribute, but from now on we were eating in common again.

Everyone went out to the rice fields, where each worker received a ladleful of liquid as clear "as tears." We were becoming weaker and weaker, and one day no one went into the rice paddies. We didn't have the energy to get up.

Met Rôn arrived at our hut. "Why isn't Met Rêth at work?"

"I haven't the strength. I fell down from exhaustion yesterday. The others are saying the same thing—we can't work with nothing in our stomachs."

"And you, Met Peuw?"

"I'm too weak."

"You're stubborn. After all, no one in your family has died yet."

She was obviously displeased that our family was still intact. She didn't go to the other huts. We didn't go outside—there was nothing left to gather nearby, and there was no point in looking for water lilies or *ptih* because everything had been picked. My older sister and I stripped some leaves from trees. At noon I tried to get some rice at the communal kitchen, but Met Rôn intervened. "If you forget to work, your stomach can very well forget to eat." So I came home empty-handed, and my father decided to go see Met Rôn himself. Calmly, without raising his voice, he explained to her that we were all too weak to work, and that with only one ladle of hot water per day we weren't able to make an effort. Without answering, she turned her back on him. Then he insisted, and when she walked away, he followed her. I experienced the humiliation of this scene; I felt as though I were watching a dog following its master, and my heart was deeply wounded. Finally, the Mekong brutally slung a ladleful of rice into the bowl—that was all she gave us for the entire family.

My father returned slowly to the hut. Putting the bowl on the ground, he sat down and bowed his head in his hands. "That rice was given to me like a knife in the heart." He didn't say anything more; behind the blanket that separated us from the neighbor woman, hostile ears were listening. When we wanted to speak at our ease, we had to go outside.

"Eat," said Mother.

"No, I can't swallow anything."

"All right, then everyone gets a spoonful."

We were all sitting on the ground in a circle around that pitiful bowl. No one said anything. Finally my father raised his head. "No one's eating? Then let Vannah have it." My little brother didn't wait for a second invitation and swallowed the clear soup in a few gulps.

The next day we felt even weaker. Gold trading was forbidden by this time, but in any case, we didn't have the wherewithal anymore: all the family's gold necklaces had already been traded away. Ten days of boiled tree leaves had worn down our resistance. Father offered to go to work.

"And the children?" asked Met Rôn.

"They're too weak."

"They're big girls, and none of them has died yet."

So my father returned to the rice field. At noon he got his three ladlefuls of watery rice and started back to the house, but it was forbidden to leave the worksite unless you emptied your bowl back into the communal pot. So he stayed there, during the work break, without eating. In the evening he brought his portion of rice, which he had kept in his bowl, back to the house.

I saw him coming home, leaning on a bamboo cane. His face was black, devoured by the beard he was letting grow to economize on razor blades. My little brother ran to greet him and carried the bowl triumphantly home.

"We've eaten some leaves," Mama said, "that's enough for us. You worked."

"No, it's for you. Eat, children. I'm going to smoke."

For some time now, he had been rolling himself a sort of cigar from banana leaves. Two weeks went by like this. Then Naroeun and I decided to go to work, too. Father told the Mekong that we wanted to work. "Fine, let them come. There's work for everyone." So I went to work with my father and older sister. The first day it was chilly in the water and I shivered from cold and fright. Toward midmorning, my ears started humming, and I had dizzy spells. Father wasn't working near me. I asked the Mekong if I might rest for fifteen minutes.

"Yes, but if you go home, come back right away. If you're not back here in fifteen minutes, you won't get anything at noon. You don't come here just to get three servings of soup."

I lay down at the edge of the field, but after a few minutes a black mist appeared before my eyes and I asked to be allowed to go home. A companion led me by the hand, because I couldn't see a thing in front of me. In the evening my father and sister returned, each bringing their three ladlefuls of food to share with us. Father continued to fast. Once, he did ask for a spoonful from one of my little sisters and she snapped back, "You're on your own!"

The Mekongs were in fact teaching the children: "You're all equal. You don't need to worry about your parents. They must take care of you, and you don't owe them anything." The lesson had taken effect.

Two days later I made up my mind to return to work. My parents decided, with Naroeun's agreement, that I should have three ladlefuls all to myself to gain strength. I ate two and kept the third for breakfast the next day before work. To my great surprise, they gave us three ladlefuls not only at noon but again in the evening. We could eat the soup at noon and bring home the rest. A feast!

Now my father's body began to swell up; his face became quite round, and his feet were icy cold. He asked Met Rôn for a day of rest. "We don't have sick people in the village. You either work or hide yourself." Of course, we could always go off to die.

That evening he came home even more tired than usual, if that was possible. His whole body was swollen, and he could no longer urinate. "Don't pretend," the Mekong told him; "everyone's in the same boat." He didn't answer, but the next morning he was quite drowsy and didn't go to work. Mother went in his place so as to bring back something for the children to eat. As for me, I had eaten some kind of leaves that I didn't recognize, and now I had diarrhea—I couldn't possibly work. Father stayed in bed for part of the morning, dozing. He was very bloated, and his chest was congested. Toward late morning he dragged himself out of the hut to find some tiny palm roots, from which I prepared a decoction for him. I saw him fall down several times outside the hut, but my decoction seemed to help: he was able to urinate, and the swelling began to go down, except in his face and legs. He stayed in the hut for two days, suffering from violent diarrhea, and then decided to go back to work. Next it was Naroeun's turn to fall sick: her old fever had returned.

I felt too weak to go with Father. It took all my strength to fetch the water we used for washing and for the pitiful "cooking" we did with whatever came to hand.

Mother hadn't been able to bear up, so she stayed home. Once more, Father was the only one working. Always on the lookout for anything that might be edible, my sister Sitha had found some mushrooms and brought a basketful of them back to the hut. Everyone was overjoyed, but Mother, fortified by her eighteen months of peasant life, said that we should be careful. Since the mushrooms didn't show any traces of damage from birds' beaks, they might well be poisonous. Sitha didn't want to throw them out. "I'll ask the Mekong; she's from the country and would know better than you."

A few moments later she returned triumphantly. "They're edible. Met Rôn said everyone knows about them." Did she want to poison us? It wasn't possible! Mama cooked the mushrooms. "Who wants to taste them?" Vannah and Sithân weren't around, they were off looking for some edible grass. Sitha hesitated. Father didn't say anything. So I announced that I'd like some, and I thought they tasted good. "Fine, we'll share," said Mother, and we started eating heartily. But after her first mouthful, Mother shouted, "Stop! They're poisonous!" Everyone stopped eating. Suddenly my head hurt, while my stomach started to rumble. I went outside to vomit in front of the hut, and Sitha came out after me. Everyone had diarrhea. Mother ran to a neighbor who knew something about herbs. She told him her story in tears, and he came over to our hut, where he gave each of us a spoonful of rice with a piece of beeswax and a drop of honey. After a half hour I felt better. Mother gave us all *koktchaï** to warm us up, then bundled us under the bedcovers. I slept straight through until the next day, but when I woke up I was still sick. Father went to tell our story to Met Rôn, without making any reproaches. She seemed to soften her manner toward us and allowed my mother to get some rice from the community kitchen, where they gave her three cans. Mother cooked the rice and ground it into a fine paste.

For three days in a row, we were given five cans of rice, of which Mother managed to put aside six cans. At that point I was able to go back to work with Father and Naroeun. Father walked like an old man, leaning on his walking stick. I held his hand, and my sister took his arm on the other side, as he stumbled at almost every step. And now it was raining! The path was so slippery . . . The Mekong woman was there to greet us at the worksite. "It's not hot today, you won't be overwhelmed by the sun. The rain will give you strength, you won't need to think about eating." The oxcart was already there with its load of rice to be planted. Everyone was shivering in the wind; luckily, the rain was just a light drizzle. At noon, as usual, they gave us rice soup, but in the evening the rice was mixed with red corn, which made it rather bitter. When I went back to Father with the bowl to be taken home, I found him lying on the ground. He didn't say anything, but his face was so sad! He had fallen, and he couldn't manage to get up. He told me to get his allotment of rice. Naroeun arrived, and together we got our father back on his feet. I took his bowl to get his ration. Met Mao, Rôn's husband, was in charge of the distribution.

"Why doesn't Met Rêth come get his own portion?"

"He fell down and hurt himself."

Mao gave me Father's serving without saying anything. The three of us set out for home, but as we climbed up an embankment Father's foot slipped and he fell: the bowl spilled, and all the liquid was quickly absorbed by the mud.

When we arrived home, Father didn't want to eat, but we shared our portions with him. After eating, he wanted to clean himself up, so we accompanied him down to the river.

---

* In *koktchaï*, the skin is lubricated and then rubbed briskly with a copper token, always in a direction away from the head, which causes the skin to become bright red as the "bad" blood comes to the surface. The coin-shaped copper tokens used are family heirlooms, and the token Nêm uses here is the only object Molyda still possesses that once belonged to her mother.—Translator's note

5   THIS SINISTER and monotonous life continued for several days. One morning, when I woke up, it was already broad daylight. I heard a bird call three times—a bad sign. I wouldn't go to work that day.

"Where's Papa?"

"He left without you," answered my mother. "He didn't want to wake you."

I felt very tired. As I made my way down the outside stairs to go wash in the river, a fit of shaking seized me and I started vomiting: my intestines emptied themselves in one convulsion, as if the contents had been sucked out by a powerful force. I collapsed on the ground. A neighbor saw me, picked me up, and carried me home. My mother gave me *koktchaï*, and I lost consciousness.

Mother told me later that the neighbor, who was an herbalist, came to treat me with herbal decoctions. My nails had turned completely black. He performed insufflations over my entire body. The Mekong in charge of girls was informed of my illness and sent for the hammock that served as an ambulance. Two men ran with me in the closed hammock to the Moung Russeï hospital, where I had been taken care of as a Daughter of Pol Pot. My mother followed as best she could, but with her poor swollen legs she lagged far behind. A passing cyclist agreed to give her a ride to the hospital, where she found me and the porters in front of the hospital gate: the Mekong in charge of admittance had refused to let us in. Mother showed her the note given to her by my supervisor. "That's not my sector. Take the patient to her sector hospital!"

The two porters protested: "We've just run five miles, and anyway, there isn't any hospital at Vat Thmey. You can see for yourself that she's dying."

"You should have treated her before bringing her to the hospital."

"But we did treat her—it's because the treatment didn't work that we brought her here."

They laid me down in the vestibule. A nurse arrived with a syringe, but when she tried to draw some blood she couldn't find a vein until she had tried about ten times.

Another nurse gave me an injection of I don't know what, after which they tried to have me swallow some capsules, but my jaw was clamped shut and they couldn't get my mouth open. Then they gave me a perfusion of coconut milk, but I didn't regain consciousness.

Toward noon they gave up hope and decided to have me carried to the crematorium, where they laid me out on a bamboo bed covered with a woolen blanket. The superintendent of the crematorium lit a fire under the bed. When my mother began to cry, the man told her that I was dying of cholera in any case. "The fire will either cure her or finish her off."

All of a sudden I came to. "Where am I? Mâ, where are you?"

The blanket was beginning to burn, which is perhaps what woke me up; licked by flames, the feet of the bamboo bed were turning black.

"Bring the hammock," said the superintendent to his assistant. "We're putting her back in the ward."

"Mama, where am I?"

"At the hospital, they're fixing a bed for you."

Two men carried me in the hammock to the entrance of a room full of sick people lying on bamboo pallets, where they set me down. "Wait here a minute; someone just died and they'll be taking him away."

I looked into this dark room full of the dying, reeking of decay and excrement. "Mama, I'm going to throw up, I can't breathe!"

My mother tapped me gently on the back, and I vomited on the ground, but at the same moment my bowels gave way, flooding the hammock with diarrhea. When I went to sit down I saw the dead man whose place on the bamboo pallet I was to have: he was enormous, swollen to a monstrous size. They took away his body and laid my blanket over this "hospital bed." I couldn't breathe and thought I was going to faint. "Mama, I want to die right now." The stench was a horrible mixture of vomit, excrement, and carbolic acid. There were about fifty people in the room, spitting, vomiting, and moaning.

My mother held my head up for a moment; I couldn't speak anymore. She ran to look for a nurse and found one who was willing to go with her. Nâ Rin, the eighteen-year-old nurse, was touched by my mother's distress and gave me an injection and a perfusion of serum before returning to her duties elsewhere. A ten- or eleven-year-old girl arrived: she was the day nurse, and her orders were to give everyone an injection.

"But my daughter has already had her shot."

"It doesn't matter, I'm to give an injection to all the patients."

And she gave me the shot. Immediately I felt very ill: my heart beat rapidly, and I lost consciousness. My mother ran to find Nâ Rin, who hurried to my bedside. She poured some palm sugar in my mouth and massaged my legs. Mother showed her gratitude by calling Nâ Rin "kohn" (daughter).

That evening I was given another serum perfusion. Mother remained crouching at my bedside. Nâ Rin came by from time to time to take a look at me. I was having trouble breathing, and the fleas were keeping me awake.

That night must have been a terrible ordeal for my mother. The next morning she asked Nâ Rin if I couldn't be moved to another room where the patients weren't dying of cholera. Nâ Rin promised to do what she could as soon as a bed became free.

I hadn't eaten anything for two days; the atmosphere was too oppressive for me. Mother had had to force herself to swallow two spoonfuls of rice; yet she must have been hungry. And the rice was served with soy sauce!

The matron came by on her rounds; this was the first time we had seen her in the cholera ward. "Met Mi," she said to my mother, "you can't stay here, cholera is contagious. If you stay here and catch it, we won't take care of you." As if they took care of the other patients! Mother begged to be allowed to stay. "If I don't stay, she'll die. I want to take care of her myself." She didn't say what we all knew, which would have offended the health authorities—if anyone had dared to say that the patients were poorly taken care of, he or she would have disappeared that very night. As for the patients, they lay in their own excrement, no one came to bathe them. Aside from the ten-year-old nurse who appeared twice a day to give injections, there was no one around. Nâ Rin had grown fond of my mother and came by several times a day, always dashing in and out. She was accompanying the matron on her rounds, and when this woman silently turned her back on my mother's supplications, Nâ Rin motioned to her not to leave.

At night, in this filthy and nauseating place where the only sound was the moaning of the sick, just one paraffin lamp was lit. Two men passed through from time to time, piling up four or five corpses in a hammock, which they then carried out to a large open grave close by, a grave which remained open until it had been filled.

I became nauseated in the middle of the night, but I couldn't vomit anymore; my belly was as round as a balloon and felt as if it would explode. I could only lie there and moan. Mother, still crouching beside my pallet, told me she was going to see if Nâ Rin was on duty. After a little while she returned with some hot ashes she had taken from the crematorium, from which she made a compress for my whole body. I was finally able to vomit, my bowels moved, and I felt some relief, but Mother continued the compresses throughout the night while I slept.

Nâ Rin came by the next morning, saw that I was feeling better, and gave me half a spoonful of rice purée with a few drops of *niok mâm*, fish sauce. I managed to keep it down. Mother kept applying compresses of hot ashes throughout the day. "Courage, my little girl, tomorrow they're going to put you in with the ordinary sick people." The night was made difficult once more by the fleas that swarmed everywhere as soon as it was dark.

On my fourth day in the hospital, Nâ Rin came to get us. "The room where I want to put Met Peuw is not for incontinent patients," she told my mother, "so promise me you'll be there to clean up immediately. Promise me!" My mother would have promised anything to get me out of that hell. "If the other patients are bothered by the unpleasant odor, I'll have to bring Met Peuw back here."

My mother went to look at my new bed. A woman had just died there and Mother wanted to hide this from me, but I guessed anyway. "Don't worry, Mâ, I'm not afraid of ghosts anymore. You can tell me the truth." Leaning against each other, we walked to the bed, made of three planks fitted together, with a straw mattress. The room was well lit with electric light, and the sheets were clean. Nâ Rin hung two blankets around the bed to make a little alcove for me; it would be better if the other patients couldn't see me if Mother was going to clean up after me. The matron made her rounds, however, and objected.

"Take down those blankets!"

"May I hang up a mosquito net?"

I was having trouble breathing, and flies kept getting into my open mouth. The matron agreed to the mosquito net. Nâ Rin brought a small pot for me to use as a chamber pot. Mother washed me and tried to make me comfortable. My stomach was still rumbling. "Try to control yourself a little," my mother said, "or the other patients will complain." The violent noises from my abdomen did astonish my neighbors, yet no one said anything.

"My daughter isn't improving very much," Mother told Nâ Rin when she arrived to administer the injections.

"After her shot, Auntie, take your daughter outside under the trees. The weather is pleasant, and you'll both be more at ease."

She gave Mother a small shovel with which to bury my bowel movements: they were still quite liquid and scummy, and we had to think of the other patients. I spent the entire morning sitting on the trunk of a fallen tree, unable to control my bowels. At noon we returned to the ward for a plateful of good, hot rice, nice and thick. This went on for three days. At night I kept the pot under me all the time. There weren't any nurses, except if a patient called for a very long time. My mother slept

curled up at the foot of my bed. On the fourth day she, too, began to
have blood in her stool. "Kohn Sreï," she told me, "I'm not well." Nâ
Rin gave her *koktchaï* with gasoline rubdowns and a few medicines, even
though this was strictly forbidden; she wasn't allowed to treat those who
weren't officially hospitalized. She advised my mother to go home, since
as a nurse she herself risked being punished for not reporting my mother's
illness, while my mother might have been sent to join the patients suffering
from cholera.

Mother asked to be allowed to stay one more night. The compresses of
hot ashes had helped me, and I was able to sleep. In the morning Mother's
face was drawn, as if her ears were coming off and her nose were shrinking.

"Do you think you can stay by yourself, my child? I'd like to stay close
to you, but you can see that's impossible."

"Go home, Mama. It's because of me that you're sick."

She placed a bamboo stick near my bed so that I could go out alone
during the day. Nâ Rin promised to look after me. I cried when my
mother left. Nâ Rin led me out under the trees, where she gave me my
morning injection. There was still blood in my stool.

Suddenly she came running back. "We have to get you inside: there's
an inspection, you have to be in your bed." She helped me to go back,
but I felt so weak! It had been a long time since I'd prayed: "Lota Proung,
come help your granddaughter. Stop my diarrhea. Give me the strength
to leave this place."

The next day I asked Nâ Rin to let me leave; I felt that I was getting
better. "Not yet, Met Peuw. If you go home to your family, they'll send
you back to work. Wait a while longer." The following night was the first
one in a long time that my intestines didn't give me trouble. Nâ Rin told
me that she had been transferred: she had been assigned to the new hospital
at Vat Chas, less than two kilometers from Vat Thmey. She was to leave
at the end of the week, and then I wouldn't be able to stay on at Moung
Russeï. I waited for another two days, and my health continued to improve. Nâ Rin gave me a handful of pills that I tied up in a corner of my
krâmar. "These are for you and your mother. I'll come to see you when
I'm at Vat Chas."

 AND SO I LEFT, leaning on my stick, to travel the four or five kilometers to Vat Thmey. I was trembling all over, my ears were ringing, my legs were shaking. I prayed, "Lota Proung, help your granddaughter. I'm not getting very far."

Sitting half-conscious by the side of the road, I heard the creaking of wagon wheels: a cart drawn by two oxen was coming in my direction, headed toward Vat Thmey.

"Oh, comrade uncle, could you let me ride in your cart?"

"Where did you come from and where are you going?"

"I'm going to Vat Thmey, and I've just come from the hospital, but I'm so sick!"

"If you're so sick, why didn't you stay in the hospital? Did you run away?"

"No, I have a note written by the Mekong."

It was forbidden to go anywhere without an official paper. "Climb up!" I didn't have the strength. He grasped me under the arms and pulled me up onto the cart, where I settled myself as best I could, leaning my back against a bag of rice. The seed time wasn't over yet.

After an hour we came to the bridge. He continued along the road, while I dragged myself over the bridge and took a shortcut across the fields behind the house of the Mekong chief, where I had stayed as a Daughter of Pol Pot.

It was almost noon when I arrived within sight of our hut. My mother rushed to meet me; her sarong was filthy, and she smelled bad. "Why did you come back? There you had rice, here there isn't any." My father was happy to see me, and he helped Mother lay me down on a mat. The hut hadn't been cleaned, it reeked of misery. The neighbors were astonished at my return: everyone had thought I was dead. The Vong family arrived with my Aunt Nang, who had come back from the hospital. I could hardly recognize her—her entire body was swollen, and she was so different she frightened me. Visitors came and went until evening.

I rested for two more days, at which point the Mekong in charge of girls came to tell me I had to return to work. It was very hard, but it was the only way to get a portion of rice. I worked for two days, and then I learned that my Aunt Vathana was ill, with all the symptoms of cholera. My grandmother was alone with her, and she needed help. She sent word to the house that she needed someone to do *koktchaï*, but Mother was lying down, too weak to go, and Naroeun hadn't come home from work, so I gathered up my courage and set out. I found Vathana unconscious, bloated, as enormous as her older sister, my Aunt Nang. Her skin was completely black. I told my grandmother that she'd have to have the same treatment as I had had—the fire lighted under her bed—and I went to get the porters to carry my aunt in their hammock to the hospital. It was beginning to grow dark out. I held the hammock steady while my grandmother, weeping and exhausted, carried the lantern in front of the men. "Oh, Grandmother," I told her, "try to give her some courage!"

They put Vathana on top of the coals, but when the blanket began to burn, my grandmother ran up with a pail of water. "My little girl will be burned, I don't want that." The fire went out. Vathana remained lying on the ground at the entrance to a room full of dying people. A little nurse gave her an injection in each buttock. Vathana, still unconscious, beat her breast and groaned. We heard the death rattle . . . it was all over.

Through her tears, Grandmother asked that her daughter not be taken to the open grave right away because she would like her sisters to be able to see her. We'd had to alert the family, because no one had had any idea Vathana had been so ill. I embraced my aunt and kissed her face. She wasn't even twenty years old. "You're leaving for the true life ahead of me."

My cousin Tôn Ny arrived shortly afterward, followed two hours later by my mother, leaning on a stick. The hammock was taken away, and the body was thrown into the pit behind the hospital. This lack of respect for the dead was hard to bear—they were treated worse than dogs.

Grandmother wasn't able to withstand the shock and took to her bed when she got home. Nobody in the family went to see her; Father was working, and Naroeun, too. Mother was lying down between Sitha and me. Vannah was out hunting edible insects, while Sithân was off somewhere looking for wood for the house. A neighboring family came to tell us that Grandmother had been taken to the hospital, but when I tried to get up to go see her, someone told us she had already been thrown into the pit. We never saw her again. She died barely three days after her daughter. We were all so miserable. That night I began to vomit, and I woke up my mother to go outside with me: I was once again afraid of ghosts.

The symptoms of cholera had returned, and my parents decided to try the fire treatment again. Father lit three small piles of embers beneath a bamboo screen, on which I lay stretched out while my father and mother gave me *koktchaï*.

And then I had a dream. I'm on an embarkation pier in a seaport in the middle of a large crowd. A great ship arrives, decorated all over with red flags. At the bow of the boat is standing a kind of giant leaning on a pitchfork, with a machete in his hand. There's a big red scarf tied around his waist, and a red bandeau encircles his forehead. Behind him I can see many people shouting and singing, and the people on the quay seem happy, too. The man leans toward the quay and calls out, "All right, all of you, come on board!" Everyone takes their baggage and hurries toward the deck in a joyous rush, carrying me along with their momentum. When everyone is on board, the giant takes a list from his belt and calls the roll. Each person named answers "Present!" The giant rolls up his paper and asks: "Is everyone on the list?" I step forward and say: "My name wasn't called." "Then get off the boat!" I cling to my father's hand, I grab my mother's arm, I scream, I dance with rage—I don't want to leave them! The giant pushes me back, gently but firmly . . . and I find myself standing alone on the quay, watching the boat disappear.

I woke up in tears. Naroeun was giving me a massage while Mother took a breather. Father had gone off to work. My sister Sitha was pulling on Mother's sarong: "You could give me a massage, too!"

I slept on top of the embers, and Mother made me more compresses of hot ashes. My Aunt Nang came to see me, using a cane and leaning on the arm of her husband, Mitia Mir, who scolded her softly: "You can hardly walk and you want to visit this child."

"It's just that I love her very much, and she's already the child of a first miracle."

She leaned over my face.

"How are you, Sreï Peuw?"

"Who's there?"

"It's Mâ Mi" (Mama-Aunt, the family's name for her among ourselves).

She gave me a kiss and left immediately, doubtless needing to lie down and rest. Her movements were poorly coordinated, and she missed the last step of our stairs, falling over backward. My uncle had a lot of trouble helping her up. They went off together.

I was still very weak, but my body was more relaxed, and I remained lying down next to my mother. Naroeun was also lying down, and Sitha and Vannah, too. Father continued to work to bring home the three ladlefuls of rice soup for the entire family. He had been absent for a whole month, forced to go to Lake Sap for a fishing expedition three days' march from our village. They had had to cut a path through the forest. His strength was so depleted, however, that the Yotears had sent him home alone through the jungle, defenseless against the snakes and tigers. His feet had become terribly swollen. The first thing he had done when he returned was to shave off his heavy beard. He had brought back just a few little fish, at the risk of his life. And now, this evening, after bringing home his bowl of soup, he didn't want to eat and smoked his rolled banana leaf instead.

"But tonight," he said, "there's an ear of corn behind the house that's ready to eat, as a celebration of my daughter's return to health."

"Why don't you eat it yourself," my mother said, "you need to gain strength."

"No, I offer it to my daughter."

He boiled the ear of corn and offered it to me, but I didn't want any, and said that it should be divided into seven shares. "No," said my father, "it's for you."

I tried to nibble on it, but I was too weak, so Father mashed the corn into a purée and had me eat it. When I told him at least to divide the bowl of rice into six parts, because I'd had enough to eat, he did agree to eat the half spoonful of rice coming to him in an equal division of portions. This is the last image I have kept of my father.

As usual, the next morning at five o'clock, before the crowing of the Mekongs' rooster, he took his staff and his bowl, and without saying goodbye to anyone, he set out for the rice fields.

At sunrise Mother woke up and asked me, "Did you see Papa leave?"

"I think he did leave, his cane isn't here."

"He left without saying anything?"

Early in the afternoon Sy Neang, who worked behind the hospital in Vat Chas, came running up. "Mâ Mi, Mâ Mi, Pâ Ohm [uncle] is lying under the trees in front of the hospital!"

"What did you say?"

"I saw him—his face is covered with mud!"

At the same moment my Uncle Vong arrived. "Sister, come and see, my wife is dead." Sy Neang ran off to his family's hut, and Tôn Ny, in tears, came out to meet him.

My mother ran first to her sister, two huts away from ours. Then I saw her pass by again in the opposite direction, going to join her husband two kilometers away. I was unable to move. Mother retraced her steps, however, to speak to me: "You stay with Vannah and Sithân, I'm going with Naroeun and Sitha to join Papa." Naroeun took her arm; I knew she'd have to stop and rest five or six times before reaching Vat Chas.

Hours went by. Night fell, and I wondered if Mother had been able to reach Vat Chas, and in what state she had found my poor father. There was nothing to eat in the hut, but I didn't think about that too much. I asked Vannah to come and lie down next to me, but he couldn't keep still. It had begun to rain, and the air was growing chilly. Lying in our house, I smelled something like the odor of the leaves Father used to smoke instead of eating with us, and I wondered if perhaps he was coming home. Then Vannah started shouting, "Come, Pâ, come here!" And he held out his arms as if to kiss someone. I held Vannah back. "Calm down, Vannah! Stay in bed, go to sleep!" Then Vannah cried, "But I saw Papa— Oh, he's going now!" I would have liked to see him, too, but I didn't. It was very late when Mama returned, alone. She was drenched with rain, and tears ran down her face.

"Papa is dead."

"Oh, Mâ, how did it happen?"

"His face was covered with dried mud, it was very hard to get that mask off him. I found some water and washed away the mud, gently stroking his face. He was groaning softly. He wanted to tell me something, but I couldn't understand him."

She had wiped off his face, cleaning the mud out of his mouth and nostrils. For more than a quarter of an hour she had whispered prayers into his ear. Then she heard the death rattle, and it was the end. The gravediggers arrived almost immediately, and took him away behind the Vat Chas hospital, where they throw all the bodies.

"When did it happen, Mâ?"

"Just when it started to rain."

That was the moment when I smelled the burning leaves and when Vannah sat up to embrace his father. Mother told us what had happened. Father's fellow workers had noticed his absence when the rice was being distributed around noon, and they found him lying face down in the mud of the rice field. Three or four of them carried him to a spot under the trees near the hospital, but since they didn't want to miss the distribution of the three ladlefuls of rice, they just left him there without doing anything else for him. That's where Sy Neang found him, and he ran to let us know.

It was the ninth of October 1976, eighteen months after we left Phnom Penh. My Aunt Nang died the same day, forty-eight hours after coming to see me. She lay all night long surrounded by her children. It was raining very hard. Her husband asked some neighbors to help him bury her, but they answered, "We'll see, after the rain." Finally, a man related to the Mekongs, Met Mân (who was later to be of great help to us), agreed to help Mitia Mir bury my aunt in the Vat Thmey cemetery, which was already quite full. The village was losing its people with each passing day.

7 THAT NIGHT Robona, Tôn Ny's six-year-old sister, had a dream in which she saw someone very like an angel who carried an armful of five lotus blossoms and spoke to her. "Don't be afraid, my little girl, I'm keeping your mama with me. But you shall go on living." In fact, one would have said that all the children were hurrying to join their mother. The first to die were the two five-year-old twins, three days apart, lying silently on a bamboo pallet; then two other brothers, Youthevy and Vouthinouk, nine and seven years old, the first at the hospital, the second when he came home from the hospital. Kosol, the four-year-old, and Robona died three months later, on the same day. All of them starved to death. After they died, Mitia Mir dreamed that he saw four columns still standing from a house in ruins. I thought that they were my uncle and his three surviving children, but now I know that the fourth column was myself. My uncle often said to Tôn Ny, "We live, we die, we live, we die; it's the law of life. Watch over your sister, she's young." Born in 1973, the little girl was three years old when her mother died. From that moment on we called her Sreï Peu, "the youngest girl."

At our house, no one had the strength to work, so we were given no more food. Those who could walk went out to look for leaves. Naroeun had fallen while going to get water to bathe me, and Sitha, who was also sick, refused to assist her. It was Sithân, ten years old, who went to help. After that, Sithân went to look for wood, but since there wasn't any more simply lying around on the ground, she had to break off or tear up young bamboo down by the riverside, where we didn't like to go because anonymous corpses were still often found floating there. Her bare feet picked their way carefully between the bevel-edged stumps of bamboo sticking out of the ground. She didn't have a machete, but she broke off the most fragile shoots, the ones her little hands could manage. There was a young bamboo, however, bigger than the others, and yet it didn't seem deeply rooted at all. Sithân strained to pull it up, and when the roots suddenly let go she fell over backward, impaled on a bamboo as sharp as an arrow. She called for help, but there was no one nearby: the remaining inhabitants of the village were busy planting rice seedlings.

Mother had just finished bathing me, and now she was washing my rags. "You must be clean and neat, my daughter. When you're well again, you can take care of us." Suddenly she became worried. "What's taking Sithân so long?" She went out in front of the hut and thought she heard someone calling down by the river. Hurrying there as fast as she could on her poor swollen legs, she found her little child unconscious among the bamboo and dragged her back to the house as best she could. Sithân's legs were covered with blood, and her back was torn by the bamboo shards. Mother boiled some of the water that Sithân had fetched barely an hour earlier, and after adding salt to it, she forced herself to wash her child's wounds. Sithân regained consciousness at the touch of the salt water and began to scream. Mama put a compress on the wound between her little thighs, and the child fell asleep.

Met Rôn chose this moment, at noon, to make an inspection. "Another sick person? So there's nobody left to work in this family? Everyone must work or go to the hospital."

"Let us stay here today. We'll leave tomorrow morning."

"All right. But you can't take any of your things. Nothing!"

"One pot," my mother asked her, "just one pot."

"The pot's okay, but nothing else! And I don't want to see anyone in this house anymore."

The next morning we drank a little hot water and dragged ourselves toward the Vat Chas hospital. My mother, leaning on a staff, supported Sithân, who walked with tiny steps, moaning softly. I moved along all bent over, unable to hold my head up, with Vannah clinging to my sarong. Sitha walked alone ahead of us. Naroeun, her body swollen to enormous size, had not been able to get up from her bed. Under her waist Mama had slipped a little cloth bag containing all our remaining valuables: a few small leaves of pure gold, some diamonds, and some medicine. She was afraid they would be taken from us at the hospital under the pretext of washing and dressing us.

Having left at dawn, we arrived at the hospital, less than two kilometers from the village, at the end of the afternoon. They were distributing the evening supper: a ladleful of fresh rice per person! Our digestive systems, no longer accustomed to such abundance, gave us all stomachaches.

They installed us on the floor in a corner of the main hall. Two days went by, during which no one took any notice of us, except to give us our ration of rice, which was freshly harvested, since the Yotears didn't take into account the customary rhythms of seed time, planting out, and harvest. As soon as a rice field had been harvested, the earth was turned over and resown. It was now December, and in the lowlands, near the river, they were transplanting seedlings, but in the highlands, above Vat Chas hospital, fields were being harvested. At noon, on the third day of our "hospitalization," we were given our ladleful of rice and a little salted fish. We had eaten and were dozing when a voice called out, "Are there any people here from Met Rôn's group?" A woman from outside stuck her head through the open window: "Rêth-Nêm's house is on fire!"

To my great amazement, I saw my mother burst out laughing, clap her hands, and start to hum a little song. "But, Mama, pay attention! Listen to me! Naroeun is burning!" Then my mother looked at me, sat up, plunged her face into her hands, and burst into tears. What could we do? A hut like ours burned in a few minutes; we had seen some flame up like torches, while those inside had just enough time to dash out into the open, without saving any possessions. Naroeun, who wasn't able to move, may not even have had enough time to realize that the hut was burning. I put my arm around my mother's shoulders. "Mama, it's me, your daughter, listen to me!" She didn't know who I was, and started laughing hysterically. I pinched her earlobe very hard, and she came to her senses.

Embracing me, she asked, "Where is your sister?"

"Mama, she burned to death!"

Mother started weeping again, but softly this time. The woman in charge of the hospital came over—it was Nâ Rin. She hadn't even known that we had been sent to the hospital. She tried to console my mother, who told her, "You understand, she was my oldest girl. She was trapped in the fire!"

At nightfall, around six o'clock, I dragged myself out under the trees, and whom did I see? A few steps away from me, leaning on a staff, catching her breath for a minute under the trees—Naroeun! Her right leg was completely scorched, the left leg of her trousers was in shreds, her back was horribly cooked, and her face was as flayed as a skinned rabbit. Supporting each other, we went into the hall where Mother was resting. "Mama, Mama, here's Naroeun!" Mama was overcome with emotion; her hands trembled as she helped her oldest daughter sit down next to her, where I had been sitting. Mama wanted to take off Naroeun's clothes, but the trousers, made of thick nylon, had melted into the flesh. "Oh, Mâ! It burns me inside, and I'm cold!" My mother had nothing with which to clean her wounds, and the nurses wouldn't be back until the next morning, so she sent me to get Nâ Rin. I didn't know where to look for her, but I tried over by the nurses' quarters, and there I ran into Sim, who had taken care of me at Moung Russeï.

"What are you doing here, Met Peuw? Are you back in the hospital again?"

"My whole family is here. We need some help right away for my sister; she escaped from a fire but she's badly burned."

Sim took charge of Naroeun and had her carried to the pagoda, where there was a special section for injured patients. She laid her down on the flagstones and painted her with Mercurochrome. When I returned to my mother, she said, "Naroeun is too far away from us—if she dies, she'll die all alone. She must be brought back close to us." I asked Nâ Rin about this, and she allowed my sister to stay with us, but only for one night.

My mother helped us bring her back, and Naroeun started to tell her story, but first Mother asked her about our little stash of gold and medicine.

"Oh, Mâ, I didn't see anything in the fire, I didn't know which direction was which, I don't even know how or where I got out."

Mother didn't say anything. All our resources for the future had melted away. There, in the hospital, they were of no use—all forms of barter were forbidden, and people didn't need to worry about getting something to eat—but once we left the hospital, what would become of us?

Bit by bit, we learned what had happened. Naroeun had stayed alone in the hut for two days. Then Met Rôn came to rummage through the house, looking through our baggage. My sister protested, "Why didn't you search through everything in front of my mother?" The Mekong slapped her, telling her to shut up.

She emptied out all our poor bundles, looked under the mats, poked around between the straw partitions; but she didn't think to search under the house, and went off without taking anything.

The next day, around noon, Naroeun was dozing when the hut caught on fire. Unable to move, she called for help, but when no one came she managed to drag herself to the threshold and roll down the stairs. It took her hours to reach the hospital. A neighbor woman said that she had seen Met Rôn throw a cigarette butt into the house. I find it hard to believe that she did it deliberately . . . and yet someone had told her, "That was the only family left in your group."

Naroeun was lying between me and Mother; she was having trouble breathing, and constantly complained of feeling cold. Her burns were beginning to suppurate. We spent the night dozing fitfully.

The next morning an important Mekong official made the rounds to separate the more seriously ill patients from those who had some hope of recovery. Mother begged him to let her daughter stay, but he ordered Naroeun moved to a bamboo pallet outside under a tree. They carried her out in a hammock, which reminded me of the hammock bearers who carried out the dead. Naroeun was still alive, however, and Mother watched by her side, while I took care of Vannah, who couldn't be left alone. His body was very swollen, and toward the end of the afternoon he moaned softly, calling for his father. I went to get Mother. Outside, there was a heavy mist, and Naroeun was shaking with cold. Mother put a bottle of hot water on her stomach and beneath her feet; then she went to her son. "Mâ, I'm hungry, I'd like some sugar, some sweetened rice." Mother gave him a mouthful of rice, but he wasn't able to swallow it. "Mâ, my tummy hurts, I want to go with Papa." His little belly was rock-hard, and his penis was swollen like a balloon so that he couldn't urinate anymore. He talked constantly.

"Be quiet, little one. Don't talk, you're wearing yourself out."

"I have to talk because I'm going to leave you."

"Where are you going, Vannah?"

"I'm going to be reunited with Loch Put" (this is the name children give to Buddha). "I'm going to see Pâ. I love you, too, Mâ" (and he called her by the name given to Buddha's mother: Kyak Mâ Daï). "I also love my sisters, but I can't stay, I'm too hungry . . . Mâ, I'm going to leave, please forgive me. I'm going to make the voyage with Papa. You, too, Bang Peuw" (that was his name for me), "please forgive me: don't remember me unkindly . . ."

"Why do you say that, little brother?"

"I'm hungry, Bang Peuw. But it'll be over soon. Pâ told me that he would come get me."

The night wore on in this manner, in somewhat incoherent dialogue. Sitha was sleeping quietly, while Sithân moaned softly; she was also very swollen. Mother had changed the dressing between Sithân's thighs, and now she moved back and forth between my little brother's bedside and Naroeun's pallet under the trees.

At around five in the morning, Vannah called out, "Papa! Papa!" Mother was next to him, and murmured a prayer in his ear. Vannah had stopped moving. Weeping, my mother covered his face so that no one could see he was dead; that way we'd still get his portion of rice.

"Let's go see Naroeun," she said, "she needs us more."

Just at that moment, Naroeun called out. "Mâ, I'm cold, I'm burning up inside, I'm hungry."

"Your brother's dead, Naroeun."

"Yes, he's dead."

She clutched my hand. "Bring me a bottle of hot water!" But there weren't any—an orderly had confiscated the two bottles we had.

Mother warmed two bricks for Naroeun. I was still close by her side. Her lips were dry, but in the pale light of dawn I saw a froth well out of her mouth. I called my mother, who ran over. "Do you hear me, darling?" I squeezed Naroeun's hand. "Can you hear me, sister?" Mother told me softly, "Let her go, she's dead."

It was time for the daily injection, but I didn't want any more shots; my arm was red all over. Every morning there were screams of pain and protestation. Mother went alone to get her shot. As for me, as I did every day, I hid behind the hospital and returned only when the rice was being distributed. It was seven in the morning. We decided to bury Naroeun as soon as we had gotten our rice, but the distribution took longer than usual and when we arrived under the trees, Naroeun's body was gone: the orderlies had already taken it to the open grave.

When we followed her there, we saw them disentangle her from two other corpses that had been piled on top of her in the hammock. We weren't allowed to approach her body. Then we sat for a while behind the hospital, and I told my mother about the dream I had had after Grandmother died, with the big boat carrying off a joyous crowd of people, from which I was excluded.

"What can that mean, Mama? I'm afraid of that threatening man." My mother was thoughtful but didn't answer me. I repeated my question several times. Finally, she said, "Keep peace in your heart, my child."

We went back inside the hospital, where Mother took care of Sitha and Sithân. A woman in a neighboring bed must have seen that she wasn't looking after Vannah and informed on us, because at noon, when the rice was being given out, a kitchen worker named Met Rî came up to us, ladle in hand, and shouted, "Met Yeï [Grandmother], you mustn't lie, you mustn't hide anything. Why didn't you say your son had died?" And she made as if to hit my mother with the ladle. "My daughter," Mother replied to her, "please. I hope your children are never hungry. Look at my children dying of hunger. We needed that extra portion today." The other woman, astounded that a patient had dared to answer back, went away grumbling, but two men came and took away my little brother. They threw him on the pile of corpses building up in the hammocks in front of the door. We didn't dare move for fear of missing the noon rice distribution.

That evening, it was Sithân's turn to talk constantly. Another night to keep vigil. At dawn, she spoke to us, "Mâ, forgive me. I was unkind when I wouldn't give you and Papa some of my food."

"You were hungry, my child, I understand."

"Bang Peuw, please forgive me."

"Sister, you know I forgave you long ago."

She stared fixedly at the ceiling, as if looking for something else to say. Mother called to her, "My dear, my dear child!" but she was past hearing.

Out of our entire family, there were three left. "Mother, I want to die too."

"You'll die when your time comes, my child. I must take care of you until the end. If I die before you now, my crossing will be more difficult."

8 SITHA, although still puffy and swollen, was the healthiest of us three. The hospital food had given her some strength, and she could walk without too much difficulty, so Mother told her to go see what was left of the house at Vat Thmey. Perhaps she'd be able to find a few of the valuables that had been left with Naroeun. There was also some silver plate buried under the house, and it was possible that people hadn't taken everything.

Sitha was quite willing to go. "But you know, Mama, if I find something, I'm keeping it for myself. I want to have something to live on later." She was now twelve years old, and the ideas of equality and independence from one's parents that the Yotears had stuffed into her head had found fertile ground in her heart. We watched her leave, carrying a staff in her hand and dragging her feet, because she couldn't look too able-bodied if she wanted to avoid conscription for work.

She was back again before the midday rice distribution, and she had found something! Arriving at the site of the fire, she saw people searching through the ashes with hooks, picking up little things and putting them in pails. Since she knew precisely where Naroeun had been lying, however, Sitha was able to go right to the spot, where she found a diamond ring of Mama's, two gold earrings that had been Naroeun's, a diamond pendant and two bracelets with stones, a few small uncut diamonds, and a crumpled plaquette of gold. Without letting anyone see what she had found, she returned to the hospital as quickly as possible. Mother asked her to show us what she'd brought. "No, they're mine." "I just want to see," said Mother, but Sitha refused. Hunger had really made her mean.

Accompanied by a nurse, a high-ranking Mekong official came to make an important announcement at the hospital that afternoon. "You know that it's forbidden to engage in any kind of commerce within the hospital, but it seems that there is trading going on. We're going to search everyone's personal effects. Be prepared." He went off to make his announcement in the other rooms, while nurses and Mekongs began to search people. Sitha became frightened. "What should we do? Come behind the hospital with me," she said, "we'll share the things." I was willing, but since she offered me only Naroeun's earrings, I told her it was out of the question. The search continued. I whispered to Sitha, "If you keep those valuables, they'll kill you for sure. Give them to me, I'll hide them." She was really frightened and slipped me the little bag she had made out of a sheet of plastic. Since everyone knew I had diarrhea, they allowed me to go outside under the trees. Innocently crouching near a brick half buried in the dirt, I removed it and slipped the packet into the hole. The search revealed nothing concealed by us.

The next day, after long discussion with Sitha, I convinced her that I should turn the valuables over to Mother, who took the bag without opening it, to avoid the curiosity of our neighbors, and attached it to the waistband of her panties with a safety pin. Perhaps someone caught a glimpse of our stratagem . . . In any case, after the midday rice distribution, Met Rî arrived accompanied by a young Yotear, and all three of us were thoroughly searched. The Yotear found the small bag at Mother's waist; he tied her arms behind her back and pushed her in front of him without a word. Mama had just enough time to turn toward me and say, "Daughter, you must watch over Sitha, you're the older sister. Don't wait for me . . ."

The Yotear boy, as proud as if he had just conquered an entire country, pushed my mother with his bayonet. I watched them disappear in the direction of Vat Thmey. I prayed and I prayed. My mother killed with a pickax? No, it wasn't possible. I stayed at the window all afternoon, waiting for her return. She had to come back. God in heaven, send her back.

And she did come back! Toward evening I saw her appear in the sheet she had removed from Naroeun and from which she had made herself a sarong. I went outside to meet her: I wasn't able to run, but my heart flew out to her. We fell into each other's arms.

"Come and eat, Mâ. I saved my portion of rice."

"No, my child, I'll go ask for my portion."

She went to find Nâ Rin, but even she couldn't change the kitchen schedule. Moreover, Nâ Rin hadn't heard anything about what had happened, and it was forbidden to talk about such things.

Night had fallen. Lying next to my mother, I listened to the story she recited to me in a monotone, her voice cracking with fatigue. The boy had taken her to the Yotear house, where she was brought before the Yotear leader. First she had to ask forgiveness for having been arrested: a waste of time, but they were running the show. Then Mother told them about the fire, her eldest daughter's death, the hidden gold. The leader said nothing and motioned to the Yotear to take her away.

Armed with a gun and carrying a pickax, the Yotear took her to the edge of the Vat Thmey forest, where there was a cemetery of anonymous tombs. There he untied her bonds and gave her the pickax. "Dig, Grandmother!"

The earth was moist and would have been easy to dig up for a person with normal strength. The Yotear helped her dig so as not to lose too much time. "Crouch down near the hole."

"Then," my mother said, "I called on Lota Proung and knelt down beside the grave, joining my hands as we do when we pray together. The Yotear raised the pickax over me and told me to stop this nonsense. 'We're through with all that stuff now.' I raised my head and answered, 'My son, let me prepare myself in my own way. I'm going to rejoin my husband, but I still have two sick children in the hospital. I must give them strength, too. My three other children are gone: my oldest daughter burned to death, my youngest girl died from being impaled on a bamboo, and my son starved.' "

The boy stood as if paralyzed, holding the pickax in the air. He'd probably never heard such a speech from someone condemned to death. "All right, enough, get up and go home." Was it all a fake, a charade? Or was he really moved to spare her? Impossible to say. Mother came back to us, with her little bag of jewelry.

Our difficult life at the hospital continued, monotonous and sad. And then one day we had a visitor. Met Mân, one of our neighbors in the village, the man who had helped to bury my Aunt Nang and who worked in the Central Provincial Administration, took advantage of a delivery at the hospital to ask for news about Naroeun. He knew that she had been cruelly burned when our house caught fire, but he didn't know that she had died a week before. He had brought her a bowl of palm sugar, which he gave to my mother. Learning of Naroeun's death and seeing our distress, he suggested that we come live with him: he had a large house all to himself and his wife, Met Vi. We'd be well taken care of and would regain our strength. After all, the hospital was just a waiting room for death.

He was right, they didn't take care of us and we all had to shift for ourselves. There was always the problem of food, but Met Mân, working as he did for the administrative authorities, had already worked out a solution.

Mother went to see the Mekong in charge of Vat Chas. "We'd like to be discharged from the hospital."

"If you leave, you'll have to work."

"Of course, that's what we're going to do."

"Fine, but you can't return to the hospital again."

9 THE FOLLOWING NIGHT we slept at Met Mân's house, but we hadn't had time to clean ourselves up or do our laundry, so when we arrived smelling of the hospital, Met Mân's wife wasn't thrilled to have us in her house. She was also doubtless fearful of contagion, so Mother asked Mân if he might be able to find us an unoccupied house. There were some around, but you needed permission to move into one.

Mân found us a hut covered with palm branches, pervious to rain, and open on three sides. The bamboo floor had holes in various places, and some old clothing was lying around in the corners.

Mân presented us to the Mekong in charge of the group which we were to join: Met Yâm, a woman of about thirty years old, with an inscrutable countenance. She warned us that we would be required to work "when you have regained your strength." We spent the day in a neighboring house that was reserved for someone. Mân promised to make a few urgent repairs in the roof, and brought a few slats of plywood to plug up the holes in the floor, but he didn't have much time to spare. We slept practically out in the open, which allowed us to see the people passing by. Tôn Ny lived nearby, and we saw her going to work: she had trouble walking, one of her legs was stiff from the hip joint down. She bore all the responsibility for her household, and her father encouraged her to walk as much as possible, fearing that inactivity would allow her leg to ossify and become completely useless.

We were permitted to get two ladlefuls of rice soup per person when the gong rang at the communal kitchen. They even allowed us to keep two pots and three spoons at home. Then Mother began to find that the rice tasted bad to her. "I can't swallow this, it's so bitter it scrapes my throat. Now if I just had a piece of cake!" One day, tantalized by the aroma of noodles cooking at a neighbor's house, she sent me over there to beg a tiny portion. Leaning on my staff, I approached the house, but then I tripped over the stairs and fell down, unable to get up again.

"What are you doing here?"

"My mother can't get up anymore; she smelled the noodles cooking at your house and would like to taste a spoonful."

The neighbor woman helped me to my feet and gave me three servings of salted boiled noodles, seasoned with herbs. Then she took me home, ready to give *koktchaï* to my mother and sister.

We were having more and more trouble getting about, and the kitchen gave us a can of fresh rice per person morning and evening, allowing us to prepare it as we liked. We couldn't digest it, however, and craved something else. "It's too late for our stomachs," said Mother, "we can't swallow this anymore." Summoning up all my courage, I went out to hunt crabs and fish at Vat Thmey pond, with a string for a line.

I asked Sitha to go with me, but she told me she didn't have the strength to move. "If you knew my heart, you'd realize how weak I am."

"All three of us are weak, but you don't even make an effort to go outside when you ought to."

It was true that she had diarrhea and was even passing blood, but I didn't want to admit to myself that she was so ill, especially after she had been so hateful to Mother over the little bag of jewelry.

So I went off alone to the pond. It had rained over the past few days, and the ground was so soft that corpses not buried deeply enough were rising up out of the earth. The stench was terrible, but I told myself, "Courage, you have to keep going!" I started praying as I walked along. There was an entire stretch of ground where dozens of crows were tearing corpses apart, while other birds wheeled overhead. Some of them landed in front of me and stared at me with their round eyes. When I threw pebbles and clumps of earth at them, they fluttered a meter or two away and continued to watch me. I thought about death, which didn't frighten me anymore. A Yotear could come and kill me—it would be a relief.

I grubbed around in the soil to find earthworms with which to bait my fishhooks: I still had three that my father had kept among his things ever since Tul Trieh. The morning passed quickly, and I caught two crabs and two fish, then returned home. Mother was pleased at my catch, but Sitha didn't react at all, which irritated me somewhat. I'd have liked to give all the food to Mother. "Bang Peuw," said Sitha, "have a heart, give me something to eat, too." Mother had no appetite for the fish, so I gave some to Sitha with a bit of crab, while I ate the rest.

"Forgive me, daughter," Mother said to me. "I'm getting on your nerves. I have no appetite for anything. I've been hard on you now and then. I've made mistakes." She asked Sitha also to forgive her for having been short-tempered. We were all crying, and each one tried not to inflict her distress on the others.

In the afternoon I went back to the pond, a twenty-minute walk, but I returned empty-handed. Two days in a row, I made the same trip, bringing back a few crabs or fish. On the third day, the Mekong came to see how we were doing. She didn't stay long, from fear of contagion, but she left us a little bag of rice bran, which was good for diarrhea. That night I soiled my sarong, and Mother washed it in some of the water Met Mân brought us every day. She bathed Sitha and me, saying, "When I die, I won't be able to take care of you. I'll look after you as long as I live." She took a few steps, then huddled motionless on the floor, holding her head in her hands.

Sitha saw Tôn Ny going by and called out to her.

"Oh, Mâ Ohm," blurted out Tôn Ny, "the three of you look so sick!"

"Tôn Ny, dear daughter, could you find us some tree-bark medicine?"

"Find some for me, too," added Sitha. "I want to get well."

"Yes, I'll be back this evening when I come home from work."

When she returned, she boiled the bark herself, and all three of us had some of it.

When Met Mân arrived with some water, Mother asked him to put the pot close at hand. "We can't get up anymore. And could you hang up some blankets to conceal us a little bit from people passing by?" He returned with some old blankets, but he didn't stay long, because his wife had told him he was risking contagion. Tôn Ny couldn't come by the next day, but she sent her brother, who brought us three fish. "You haven't any little boy to get fish for you, Mâ Ohm. My father's lucky, he's got a little boy who can fish for him."

While our sarongs were drying, we all lay naked on our mats. Flies tormented us, drawn by the foul odors and the filth on the floor. It was unbearable. When I called out to a passerby carrying some pails of palm milk, he pretended not to hear. I dragged myself across the floor, sitting down, to give my mother something to drink.

That night I heard my mother get up, murmuring, "I'm too hungry." She cooked a bit of rice bran, and then she wanted to make some more, but I told her, "Mâ, tomorrow you'll still be hungry. Save a little of it." Still, I left the pot on the fire and went back to sleep. Toward morning I woke up. "Mama, I'm cold," I told her, pressing closely against my mother's body, but I heard only an inarticulate moan in reply. "Mama, Mama, what's the matter with you?"—as if I were discovering only that minute that she was sick.

"I'm hungry," she answered, "hungry for some of the cake from yesterday."

"Wait until tomorrow, Mâ, I'll make some more for you. And maybe Mân will bring us something to eat."

"I'm hungry, I'm . . . hungry."

I continued to doze, when suddenly I heard someone falling. I felt next to me, but Mother's place was empty. I called out, "Mama! Mama!" No reply. At this moment someone passed by in front of our hut, probably going to work, carrying a straw torch. In that faint light, in the space of a few seconds, I glimpsed my mother lying on the ground, her head on the hearth, the pot of rice bran overturned beside her. Her feet were still on the mat. Sometimes she sighed, and sometimes she moaned softly.

Unable to move, I told her, "Speak, Mama, I hear you. Speak!" Her only answer was one last sigh. I called for help, but no one replied. Day broke. I called out again—if only someone would come, relight the fire, help us! But no one came.

Gathering my strength, I dragged myself toward my dead mother and lifted her head out of the ashes, but I wasn't strong enough to move her. I washed her face, then her whole body. Since our stay in the hospital she had kept ready a clean white blouse and a sarong of moiré silk, saying, "If I die, dress me in these." I found her things, but how could I dress her alone? I called for help again. I didn't believe that my mother was dead. We had all fainted before so many times. She couldn't be dead!

At last a neighbor came over to our hut. "Why are you screaming like that? Is someone cutting your throat? I heard you calling before, but it was dark out, you understand." So she had waited until sunrise to show up.

"Could you do koktchaï for my mother?"

"But your mother's dead."

"Would you help me dress her, then?" She went to get her son, who brought my mother over next to me. Then, with the neighbor woman, I dressed her as she had wished. The son left immediately, but the woman stayed for a moment and promised me that she'd take care of having my mother buried.

No one came the entire day. I covered the body with a blanket and fell asleep, with my dead mother on my left and my dying sister on my right. I slept all the next day, and then all night. No one came.

On the third day, Mân came to bring us water and discovered what had happened. He went to fetch a Mekong, telling me they would surely bury my mother that morning because the body was beginning to smell.

The Mekong arrived and lifted up the blanket. "What are all these fancy clothes?" He tore off the blouse and the silk sarong and threw Mama naked into the hammock.

Toward noon Sitha roused herself from her torpor. "I'm thirsty, Bang Peuw."

"Do you want to eat something?"

"No, I'd like a little coconut milk. A drop of milk . . . just a drop!"

Met Mân, whom we'd begun to call Pou Mân (Uncle), came by to see us. I asked him if he could find a coconut for Sitha, and he came back around two that afternoon with three green coconuts. "You mustn't give them to Sitha all at once, you must keep some for later. Your Mekong scolded me, because we must be sparing of food."

After he left, Sitha begged me for some coconut milk. "A drop, Bang Peuw. One drop before I die." She was talking, she couldn't be dying, and I, like an idiot, did what Pou Mân had said and didn't give anything to Sitha. She asked me again, "Why don't you want to give me something—don't you have any feeling for me?"

I was so hungry my ears were humming. I told her to stop talking. Tôn Ny came by, still limping.

"I'm afraid of Pou Mân," I told her. "He told me not to give anything to Sitha. What do you think? Do you think I can give Sitha a coconut?"

"But of course you should give her a coconut. You don't have to listen to Pou Mân."

After Tôn Ny left, I cut a coconut in half and poured the milk into Sitha's mouth, but she didn't react, she just stared fixedly at the ceiling. "Swallow, swallow it!" My little sister was dead. When they carried Mama away, I had said to her, "There are only two of us left now. We must love each other, Sitha. We must live in peace together." And now she was dead. And I, I had refused to give her the last thing she had asked for, when I could easily have given it. "Sitha, forgive me!"

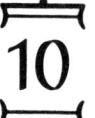 NOW I was alone. "Mama, come get me!" I dozed all afternoon. Toward evening Tôn Ny, returning from work, stopped at our hut. "Oh, Tôn Ny, Sitha's dead . . . I want to die too! Why must I be left all alone?"

Tôn Ny helped me to get up. Leaning on her shoulder, with a staff in my other hand, I went out to the stairs in front of the hut. Tôn Ny bathed me as I sat on the top step. I felt so weak! She gave me *koktchaï*. When I told her I felt as if I were deaf, she pulled on my earlobes, massaged my head, and pulled locks of my hair. I felt better, and my ears opened up again.

It was the tenth of January 1977.

I stayed alone in our hut, with Sitha lying dead beside me. Nobody else came that day. The village was a mournful sight, with barely a hundred inhabitants left of the thousand we once were in the beginning. Of the group of ten families in our sector, I was the only survivor.

Pou Mân came by the next morning. "You'll have to be patient," he told me. "The Mekongs are overwhelmed; there aren't enough people to dispose of the bodies." He didn't offer to take me to his house, since I was probably contagious. I asked him to wrap Sitha's body in mosquito netting to protect it from the swarms of flies crawling all over her. I spent another night next to her, asking again for her forgiveness for not having taken better care of her.

Toward eight in the morning, two men arrived with Pou Mân to take away Sitha's body. Mân brought me some water, but the next day neither he nor Tôn Ny came to see me. Had they abandoned me? In the evening I saw a man passing by with two cans of palm milk who stopped when I called for help. "I may die," I told him. "Give me a bit of palm sugar. I'll pay you for it." He gave me a little pot made from a section of bamboo, full of liquid sugar. In exchange, I gave him my mother's small treasure: why keep that jewelry, when I was going to die?

That night I slept with a full stomach, and the next day, filled with new strength, I dragged myself out of the hut, one step at a time, on my rear end. On each step of the stair, I called my mother—let her come and get me! Still dragging myself along on my bottom, I came to Tôn Ny's hut; she was probably off at work. I called softly, in an almost imperceptible reedy voice, "Mitia Mir!" My uncle was lying on a mat: he seemed just as exhausted as I was. Lying across his stomach was his youngest daughter, Sreï Peu. She was asleep.

I went on to Pou Mân's house, but he wasn't there. It was his wife, Mi Vi, who lifted me up under the arms and carried me inside. She took off my dirty sarong, covered with a carapace of mud, and put me to bed naked, with a blanket over me. While I fell asleep, worn out from my efforts, she went outside to pour boiling water over my clothes.

Pou Mân was there when I woke up, back from "burying" the dead, which meant throwing them on the heap of dead bodies piling up near the Vat Thmey cemetery. He asked his wife to bury my clothes while he went to fetch water. Mi Vi boiled the two buckets of water he brought back, and then both of them washed me with soap from head to foot. I was as thin as a three-month-old bamboo.

"You'll stay with us," Pou Mân told me. He went to get my belongings, and to find the Mekong to ask for a sarong and to have me registered as a member of his family.

I was placed in a corner, near the wall, and behind my head was a bundle wrapped up in a blanket. Taking advantage of Mi Vi's absence at one point, I looked inside and found silver articles from our burned-out house: goblets, cups, ladles, a dish. All these things had been buried under the house "for later," my mother had said. Tears of emotion came to my eyes—there was still something left that had belonged to the family.

Fed and cared for, I was able to begin walking after a week. I started to think I was well again, but I noticed that after I'd been on my feet an hour or two, they would begin to swell. I wouldn't be going to work just yet. I suggested to Pou Mân that I plant a garden. "If you bring me the seeds, I'll plant some vegetables." Quite pleased at my initiative and encouraged by permission from the Mekongs, who allowed small kitchen gardens to be planted near the houses, he brought me what I needed. The soil was very fertile, and in less than a month the garden provided tomatoes, lettuce, gourds, and cabbages. The river wasn't far away, and Pou Mân brought water for the garden. He also brought provisions given to him by the Mekongs. I even had some cake to eat. But I had the feeling that Mi Vi wasn't too happy with my presence in her house.

11 JUST WHEN the vegetables were at their peak, the authorities announced the reorganization of the village: all former inhabitants had to go down to Vat Chas, build new huts, and work in the rice fields. Tôn Ny's family had to vacate their house. My Uncle Vong had three children left: Tôn Ny, Sy Neang, and Sreï Peu.

Only Pou Mân was allowed to remain behind, to organize the village. All our neighbors were gone. The vegetables were abundant, but Pou Mân warned his wife and me that we must quickly harvest, eat, and even hide them, because the Mekongs were going to clear the entire area before resettling the village. Luckily, Pou Mân had been appointed head of the kitchen for the new groups that would be moving in around us. I was beginning to enjoy being alive again.

The people returned to their former houses, and soon afterward the Mekongs made the rounds of the huts to collect kitchen utensils and provisions. "Everything must be kept in common." Once again it was big Met Rôn who was in charge of our group, and she came into Pou Mân's house. "You, too, Met Mân, you have to donate all your pots and pans— the leader must set a good example." And that's how the silver goblets, cups, and ladles that once belonged to my family became part of the national heritage.

Suddenly Met Rôn noticed me standing in a corner of the hut: our eyes met, and I stared at her without flinching.

"She's the only survivor of the ten families in your group," Pou Mân said to her.

"Oh, I know that one," she answered.

All the vegetables left in the garden ended up in her basket, which she placed on her head and carried away, swinging her strong hips.

Pou Mân told me the garden would have to be abandoned.

"But there'll be more vegetables," I protested.

"They're for the entire community."

"Yes, but at night . . ."

"Be careful. They still have plastic bags for stubborn cases."

At the end of February I fell ill again. My feet swelled up like little balloons, and the swelling rose progressively to my belly, chest, neck, and face. Pou Mân didn't understand what was happening; we didn't have a lot to eat, but we weren't really suffering from hunger. I was eating rice, a little fish, fresh vegetables. Pou Mân was a strong young man, about twenty-five years old. Working in the kitchen, he dealt with the Mekongs every day. He dared to ask for medicine for me, and tried to take care of me. Since I couldn't get around anymore, he ordered Mi Vi to fetch my portion of rice soup at noon, which she did unwillingly, scolding me for not making the effort to go there myself. She was convinced that Mân would have given me bigger portions, which wasn't true at all, because he was closely watched, and there was no lack of interested parties who would have been glad to use his slightest misstep as a pretext to take over his position as kitchen superintendent.

Tired of Mi Vi's reproaches, I asked her for the bowl and went off toward the kitchen, which wasn't far away, but I hadn't taken more than ten steps when I became dizzy and fell down. Seeing my fall from the kitchen, Mân ran out to help me up. He scolded his wife, and when she argued with him, he slapped her.

That didn't improve her opinion of me one bit. Every day she begrudged me the little food she gave me. When there was fish soup, she gave me the clear liquid skimmed from the top and kept the bits of fish for herself. When she went out in the afternoon, I went behind the house to dig up and roast the big white worms near the anthills.

Inexorably, the soup became thinner and thinner, so Pou Mân came home to eat in the evening: he always brought a few tag ends of fish to add to the meager communal fare. Mi Vi grabbed my plate and ladled out the liquid, grumbling that I didn't do anything, that I ought not to eat with them, that it would be better if I left. After serving me, she stirred up the contents of the pot to serve her husband, complaining that he ought to find a way to bring more food home with him. Mân told her to be quiet, and when she not only continued talking but became rude, he got up, took a bamboo stick, and started hitting her shoulders and back.

I couldn't stand this scene. Unable to intervene, I escaped to Tôn Ny's hut, where her father greeted me affectionately: "A Peuw, welcome!" I told him what had just happened.

"You'll sleep here tonight, then."

"Thank you, Mitia Mir."

"Don't call me Mitia Mir, it's dangerous. Use the word the peasants use among themselves: Pou."

He wasn't sleeping at home that night, doubtless fearing a raid by the Mekongs on some pretext or another. He avoided them as much as possible and tried not to draw attention to himself. The next day Tôn Ny and Sy Neang left for work, while I stayed with Sreï Peu all day. My uncle was the first one home. He told me he would willingly keep me with him, but that I would certainly have more to eat at Mân's house, and that it would be easier to find the medicine I needed with Mân's help.

We went to bed that night lying under their only mosquito net: myself against the wall, Tôn Ny next, then Sy Neang, Sreï Peu, and Uncle Vong. My uncle asked me if I remembered to pray every day, and I told him that I did. "Never forget to pray," he said to me. And before falling asleep, we were all silent for a moment, praying in our hearts. There was no question of praying out loud: the neighbors could hear us, and such news traveled quickly to the Mekongs' ears.

I wasn't sleeping, it was too hot; I was thinking of what had happened at Mân's house and how I could ever bring myself to go back there. Then my uncle spoke: "You're still awake, A Peuw? Listen; if I die one day, you're the biggest of the children, so you live with my children. There'll be good feeling among you. Whatever happens to you, try to stay together, all four of you, as brother and sisters." We heard footsteps outside and stopped talking.

A few days later Mân came over to Uncle Vong's house to ask that I return with him, because Mi Vi had calmed down. My uncle didn't object, and I went back to Pou Mân's house, still swollen and unable to work.

Mi Vi didn't say anything; she fed me, helped me to bathe and dress. Her husband tried to cure me with honey from wild bees. During the rest hour he went off into the forest, returning an hour later with honey still warm from the heat of the forest.

In three days the swelling was gone from my entire body, except for the feet, but someone must have reported that I was staying there doing nothing, because the Mekong came to the hut to summon me to work.

"Wait a little longer," said Mân. "Her swelling only just went down, she's not well yet."

"You want to keep her in your house without working? Then she doesn't eat!"

Mân showed her my feet, my legs. "All right, she can stay here, but she'll weave grass mats for the roofs." I had avoided going out to the rice field, but crouching all day weaving long grasses didn't help my condition. I started to swell up again. Unable to get up in the morning, I was treated to a visit from the Mekong, who was forced to admit that I was in a bad way. "She won't live much longer." She came back an hour later, however, with a bitter potion that she had me drink. I heard crows cawing above the house; Mi Vi was frightened. Mân made her give me a rubdown, and after a little while I vomited, which made me feel better. At night, Mân put a bottle of hot water at the soles of my feet and one on each side of my stomach. I was gasping, it looked like the end for me. Neighbor women came to help massage me. Mân touched me from time to time to make sure that I was still breathing. In the morning I felt better. If my mother and Sitha had received the same treatment, perhaps they would still be alive.

12 FEELING MY STRENGTH returning once more, I went back to weaving grass mats. A month went by; then one day a Mekong woman arrived. "At dawn tomorrow there'll be an assembly of all young girls—there's rice to harvest in fields where the water is rising." These people paid no attention to the seasons. As long as the earth could provide, they sucked the life right out of it.

We set out the next day, about a hundred girls gathered together from different regions. Our destination was Sroko Trobek, in Don Trieh Province, supposedly a day's march away. Around noon they called a halt and distributed bowls of rice. In the evening it started to rain, but we kept walking. Finally, they let us stop at the edge of a wood, where we all took whatever shelter we could find. One of Mân's friends recognized me and asked if I needed anything; the mosquitoes had been plaguing us since the rain stopped, so I told him I'd like a mosquito net. He generously let me have his net for the night, but the next day, before going back to Vat Thmey (he had accompanied our group with provisions for the trip), he asked to have it back again: he only had the one and the mosquitoes had tormented him all night long.

We continued on into the forest, where each of us would have to build her own hut, but we still hadn't arrived at our destination. The earth was spongy at first; then water rose up to our ankles, and soon it was over our knees. We walked four abreast, holding hands. When the water reached chest height, I felt like letting myself slip under, but the others held me up. Soon we came to a little island where the ground was almost dry, and we were given something to eat. Red ants took their share of the meal from our hide, however.

After we'd eaten, they gave us our orders: "You have from now until this evening to build yourselves shelters from branches and leaves. Tomorrow you go to work." What kind of work would it be? They had told us that we'd be cutting rice, and that we girls had been chosen for our skill with a sickle. Finally, we learned that the rice was under water and had to be harvested quickly before it rotted. At Vat Chas, Tôn Ny was sowing rice, while here we'd be harvesting it under water; it was beyond me.

The next day they divided us into groups of ten, and each group was assigned to five boats under the supervision of a Mekong. All the Mekongs shouted at us, "Don't pretend to be sick—you're young, work quickly!"

They had told us that the rice was sticking up about an inch out of the water, but in fact we couldn't see the rice at all. We had to thrust our arms into the water, groping for the rice stalks, then cut them under water in little handfuls. I've no idea if peasants have ever harvested rice this way. We filled our boats with damp bundles that we unloaded on the island. Toward noon the head Mekong shouted, "You've worked wonderfully, you caught on quickly, but we mustn't lose momentum. We're not going to stop just yet. You're not afraid of the rain, you don't need to eat. Keep working—let's forge ahead!"

Their slogans got on my nerves. If I hadn't been so tired, I'd have felt like laughing. We continued working until the middle of the afternoon, but we were exhausted, and there wasn't much to show for our labor. The Mekongs sent us back to camp, where they gave us one ladleful of rice and subjected us to yet another educational session. The weather was damp, and it started to get cold. I shivered in my hut of leaves.

At dawn the next day, it was the same scenario. The water had risen even more, however, our sickles had rusted overnight, and the rice piled up on the island had started to rot instead of drying out, so we stopped work at noon. They made us walk four or five kilometers toward Highway 5, a difficult march through water up to our knees. I thought of Tôn Ny: I'd have liked to be with her, planting rice at Vat Chas. Her group slept in the hospital at night; the patients were all dead and gone, so the workers had taken their place. Her brother, Sy Neang, was an oxherd for the Mekongs. He would come back at noon to get rice for himself and Sreï Peu, who spent hours sitting in front of the straw hut waiting for the kitchen gong to sound. Their father worked somewhere in the rice paddies, coming back only in the evening.

We reached the road at the end of the afternoon. "You'll build your huts here, you won't need to cover all that distance every day." No one asked any questions; they'd explained to us that a road had to be built between the highway and the island where we had left the rice, so that oxcarts would be able to reach it. We looked at each other without laughing. A truck had brought pickaxes and rush baskets. Each girl was given two baskets, which she attached to the ends of a bamboo pole. I would have preferred a pickax, and said so, but the Mekong woman scowled at me and handed me two baskets.

Going up the highway we came to a spot where the sides of the road were a bit wider, sloping gently down to the flooded fields. A Mekong stuck long bamboo poles with little flags on top into the ground in two lines, two and a half meters apart, to mark the width and direction of the future road.

Our job was to remove the mud by hand and pile it up on each side. The principle was childishly simple; they didn't see why engineers would be needed to build roads. The mud fell back where it had come from, but a hundred pairs of hands tirelessly brought it back up again, while the Mekongs shouted slogans of triumph and encouragement: "Let's forge ahead! The Angkar is watching us! We love our country!" After five days of standing constantly in water up to our knees, our feet began to feel more solid ground. Then we were ordered to bail out the water . . . with our rush baskets. We lost a lot of water along the way, carrying it over the embankment, and the fragile mound of dirt crumbled a little, but finally the water level dropped in the canal that we had excavated to serve as a road. It had taken three weeks. But then it seemed that too much earth had been piled up, so, using our baskets, we moved dirt from the area around the new "road" and carried it out into the flooded fields. An endless task. Silently we wondered if these people were insane. For their part, they harassed us constantly: "Faster, faster! Forge ahead!"

This went on for another two or three weeks; it had been more than two months since we had begun this useless and exhausting project. Useless, because heavy rains began to fall, causing the walls of our "canal road" to collapse in places. We couldn't possibly be going to start all over again! That night there was a long educational session in which we learned that our work had produced nothing and that we were all incompetent. The Angkar granted us one day of rest, however, to allow us to return to Vat Thmey or the other villages, where we might get some vegetables or collect our personal belongings from our straw huts.

13

A GROUP OF ten girls left for Vat Thmey, and I went along with them to see Pou Mân and my Uncle Vong. We walked on muddy paths, crossing flooded fields, but the joy of not working gave us wings. Having left before sunrise, we arrived around noon. I went by Pou Mân's hut, but he wasn't home, so I continued on to Tôn Ny's hut, preferring not to confront Mi Vi's bad disposition all by myself. I knew that Uncle Vong was never there at noon, but Tôn Ny wasn't home, either. A neighbor woman told me that she had been taken to the hospital at Moung Russeï because of a particularly serious attack of malaria.

I found only four-year-old Sreï Peu, all alone.

"Where's Sy Neang?"

"He's not here yet."

"And Papa?"

"I don't know where Papa is."

"What do you mean? Didn't he sleep here last night?"

"Yes, but during the night a Pou came to get him for work."

"What work, where?"

"I don't know. Ask Sy Neang."

"But where's Sy Neang?"

"He takes care of the oxen. He's going to bring me something to eat."

I was worried—Sy Neang should have been there. The bell for lunch had already rung, but I didn't have the right to get any food. Then Sy Neang came running up, bringing two bowls of rice.

"Sy Neang, where's Mitia Mir?"

"He left last night. The three of us were sleeping when all of a sudden 'Grandfather' Rem [an old Yotear of about forty whom we all knew, who was in charge of policing the village] came to call him: 'Met Vong, come out!' 'Are you looking for me?' Father said, and then he turned to me: 'Take good care of Sreï Peu.' And he went away, wearing just his white shorts. I shouted after him, 'Where're you going, Papa?' 'I'm going to work at Moung Russeï.' That's all."

"I'm sorry, I can't stay very long, Sy Neang, I have to go back to Sroko Trobek. We have only this one day off."

"That's too bad—our corn isn't ripe yet, and you could have taken a little back with you. But perhaps in a month we'll be eating it together."

"You should leave a bowl with Sreï Peu, so that if you don't come home on time she can get her meal herself. I'll come back and see you when I can."

I left with a heavy heart, worried by the knowledge that Sy Neang and Sreï Peu were on their own. Sy Neang was a boy, true, but he was only eleven years old. I felt much older at fourteen. I rejoined my companions at the end of the bridge where we had agreed to meet again. We had to run almost the whole way back, arriving at Sroko Trobek in the middle of the night. By the end of our journey, I was limping: during the senseless work of bailing out our "canal road" I had scratched the calf of my leg, and now it was swelling, sending shooting pains all the way up to my stomach.

When the reveille whistle blew the next morning, my leg hurt and I told our Mekong about it.

"You walked well enough yesterday, Met Peuw. If you don't work, then you won't eat."

"Yes, but my leg wasn't all swollen yesterday like it is now. Look at it."

"You won't need to walk if I push you into the bag with a few swipes of a pickax."

I kept quiet. Afraid and hungry, I dozed throughout the entire day. In the evening the girl who shared her mosquito net with me brought me a cold rice ball that she had kept in her sarong. I waited until night fell to eat the rice, hidden under my blanket. Just as I was dropping off to sleep, my companion started to shake me. "Wake up, there's an educational session!" She had never done that to me before, but I saw a flashlight behind her—it was the Mekong, who spoke harshly to me: "You have to come, Met Peuw, for at least five minutes, even if you can't stay any longer than that."

My friend took my arm, and while we walked, she explained to me what was happening. "There's someone important coming from Vat Chas. It seems we have to see his face."

We were all seated in a circle under the trees, and the mosquitoes attacked our arms and necks. The important Mekong official began to speak: "Today no one can stay at home, you must all see the face of a bourgeois who has betrayed the people's cause."

I didn't understand a word of what he was saying, even though I knew all their speeches by heart. I'd taken a place close to the Mekong woman to make sure she could see that I had come; softly, I asked her if I could go back to bed, because my leg hurt.

She spoke up in a loud voice to the head Mekong: "I have a sick person in my group. May she return to her hut?"

"Why do you bring sick people here? There's no room for them."

I didn't wait to be told twice and slipped away. The moon had just risen, there was a soft half-light floating under the trees. Suddenly I heard shouts: "Here comes the king! Here comes the king!" And what did I see? A Yotear all in black carried a candle held out stiffly before him; next came a bare-chested man in white shorts, his hands tied behind his back, with a pot and a spoon hanging from his bound wrists. Two men behind him were beating him on the shoulders with their rifle butts in time to the rhythm of the clanking pot. I recognized his voice when he cried out: "Kill me now, you pack of savages!"

It was Mitia Mir, my beloved uncle. "The king is here, the king is here!" Our Mekongs clapped, and all the girls applauded after them. "The king is here, the king!" I was so thankful that I had left the circle in time. I could never have clapped or shouted.

Crouching down quite close to my hut, I could see another prisoner, led by two other Yotears behind my uncle. "And here's one of his accomplices." They were hitting him with their rifle butts, too. I could hear my uncle shout: "You're the enemies of heaven, evil spirits! Why don't you just kill me and be done with it!"

They disappeared inside the circle, and I couldn't see anymore. I hid under the mosquito net. When my friend returned to our hut, she told me what happened. "It's Tôn Ny's father—they hit him on the head, they

rubbed the pot of soot all over his face, and now they're taking him to
Vat Chas to show him to other groups. We mustn't say anything to Tôn
Ny, above all—it's too horrible."

Later, some people at Vat Chas told me how the sinister procession
had arrived the following morning around nine o'clock. They had wrapped
truck chains around my uncle's hands and shut him up in the pigsty with
the other man.

That night, holding candles in their hands, the Yotears made them
come out, shouting, "Here's the king!" They struck his head with a rifle
butt. He cried out several times:

"Just kill me now!"

"Not right away. Where are your children?"

"They're all dead, go look in the cemetery."

"Where are your brothers?"

"I'm all alone."

The Yotears rolled the two of them in the dunghill until the poor men
were unrecognizable, indistinguishable one from the other. Four men took
them out of the village into a little wood. I know that on that night a
Yotear brought Met Ban, the village medicine man, two livers and two
gall bladders to use in his preparation of medicines. I also know that this
same Met Ban stole everything of value from my uncle's hut. Coming
back from the kitchen with their bowls, my cousins surprised him as he
was leaving their hut. "I saw a snake on the roof," he explained, "I chased
it away." But in the hiding place my uncle had arranged under the main
beam of the ceiling there was nothing left but a statue of the reclining
Buddha. Missing was a mysterious stone as big as a man's forearm, en-
dowed with excrescences that turned white or red according to the fa-
vorable or hostile aspects of fate. Several diamonds had been hidden inside
the stone.

Tôn Ny had left the hospital at Moung Russeï the day after her father's
murder and gone immediately back to work in Vat Chas. One of her
companions, whose brother-in-law was in charge of the group of workers,
informed her of her father's death. "You've just gotten back from the
hospital, Tôn Ny. Yesterday your father was paraded before everyone
with his face all blackened from soot. He said he had no more children,
and he died. Don't say anything to anyone. And if anyone talks to you
about it, pretend you don't know anything. It's safer that way." Tôn Ny
cried all night under her blanket. The most difficult part was not being
able to ask anyone about it; that would have meant certain death for herself
and her little brother and sister. The Yotears who had killed her father

weren't from Vat Thmey, and they had to be prevented from learning that Met Vong had left three children, because they would have wanted to annihilate the family, to eliminate even their friends, to erase all trace of their existence. With swollen eyes, but without saying a word, Tôn Ny went off to work as usual.

Four

TIME WORN AWAY

1 THE SPECIALTY of our group of young girls at Sroko Trobek seemed to be the construction of dirt roads. In a country where the soil is sometimes simply mud a meter deep, if not more, and at other times a covering of dust swirling around our ankles, such an enterprise required the permanent mobilization of an army of specialists such as ourselves, armed with our rush baskets and tireless hands.

For the moment, however, I was immobilized by my infected leg and had no hope of finding the least medication. But then my father appeared to me in a dream and told me, "Take some cerumen from your ear and put it on your infected cut. Don't use anyone else's earwax."

When I followed this astonishing advice, the result was undeniable: in three days my leg was well again. My Mekong was taken by surprise at my return to health, and convinced that I'd been cleverly faking my illness, she seemed resolved not to let me get away with anything else. When I told my companions how I had cured myself, they laughed like crazy, and thought I was teasing them, but I couldn't help that. It was back to work for me: there was a new road being built in the direction of Don Trieh.

The Mekongs were always right on top of us: "Come on, get going, you've got to hurry up. The road must be ready by the time we plant the rice." And of course, "Forge ahead!" It was their favorite slogan.

They made us work even at night, as soon as the first moonbeam appeared, and often in the light of gasoline lanterns. If only they'd given us something to eat! One ladleful of liquid at noon and another in the evening were all we got.

After a month or so, it seemed to me that I was going blind. I was digging up the earth with a pickax, and it wasn't necessary to see clearly all the time, but at night, when I had to gather up the dirt in my basket and carry it to the embankment, I needed to be able to guide myself and I couldn't see a thing. I was reduced to feeling around on the ground, risking a pickax blow on the head. "Met Peuw is just pretending," the Mekong said. "Met Peuw says she can't see, the way she claimed she couldn't walk. Come with me." She took my hand and led me to the middle of the road. I thought I was going to end up in the plastic bag, but I couldn't have cared less. The Mekong left me in the road, telling me she was going behind a bush for a minute to relieve herself. I didn't know where I was. I waited. Then I felt the ground: it wasn't grass or gravel, it was earth. I felt around the place where she'd left me, and my hand encountered a small mound—a tomb! I sat down on the edge of the grave to wait for the Mekong's return. But she didn't come back . . . An hour went by, then two. It was getting close to dawn, the hour when the workers returned for about four hours of rest. I heard a group go by and called out to them, and one of my companions led me back to my hut. "You were in the middle of the graveyard," she told me. "The Mekong must have wanted to find out if you could see. If you'd been afraid, you'd have run to your hut, and then you'd have found her waiting for you with a pickax . . ."

That evening, after I'd done my usual stint of work during the day, the head Mekong announced publicly (everything was public) at our educational session: "Met Peuw is excused from night work because she really can't see."

Three days later, after we had finished a section of the road, everyone was given a day off to visit their villages. I would have liked to go to Vat Chas to see Tôn Ny or obtain some news of her, and learn how Sreï Peu was doing, left alone all day long. But my poor eyesight made me afraid to attempt the trip.

Later that night a few of my companions who had been to Vat Chas said that people ate better there; the workers received rice regularly, and sometimes even pieces of pork.

At the educational session the next evening the head Mekong announced that if anyone wanted to work at Vat Chas they had only to say so. He knew that the food was better there and that there was no need to work at night, either. He understood why someone might want to work there.

"Besides, the girls who went to Vat Chas yesterday can tell you all about it. Who was there?"

"Me, I was," answered several voices.

"Do they eat well there?"

"Yes, yes."
"Who wants to go to Vat Chas?"
Five hands were raised.
"You really want to go?"
"Yes! Yes!"
"All right, get your things."
The Mekong went with them. They never arrived at Vat Chas.

2 THE ROAD had now reached the village of Don Trieh. We returned to our huts to sleep, happy to be using the road we'd built with our own hands. It looked out over vast sheets of water on either side. At dawn we went back along the same road to Don Trieh, where we were fed and permitted to rest for an hour before continuing on toward Bat Tnât, across country this time. Halfway there, in the hamlet of Kat Holet, we were to construct new huts: we were going to build another road! The hamlet was only two hours' walk from Vat Thmey, and it was only five o'clock when they distributed our evening meal; work wouldn't begin until the next morning, since we couldn't start a new section of road at night. So we all—myself included, for the sake of unanimity—asked the Mekong for permission to get some fruit and vegetables from Vat Thmey.

"We'll put them all together, we'll share everything."

"All right, if you're back in time for work tomorrow morning."

I asked one of the girls if she'd go see Sy Neang and ask him for a bit of corn for me, because I still couldn't go anywhere on my own; I couldn't see a thing. "If you meet Met Mân, ask him for some, too."

She returned at dawn. "I saw Sy Neang, but the corn isn't ripe yet. I also saw Met Mân, he had come to see Sreï Peu. He comes from time to time."

Met Mân had sent me a mosquito net, and I found a little cooked corn and a few cucumbers discreetly rolled up inside. It heartened me to think that I wasn't forgotten in Vat Thmey.

In a few days the road had reached Kat Holet. The Mekong gave us a half day off, with permission to visit our villages. This time, I set out with a companion who was willing to lead me by the hand. I could see a little bit, just a blurred white band in front of my eyes.

Halfway there, we met Sim, the nurse I knew at Moung Russeï, taking medicine to the Mekongs at Kat Holet. I didn't see her, but she recognized me and stopped. "What's going on, Met Peuw?" She probably saw that I was being led by the hand. My companion quickly spoke for me: "She's blind, but she can see a little in the daytime." Met Sim rummaged through her bag and gave me three gelatin capsules. "Swallow these quickly," she said, without lingering any longer. In fact, a Mekong was running up, shouting at me and my companion: "Come back, girls! Let's go, there's water on the road. You have to come right away and repair it." Back we went to Kat Holet. All day and all night we built the embankment higher and higher; half the time we were in water up to our armpits. It was cold, and no arrangements for food had been made, since we had been planning to go to our different villages.

The next morning, we dried off for an hour in the sun, and then there was a new change in plans: the road wasn't going to be built in the direction previously decided upon. We were off to Moung Russeï! I was beginning to see a little better: the white film before my eyes was starting to dissolve. At night, I could see more or less as I had before. It was almost ten in the evening when we reached Moung Russeï, without having eaten anything all day or the day before. We collapsed under the trees to wait for the head Mekong, who arrived an hour later. "Follow me." We all staggered to our feet and followed him to an animal pen with buildings down at one end. A peasant came forward, carrying a lamp.

"What's going on?"

"Get the cows out of the pen—these girls need sleep!"

The peasant brought the cows out into the yard, and the Mekong told us that we could sleep after we had cleaned out the pen. We carried out the manure by hand, while the peasant brought us fresh straw. When we were ready to go to bed, we still couldn't sleep until the Mekong had given us a lecture. Settling down in a circle, we huddled around the Mekong looming over us in the moonlight. "I must explain your work to you, and then you can go to sleep. You must be ready for action at any moment. You are the emergency intervention group for roads in danger of flooding. You did very good work at Don Trieh. The Angkar needs you here." He hadn't even really gotten into full swing yet when the gong sounded. "You see, there's an emergency, we have to go out to the road."

Nobody dared protest, nobody asked for something to eat. We covered two or three kilometers, arriving to find other "elite" emergency groups like ours already at work, a crowd of people thrashing about in the water to replace earth on the embankment where it had collapsed in several places. In water up to my neck, I dredged up shovelfuls of muddy earth that other girls carried away in rush baskets. New girls came to relieve us at around six in the morning. Shivering and famished, we returned to the pen and buried ourselves in the straw. At eight o'clock the gong sounded. Everyone got a ladleful of real rice, and a few minutes later— off we went again! The road had to be reinforced where we had patched up the breaches during the night. We built up the earth a meter thick along a stretch of several kilometers; this project lasted for a month. But we did get a ladleful of good rice at noon, half of which could be set aside for the evening. Our stomachs weren't famished any longer, but our muscles ached all the time.

When the work of patching and reinforcing was completed, we began a new road toward Okrirt, about fifteen kilometers from Moung Russeï, at which point my body had had enough. The flood waters had begun to recede and we were submerged only up to our waists, but I had fits of shaking; I vomited, I was cold, I was burning up. I couldn't get up off the ground. Met Soen, the Mekong, came to find me in the pen when she didn't see me in the morning lineup. "So, you're sick, Met Peuw? You know we have no use for sick people here. Perhaps you'll get better if we put you in a bag!" I kept quiet, but I didn't care if I died or not.

I spent five days like that, shaking with fever. The Mekong paid no more attention to me. When the Yotear chief arrived on an inspection tour, she brought him to see me.

"Here's one who's been sick for five days."

"Sick? How is she being treated? What? There's no nurse here?"

He and the Mekong left. A nurse from the hospital at Moung Russeï arrived an hour later and gave me an injection and several tablets to swallow. One of my workmates brought me something to eat. The Yotear chief came by again during the afternoon. "You must work, but the work here is too hard for you—you'll go to Vat Thmey. Hurry up and get well."

After the educational session that night, which I wasn't well enough to attend, the Mekong came to tell me that I would be leaving for Vat Thmey as soon as I was able to walk.

3 THAT NEWS was probably all I needed to make me well again, but I spent a horrible night. I saw snakes hanging from the ceiling and the shining eyes of people mesmerized by them, walking softly toward the snakes as if in a trance. I screamed and called for help while my companions tried to calm me down.

The nurse returned in the morning to give me another shot. They tried to feed me, but I couldn't swallow more than a spoonful of rice. The next day the nurse came back to tell me that I ought to be getting better and that she wouldn't be back again.

At this point, I summoned up all my courage, and without going to see the Mekong again, I set out for Vat Thmey, only three or four kilometers away. At eleven o'clock, I arrived at Pou Mân's hut, but only Mi Vi was there, so I went on to Sreï Peu's hut, where she greeted me with indifference: "Are you coming to sleep at our house?" Without bothering to explain, I lay down in a corner of the hut.

I spent three nights with Tôn Ny, Sy Neang, and Sreï Peu. On the fourth day, the neighborhood Mekong told me that I had to plant rice at Vat Chas. A second Mekong added that I couldn't live with my cousins, it wasn't my house, and, in any case, I had to live near the place where I'd be working. I had to build a hut just for myself down by the river.

I went to tell Mi Vi that I was having some trouble and had to speak with Pou Mân; when he came home, I told him my story. He informed me that he, too, had to leave Vat Thmey and build a new hut. "Don't worry, I'll take all four of you with me."

During rest hour he went over to the Mekongs' house. They allowed him to take us all with him, and in the meantime, I might stay with Sreï Peu. Shortly after hearing this news, however, I was called out by a Mekong. "Let's go, off to work!" I set off for Vat Chas.

Out in the rice fields I followed the water buffalo as they turned over the earth, breaking up the clods of muddy dirt. At night I joined Tôn Ny in a damp little hut, but the gong called us almost immediately to the evening lecture.

Five Mekongs were there, strangers to the village. The headman told them, "Pick the girls you need. Each of you take any five faces that strike you." Wondering what all this meant, I prayed silently. Tôn Ny's Mekong came up to me and said, "You, you're as sick as a dog—we need strong girls," and she started to laugh, the others all laughing with her. I couldn't tell if that meant I was saved or in worse trouble.

The Mekongs made their choices; Tôn Ny was picked. There was one Mekong left. With a half smile that showed her pointed teeth, she announced: "I'll take all the sick ones. You, Met Peuw, first of all. Why are you sick?" She turned toward the others. "She's worked a lot, we have to take care of her." I didn't know what to think. She took five of us to another hut, not much more comfortable than the one I had just left.

The next morning a whistle awakened us at four o'clock; loudspeakers blared revolutionary songs. There were at least five hundred people in the village square, with more arriving from all directions. Where were they coming from? They regrouped us by hundreds. I caught sight of Tôn Ny in the group next to mine. A smile played over her thin face, but she was astonished to see me there, since I'd been among the sick girls. She didn't understand any more than I did. Or else we understood all too well.

The groups set off one after the other in single file along the little dikes that crisscrossed the rice paddies. At the waist of my sarong I had a little handful of salt, given me by Pou Mân a few days before, that I carried with me all the time.

"Quick march! Let's go, close up those spaces!" If a girl lagged behind, the Mekong hit her with a little whip, striking her on the head and shoulders with the stinging lash. If a girl fell into the water, no one stopped to help her up.

An hour later we were all gathered on an earthen terrace, where they counted heads. There again I glimpsed Tôn Ny, and winked at her. "Let's hope everything goes all right." They handed out the seed rice and sent us out into the rice paddies, where the mud came halfway up our calves. We were forbidden to catch crabs or fish. I felt dizzy, and I didn't want to end up buried in the mud. When the sun was at its zenith, a blast on a whistle called a halt. We rejoined the Mekongs up on the dikes, where they provided a pot of rice for us to eat our fill. After fifteen minutes, work picked up again and continued on until sunset. Then we went back to our huts, where we received another ration of rice. I was completely exhausted, and the skin on my legs was as hard and wrinkled as a crocodile's from having soaked in the mud all day long.

When we finished one rice field, we went straight on to another without a moment's rest. One evening we had our educational session out in a rice paddy. "I'm your new Mekong. It seems that you're tired, that you don't have enough to eat. We're going to change all that. We're going to help

you. From now on you'll have a leader with a flag at the head of the line
to set the planting rhythm for you. If you catch fish or crabs, we'll make
sure you join them under water. And we have to move fast. If we don't,
others will move even faster: we'll become slaves of the Vietnamese!"
What did the Vietnamese have to do with all this?

The session lasted until midnight, and we had to get up again at four
in the morning. Did they want to wear us out? What would be the point?
A Mekong man or woman now carried a white flag at the head of each
planting line, shouting slogans of encouragement. One morning the girl
on my right collapsed into the mud, and I bent down to help her. When
the Mekong came running over, I told her, "Look at her fingernails, they're
all black—it's cholera." By the time they got the girl out of the rice field,
she was dead.

That night, another session lasting until midnight. "We're going to leave
this sector—we can't have you dying of cholera." And we set out during
the night for new quarters that turned out to be not too far away, the
former warehouse of what used to be the hospital at Vat Chas. The next
day off we went to transplant rice seedlings near Tiens Deï. A few days
after that, we planted rice near Don Trieh, with just a tiny piece of fish
as our only meal. After work, they searched us; the Mekong woman had
one pail at her feet for the confiscated crabs, another for the fish. So my
companions started eating the crabs raw out in the fields while they worked.
At first I thought I'd never be able to eat those things, but goaded by
hunger, I soon followed their example.

4 AFTER Don Trieh, we came back toward Moung Russeï to work.
We had to follow the water buffalo, tearing out the weeds still
sticking to the clods of earth. We didn't need to plant any rice
here: instead they posted us near the river, where we fished out
the rice plants thrown into the current by the Yotears in Battambang and
carried downstream to Moung Russeï. When we'd "caught" fifty plants,
they had to be rolled up in a banana leaf and carried on our heads to all
the rice fields spread out between Moung Russeï and Vat Thmey. The
muddy water dripped down our necks and all over our bodies, and when
the leaves tore, the seedlings fell all over the ground. At night I had a
stomachache from having spent the day in the water, because in certain
spots we had to swim in order to get from one rice field to another. Since

most of us didn't know how to swim, the Yotears installed a kind of handrail of bamboo to which we could hold on, immersed up to our necks. And since the water was warmer than the ambient temperature of the air, we shivered with cold getting out of the water. Toward noon, when we were ready to climb out to eat, what did we hear? "Ah, you're in a hurry to eat! Well, we're going to work another hour." Seated on the embankment, we got a mouthful of fish, and when there wasn't enough fish, a pinch of salt. Then it was back into the water.

This work near Moung Russeï lasted for about a month. We'd lost all sense of time, however. I do know that the water level was receding, so it must have been sometime in February or March of 1978.

Now and then they would give us a day off. We would go in ranks to the bridge at Vat Thmey, where everyone would disappear in different directions. Tôn Ny and I would run to the hut where Sreï Peu was waiting. Sy Neang would come by at noon, or perhaps return only in the evening, when we had to leave. The corn was taking its time ripening. Sy Neang was planning to bring us some later on at Vat Chas, where we lived in the warehouse.

Actually, we weren't supposed to stop off at Vat Thmey but go on directly to Vat Chas. After our third visit, Pou Mân told us not to come back. "Someone has informed on you. If you come again you'll end up in a plastic bag, and me too, since I'm in charge of Sreï Peu. If you love her, you mustn't come to see Sreï Peu anymore."

I was worried about the child—she'd soon be four and a half years old, but she didn't look older than three, she was so tiny. Some neighbor women told me that Mi Vi beat her every day. When she was cleaning vegetables, she would hit Sreï Peu on the head with the flat of her knife, simply because she wouldn't go outside to play. She didn't have the strength, poor little thing! And Sy Neang wasn't there during the day.

When we left Vat Thmey, Sreï Peu wanted to follow us, and cried— she was so afraid of Mi Vi. When Tôn Ny tried to reason with Mi Vi, she answered, "But I hardly touch her, and she has such a bad disposition!"

Another month went by; the water was at its lowest level. We were given three days off. Tôn Ny and I went to Vat Thmey, where Pou Mân told us that our new communal hut was ready. We moved in right away: our belongings were quickly packed, and it was only a few hundred meters to our new hut, near the former pagoda that dominated the riverbank. We spent our first night there, with Mi Vi and Pou Mân by one wall, Sy Neang, Tôn Ny, Sreï Peu, and I by another.

We had been warned at an educational session that we would be given food only in exchange for a pot of night soil that had to be brought behind the communal kitchen. We had to be checked off a list, and those not checked off wouldn't receive that day's rations. Well, our neighborhood Mekong couldn't bear to see us without anything to do: the law of communal life was Work! She made Tôn Ny and me gather tree leaves, chop them up, and mix them into manure.

The first day passed well enough: we spent the morning gathering leaves, which were then chopped up by a group of married women. Since there were too many leaves, the women asked us to help them, but one woman complained to the Mekong: "Do you think that mixing manure is girls' work? We need a man here." I don't know if the complainer stayed long at her post, but the next day a man arrived to replace us, so we just continued to gather leaves, going farther into the forest each day. At the end of a month, there were no more leaves to gather or we would have ended up stripping the trees bare. The Mekong told us to go to Vat Chas, to the burial ground of the former hospital.

I walked over this mass grave where all those I loved lay rotting. I wasn't afraid of the dead anymore. From time to time I tripped over a skull or a tibia sticking up out of the earth; the terrain wasn't very steep, but the violent rains eroded the surface rapidly, and the last bodies hadn't been buried very deeply. There was an abundant harvest of weeds, and from one day to the next they grew back thickly. Mi Vi was there, too, since the Mekong didn't want anyone to be idle. As for Pou Mân, he was now a blacksmith: everyone's job changed according to the Mekongs' moods.

The Mekong in charge of girls at Vat Chas had tracked us down, and she arrived at our hut. "Does the Mân-Vi family live here?"

Having seen her coming, we tried to hide, staying in a corner of the hut without answering. She climbed the ladder and found only us, alone at the end of the day.

"Why didn't you answer?"

"We don't belong to the Mân-Vi family."

"I know. Get your things together right away. Assembly at the village square in Vat Thmey!"

We each took our mosquito net, a tin plate, and a spoon. We didn't have any other belongings. A few dozen girls were already gathered in the square. The head Mekong explained to us at length that we'd be building dikes between the rice fields to serve as roads. I knew the speech by heart and didn't listen to him going on and on. Suddenly I heard him ask a question: "Does anyone here have very young brothers and sisters?" Tôn Ny raised her hand.

"I have a little sister, may I bring her with me?"

"No, no, leave her with some neighbors. Little children would just be in our way."

We set out for Phum Mras Preu, at the border of Pursat Province, toward the south. We walked for part of the night, and when we arrived, there was another speech from the Mekong in charge: "You'll set up huts here, at the entrance to the forest. There's a camp of boys a bit farther along—you're not allowed to go to their camp. Even if you have a brother there, you may not visit him. You're here to work. We must become a rich country. Soon we'll have machines, but don't think about that now. In any case, it's useless to think. The Angkar thinks for you. You, you just work. We're going to win!"

Tôn Ny and I were too weak to build a hut, so we just lay down under the trees; it was dark out, and no one paid any attention to us. We'd see about a hut the next day, which turned out to be right away: hardly had we fallen asleep when we had to get up again. It was perhaps four in the morning, and sunrise was still far away. We walked and walked: construction was to begin at the far end of the projected road. That way, we'd be getting closer and closer to our camp as we built the road. The workday was over at six in the afternoon, but we still had to return to camp, and they hadn't given us anything to eat at noon. Luckily, the evening ration of rice was a big one. Shortly after our meal, however, there was another assembly and an educational session lasting more than two hours. I didn't usually listen, since they always said the same thing, but this evening they talked about the Vietnamese, who had been driven out of the country . . . there must have still been some left, however, since we were warned against them. "No contact with the Vietnamese. And you're not allowed to be sick. You're healthy young girls. If you're sick, it must be because you're thinking about boys. Perhaps you'd like to get married? Then say so. Does any one of you want to get married?" No one answered; we knew how that could end up. And how could anyone be thinking about getting married when we were all dying of hunger and rotting in stagnant water? Anyway, not one of us had her period: we wouldn't menstruate again until after we'd left this land of death.

We worked for two weeks. Most of us slept under the trees, but the rains could come at any time, so our leaders arranged for some boys to build a sort of hangar, covered with grass but without walls or partitions, like a covered market, open to gusts of wind. We slept in the center, huddled back to back.

And then there was a full moon! We worked through the night. During the day we had to watch out for rough spots and holes in the paths; snakes often curled up in the imprint left by a water buffalo's hoof. There had been snakebites, but there was no medicine for them, and two or three girls had already died. At night the shadows of the moon were deceptive, and we couldn't see where we were putting our feet. Tôn Ny and I held hands and prayed that we were stepping in the right place.

After six weeks, the road was almost finished; perhaps another week or so would be enough to complete it. But then my eyes began to give me trouble again; they ran constantly, and at night I couldn't see a thing. Tôn Ny held my hand when we went to work at night because I was afraid of getting stuck in the puddles; she told me to be confident, but she was smaller than I was, and sometimes the two of us went sprawling in the mud. Then Tôn Ny started having the same symptoms as I, and the other girls began to get sick, too.

At an evening educational session, the Mekong designated ten girls to be in charge of leading the blind girls to work. "Comrade sisters, you've been chosen to guide and assist your blind sisters. They need you, because the Angkar needs the strength of every one of you. You'll dig with pick-axes, while the blind ones collect the dirt in baskets."

But the "superintendents of the blind" didn't particularly relish their task and limited themselves to pulling us by the hand when we went off to work. What else could they do?

We usually left the worksite around midnight. One night, after falling down a few times on the way, with my knees all cut up and my clothes soaking wet, I was left on my own under the hangar. I felt around for my bag, but there was no one to give it to me. I'd have liked to wash my legs and feet, but there was no one to lead me down to the river. I called for Tôn Ny, but she wasn't around. There was no one to take me to get my rice ration. I called out several times, "Will someone get me a little rice?" No one moved. Finally, the cook came herself.

"Where's your bowl?"

"I can't find it. Perhaps it's on the roof."

That's where we kept our bowls so they wouldn't be stepped on. I didn't know in which part of the hangar I was, though . . . Finally, one of the "sighted" girls led me over to Tôn Ny, and I found my spoon in my bag.

After ten days of this charade, a nurse from Moung Russeï came to give us medicine, since still more girls were going blind. Most of us were able to see again within two days, but the nurse stayed on with us.

"Met Peuw," she told me, "you're always shaking, you've got a high fever, you're thinner and weaker than the others—you can't stay here."

"That's fine with me, but it's up to the Mekong."

5   THE NURSE ARRANGED for me to be sent back to Vat Thmey. Tôn Ny was pleased: now Sreï Peu wouldn't be alone, exposed to Mi Vi's abuse. I was the envy of many girls when I climbed up on an oxcart with the nurse, who was being taken back to Moung Russeï, while I would be dropped off at Vat Thmey. Tôn Ny was staying on at Phum Mras Preu without me.

Sreï Peu ran to meet me at Vat Thmey, calling, "Where's Tôn Ny?"

"She can't come, she's working. But look at you—what's the matter with you?"

Sreï Peu's little skull was shaved, full of bruises and bloody sores. She told me that Mi Vi had shaved off her hair because she had lice. "You're going to give me lice," she would say, and hit Sreï Peu on the head with the back of a spoon. Pou Mân had tried to save her hair by presenting her with a little monkey borrowed from some neighbors. The creature played with the child and looked for lice on her head, but Mi Vi wasn't satisfied and cut off all her hair. Sreï Peu bore up very well under her ordeal; her father had already shaved off her hair once before, after her mother's death, when he had placed her under the protection of Buddha.

Sreï Peu went with me to the Mekong, to whom I had to give a note from the nurse in order to be eligible for my rice ration. When we got back to the hut, I lay down in a corner with Sreï Peu close to me. "Tell me, Sreï Peu, what happened with Mi Vi?" She told me that Mi Vi often knocked her head against the ground and that she pinched her on the thighs and stomach. Carefully I took off her shorts to see: her lower abdomen and genitals were covered with bruises.

"Don't you ever take a bath, Sreï Peu?"

"Mi Vi took me down to the river a few times."

"And does she wash you?"

"Yes. She throws a bucket of water on my head and tells me to go back up to the house."

Mi Vi returned from work around noon. "What are you doing here? And Tôn Ny?" She was obviously afraid that we'd be coming back to live in her hut. Sreï Peu began to cry from fear.

"And you, what've you been telling her?"

"She hasn't told me anything."

"If you tell lies, Sreï Peu, you'll be sorry!"

"But why are you screaming at her, Mi Vi? She's my little sister, and she's only a child."

"If you talk, watch out. Your sister won't be staying here all the time, she'll be going back to work, and then you'll have to deal with me! And you, Met Peuw, go get our rice at the kitchen."

She obviously wanted to be alone with the child, but I refused to leave them together. "Sreï Peu hasn't seen me for a long time, and I want to spend as much time as I can with her. She'll come with me to get the rice, or we'll both stay here." Mi Vi gave in, and we went off to the kitchen together, leaving Mi Vi bustling about furiously in the hut.

We brought the three portions back in one pot. Mi Vi divided the rice. "Sreï Peu's stomach is tiny," she said, "a half portion will be enough for her—the rest is for me." The child didn't complain; the same scenario was played out every day.

After Mi Vi returned to work, I asked Sreï Peu when Sy Neang would be back.

"He doesn't come back here, he sleeps with his group. Once in a while he brings some fish."

That afternoon Sreï Peu and I went to bathe at the riverbank, where I carefully washed her head to remove old scabs and the dirt encrusted in her skin. We stayed down by the river until the evening, watching the clouds chase each other across the sky.

Unfortunately, a Mekong woman came looking for me the next day. "The Vi family hasn't turned in its night soil, you'll have to see to that. And you, what do you do all day long? You're eating, you must work." I told her about the nurse's letter that I had given to the other Mekong, but she wasn't impressed. "And you, too, Met Peu; tomorrow you go to work!"

We enjoyed our last free day, and the next morning, armed with pickaxes, we went off to break up and pulverize the anthills at the edge of the forest. There were hundreds of them, baked by the sun until they were as hard as stone. Sreï Peu could barely lift her pickax, even though it was smaller than mine. When I saw the Mekong coming, I whispered to her, "Work, little sister, work." The bad-tempered woman passed by without saying anything. "Before you arrived," Sreï Peu told me, "I already had to work, collecting cow dung. We were supposed to carry it on our heads, but it was too heavy, I kept dropping it along the way and losing half of it, so they told me to stop." She wasn't yet five years old.

The Mekong returned around noon. "Stop working! The oldest girls will come back at one o'clock, with baskets to collect the dust from the anthills. They'll carry it to the dunghill to help fertilize the rice fields. The younger children [there were five or six, from five to seven years old] will collect cow dung."

I rejoined Sreï Peu at the hut in the evening. She told me how she had managed to escape from her work for a few minutes and return to the hut. "The Mekong said we have to save our poo-poo, so I come here to do some. I leave my basket full of cow dung in front of the hut, and when the Mekong calls, I go back." This routine continued for a week or two.

When the powder from the anthills had been mixed into the manure pile, the Mekong gave us a day to plant manioc behind and in front of the house. I also planted ten kernels of corn and a few cuttings of sugar cane.

One day, another girl from Phum Mras Preu came back to the village and told me that Tôn Ny was sick in the hospital at Moung Russeï. I informed Pou Mân, who had come to spend the night at the hut, and he promised me he would go to see her. He would even take her some palm sugar, which we carefully saved up for the days when we might be sick. He asked Mi Vi to get a pot of sugar ready, but she told him that we'd eaten all of it since I had begun living at the house. This was a lie—we hadn't eaten any of it, Mi Vi had saved it all. I saw her put a little sugar in a pot anyway, and Pou Mân set out on his bicycle at four in the morning to stop at the hospital before going to work.

That evening Pou Mân announced that Tôn Ny would visit us in a few days, and in fact she did come by, three or four days later, to get some green vegetables, since there were none at all at the hospital. I went off with her during the noon rest hour. "Here, you gather some herbs while I get you some bananas." Pou Mân had planted a banana tree, which was now full of fruit, but the Mekong had put them off limits. I was able to knock off a dozen bananas without being noticed by anybody. I gave half of them to Tôn Ny, who was going back to the hospital, and cooked the others in ashes for Sreï Peu and myself. We were just too hungry.

Pou Mân came back again to spend the night, and Mi Vi complained that someone had stolen some bananas. She had already spoken to me about them, but I had absolutely denied being involved in any way. Pou Mân asked me if it was I who had picked the bananas, and in front of Mi Vi, I told him no. But after Mi Vi had left, he asked me again, and I admitted that I had given some to Tôn Ny and eaten the others with Sreï Peu. He scolded me a bit, not for having taken the bananas, but for having taken such a risk. "If the Mekong had seen you, you would have ended up in the cemetery. Don't do it again, if you want to stay alive." But we'd spent so much time with death we weren't afraid of it anymore. Death was easier than the torments of hunger. Tôn Ny told me that many of the people in the hospital poisoned themselves to escape the horror there.

6 WITHOUT Mi Vi's help, I took care of the house and made sure Sreï Peu got a bath every day. Her cuts were healing. It was too good to last, though: the Mekong came back to get me for work near Don Trieh, where the rice was ripening. Once again, Sreï Peu would be left alone with her jailer. She was so unhappy! I promised her that I'd come back as soon as I could, but we never knew what the Angkar would decide for us. She stood there crying while I made some last-minute suggestions to Mi Vi.

The Mekong was waiting for me in the square, looking in our direction. I tore myself away from Sreï Peu, who clasped me around the waist with her scrawny little arms, sobbing. I felt the tears come to my eyes, but I had to control myself in front of the Mekong. When I steeled myself to turn around for one last wave goodbye, I saw Sreï Peu wiping her eyes with her sarong; then Mi Vi pulled her savagely toward the hut. The child missed a step and fell over backward on the stairs; Mi Vi picked her up roughly, and they disappeared inside. The Mekong watched me but didn't say anything. I couldn't help wondering what life would be like for my little sister, even though the Mekongs told us over and over, at all the educational sessions, that we mustn't think. But I couldn't stop thinking.

It was a day's march to Don Trieh. Once again there were about one hundred girls. Without lingering at the outskirts of the forest, we went down toward the rice fields and set up our straw huts in the middle of the paddies. Sometimes I worked at harvesting; at other times, when a field wasn't quite ripe yet, we shouted to chase away the birds landing in it, and we caught crabs, which devastated the tender plants by cutting the stems to pieces with their claws. We were supposed to collect the crabs in buckets and give them to the communal kitchen; anyone who kept some for herself was asking for trouble.

One day, however, when they told us that there wouldn't be any rice distribution at noon, I went off alone between two rice paddies to heat up some rice that I'd saved from the day before, and I cooked myself a few crabs that I'd caught. There was plenty of straw to feed the fire, but it had to be done discreetly. Suddenly I heard Mekongs shouting in the distance that there was a fire, so I quickly put it out, scattered the traces in the rice, and crawled furtively away to another corner of the field. A Mekong arrived at the spot I'd just left and found some crab debris. "Who was eating here?"

He came toward me. "Was it you eating over there?"

"Me? No!"

I had already plunged my bowl into the cold water.

"Show me your bowl."

"Well, I just washed it. I ate right here."

He looked through my bundle, but he didn't search me or my clothing. A Mekong woman wouldn't have hesitated to frisk me, but he was a young man of twenty, and he hadn't the right. It was lucky for me, because he would have found the lighter that I kept hidden at my waist in a fold of my sarong. It was a narrow escape.

As soon as the moon was bright enough, we worked every night taking the sheaves of rice directly to a platform of earth where oxen trod them out with their hooves. There was no place left for us to sleep because of the rice everywhere. We stretched out on rice straw, eaten alive by mosquitoes and fleas, surrounded by the water in the fields. I was very afraid of snakes, which love to nest in sheaves of rice, but I wound up getting bitten by a huge centipede instead: it attached itself to my finger and I couldn't shake it off. My screams in the night brought help from a man who was treading out rice. He detached the insect, crushed it, and then tried to bleed the poison out of my wound, putting a tourniquet just above the elbow. The next day my arm was all swollen and weighed a ton. Shaking with fever, I couldn't possibly work. One of the Mekongs brought over a man said to be a sorcerer: he blew on my hand, murmuring incantations; then he gestured as if he were throwing something away and gave me a pharmaceutical flask to hold in which to trap the sickness.

I was a bit astonished, but I let him go through his routine. True, my hand did stop hurting; my arm remained swollen, however, so that I couldn't hold a sickle. Luckily, the harvest was almost over in this region and they sent me back to Vat Thmey.

My happiness at being with Sreï Peu once again was cut short by a bad attack of malaria. My fever came on every morning at around nine o'clock. Sreï Peu would sit on my stomach to give me some warmth and to reduce the shaking of my body—that was all she could do. She hadn't been requisitioned for work since I had left her a month earlier, but she was still just as thin and weak as before. She would spend entire days sitting at the top of the ladder, waiting for the moment when rice would be doled out, but she was dying of hunger, because Mi Vi was eating half her meager portion.

As we were in the midst of the dry season, the river at Vat Thmey was now only a big snake of mud. I had to go to the well at the former pagoda to get water for our baths, but I hadn't the strength to draw up the bucket, so I called Pou Mân, who was still working at the forge in the courtyard. He asked permission from the Mekong, who allowed him to help me carry the bucket back to the hut. From then on, Pou Mân brought two buckets of water to the hut every day, making sure that Mi Vi understood that the water was for me and Sreï Peu.

Sreï Peu had begun to enjoy life a little bit once more. One day when I went off at three in the afternoon to the communal kitchen with the family's night soil, I left her sitting at the entrance to the hut, dangling her legs over the edge of the elevated floor. When I returned, I heard her singing some of Pol Pot's revolutionary songs in her very pretty little voice. People stopped to listen to her. "That little girl never sings, one of her sisters must be there." When she saw me, the child got up, stretched out her arms, and started to come to me, but she either tripped over a step or had a dizzy spell—we weren't very steady on our feet at that time—and tumbled down the ten steps in front of the hut onto the stony ground. When I ran up to her, she was unconscious. I called for help, and a neighbor, a pregnant Mekong, told me to get Pou Mân at the pagoda. When he returned with me, Sreï Peu was still unconscious at the foot of the stairs with the pregnant Mekong. Pou Mân carried her back to the pagoda, where he cleaned a wound on her head with gasoline taken from his workshop. Gasoline was the Mekongs' all-purpose disinfectant. Pou Mân pulled on Sreï Peu's earlobes and shook her until she let out a cry. Then he put a dressing of honey on her head and wound a piece of mosquito net around it as a bandage. We undressed her, and I washed her poor stained underwear. Sreï Peu felt better the next day. A visit from Sy Neang also cheered us up. He would come by now and then, bringing a bit of fish, but this time he hadn't been able to bring us anything because of the drought. Mi Vi reproached him for coming empty-handed, even telling him that he needn't come if he hadn't anything to offer. "But I come to see my sisters," he replied.

7   THE WEEKS dragged by, and the months. Nothing relieved the monotony of our misery. One day a Mekong in charge of girls came to get me to go plant rice at Phum Po, somewhere in the direction of Battambang. Off we went, sleeping under the trees at night. At Phum Po, they put us in huts belonging to workers who had arrived at the site before us.

During that evening's educational session, they explained to us the difficulties of provisioning—this in a country where we were constantly planting, transplanting, and harvesting rice! We were to be given only three spoonfuls of corn, sometimes with a pinch of salt. The other workers weren't thrilled at the new arrivals, because the huts had been crowded even before we came. There was an open shed that was used as a kitchen for the girls, and I decided to sleep there, along with other girls who had been made to feel unwelcome. Those who couldn't find a quiet corner there went off to sleep under the trees.

As the work progressed, we had to walk farther and farther each morning. After two weeks, we were more than three kilometers away from the worksite, and we had to cross a bridge. The water was beginning to rise again. Enormous leeches clamped themselves to our legs, then to our buttocks, and we spent lots of time picking them off each other.

After we'd planted rice on all the available arable land, they ordered us to cut down rushes to clear new fields. We were short-handed, so the Mekongs went to get girls who were "hiding" in the hospital. When they asked me where Tôn Ny was, I told them I didn't know. "All right, I'll look in the hospital," the Mekong said, and the next day I saw my cousin arrive with her bundle. Everyone turned to look at her: compared to the rest of us, sunburned and tanned by the wind and rain, she looked so beautiful, with fair skin, although she was somewhat thin because of her illness. I found her a place next to me in the kitchen shed, where we slept in our wet clothes.

We were up to our shoulders in water as we worked cutting rushes. The corn ration was smaller now, only one spoonful per person, about seven or eight kernels. Look as we might, we couldn't find any of those good fleshy plants we used to gather close to the villages, so we cut vines instead. We cooked their leaves with the few kernels of rationed corn, and wound up with diarrhea. Unable to go to work, we asked for a day off.

"You ate any old thing just to get out of working! Get out there! And if you dirty the water, they'll carry you away in a hammock!"

Obviously we arrived late for work. They ordered us to pull weeds from the mud where the young rice seedlings were going to be planted. When we bent over, our bodies were completely under water, but there was something in it for us, because we found lots of water lilies and filled our trouser pockets with their edible seeds—out of sight of the Mekongs. There was no point in going to collect the spoonful of corn, because what we'd found was better. All we had to do was gather a few branches while the Mekongs weren't looking, build a fire under the trees, and cook our meal. That evening, a girl who slept with us brought home a gourd she had pinched from a little vegetable garden near the kitchen. We refused to share it with her, though, because if the theft was discovered, all three of us would end up in the plastic bag. Nothing ever came of it, but the village Mekongs did ask that we be moved farther away from their neighborhood.

Our Mekong found a little wooden house near the bridge with room for her entire group of ten girls, but we didn't stay there for more than a week or ten days. They brought us back to Phum Po, where we spent the night in a big drafty shed along with a hundred other people. After an hour or two of sleep, off to work! At noon they gave us a full ladle of corn as a reward for our efforts, explaining that this unusual largesse was due to the fact that we had spent part of the night walking.

We were preparing the ground for planting. Because this area was infested with rats, the Mekongs organized a rat hunt, arming us with sticks to beat the poor animals' brains out. My aim wasn't very good, but I did manage to knock one of them cold. Quite proud of myself, I picked it up by the tail and waved it around triumphantly, but suddenly the tiny beast started twisting around, lifted up its head, and bit my finger three times with its sharp little teeth. I should've dropped it immediately, but I was too startled. Blood gushed from my finger, so a Yotear tore his scarf to make me a dressing of tobacco and saliva, their standard remedy.

When I asked the Mekong for permission to rest, she "advised" me to stay where I was for the distribution of rations, and—what a surprise! Along with the spoonful of corn they gave each of us an orange, the first orange since Tul Trieh.

Since I was injured at work and wasn't just foolishly sick, I was allowed three days to recuperate. I used the time to forage, and found a few plants and edible leaves to add to our spoonful of corn. All I had to do was turn up at noon when they distributed the corn ration.

On the day I was to return to work, the Mekong appeared in our hut at first light and poked at us with a long bamboo stick. "Let's go, get up!"

"What's going on?"

"They could be up to their ears in water," she said, "and they'd still be fast asleep! Come on, get up, lazybones."

The water level had risen, flooding most of the huts. We moved all our things to higher ground, in a grove of mango trees that had been off limits to us until now.

While we got back to planting out corn seedlings, a group of boys set up huts thatched with marsh grass for our shelter at night. It rained every evening. During the day we went back and forth from a holding pool a kilometer away where the rice plants were stored. Every evening there was an educational session on the same old theme: we must force ourselves to work for the future of our country.

Our hut was a joke: the earth was damp, the wind blew in the rain, our bundles of clothes were soaked, the ants ate us alive, and the mosquitoes wouldn't let us sleep. We shivered all day long. At noon we stopped for two minutes to share an ear of corn among the entire team of ten people, standing with our feet in the water in the pouring rain without anything to cover our heads. Girls were collapsing from exhaustion every day; God knows where the Mekongs took them. The water kept rising until all the huts were flooded. Tôn Ny and I decided to take refuge in the kitchen hut, which was still dry; only the Mekong and the cook lived there.

The Mekong sent us away roughly. Choking down my shame and anger, I begged her to let us stay in the kitchen just for that one night. When we arrived, the two women had been busy eating; they had hidden their bowls, but the smell of hot rice still lingered. Sniffing the air, I asked them, "You wouldn't happen to have a pot we could scrape clean?" With very ill grace, the Mekong handed each of us a rice ball. "But don't take it into your head to go around saying I feast at night!"

"Oh no! We didn't see a thing."

The next day, before work, we all had to scrape the mud around the huts into a little dike—as if that would be of any use! The water was simply welling up out of the earth. We hung our bundles from the crosspieces of bamboo holding down the grass on the roof.

The planting out had lasted a month, and now we moved on. This time, there were no huts at all, and we slept out under the trees. There was just a skimpy shelter for the kitchen; the menu was still one spoonful of corn, and there was always rain to add to our enjoyment of our work.

For our sleeping pleasure, the Angkar provided us with a plastic sheet to be used as a ground cloth on the damp soil. We anchored it with stones, but all it took to drench us was someone running by through the huge puddles, and anyway, the plastic cloth rustled and woke us up at the slightest movement. When there was just too much water, we got up onto the roof of the kitchen shelter, where we'd hung our bundles, and slept on a slant, our hands gripping the bamboo poles of the roof. One night I leaned my forehead on a sack hanging near me and felt kernels of corn. I nudged Tôn Ny in the ribs with my elbow and whispered, "Lean your head on the other side." While she held the bag steady, I fished out a small handful of kernels. It was child's play to slip them onto the kitchen griddle, which was still warm, and wait for them to toast a little bit. Worn out by their long day, our companions were oblivious, so Tôn Ny and I quietly treated ourselves to a small dietary supplement.

8 WORK, RAIN, HUNGER. It was hunger that tormented us the most: all we could think of was finding something to appease the gnawing of our stomachs. I was fifteen years old, Tôn Ny was fourteen. One day she came to forewarn me that she was leaving for Vat Thmey without permission from the Mekongs.

"Arrange things so that they don't notice I'm gone. I'm going to try to bring back some vegetables, and there should be some ripe papayas behind our hut, the ones you planted before we left. If I'm not back by nightfall, it'll mean I didn't have any luck."

"I want to go with you."

"No, I'm smaller, I'll be able to hide more easily, and besides, I know how to swim—you remember, there are flooded stretches where you have to swim across."

As soon as the 4 a.m. roll call was finished, Tôn Ny slipped away as if to relieve herself; it was still dark out and the Mekong didn't notice anything. The day seemed to last forever, and I tried not to attract any attention as I worked. When the last whistle blew, I ran to our hut. Tôn Ny should have been waiting for me there, but she wasn't back yet!

The Mekong passed by. "I haven't seen Met Tôn Ny. Did she work today?"

"Of course, but she must have gone out to get some *ptih*. She just left."

I began to worry. I prayed. I hadn't touched my spoonful of corn; Tôn

Ny would be even more famished than I was, she'd eat it. The sky was
full of clouds that night, but no rain fell.

Suddenly I heard the whistle for the evening's educational session. After
rolling up our two mosquito nets to make it seem as though Tôn Ny were
asleep, I went off to the meeting. When her name was called, I answered
that she had a stomachache, had stayed in bed, and asked to be excused.
The Mekong never failed to check our absences, but that night she didn't
budge. The meeting lasted until about eleven in the evening. When I got
back to the hut, Tôn Ny was there, soaking wet, petrified with fear. "I'll
never ever do that again!" She had brought six little papayas picked at
Vat Thmey, a few leaves of *ptih*, and some edible vines. On the way
there, she didn't have any problems, but on the way back, she took the
wrong path and was lost by nightfall. Attracted by a distant light, she
started to swim, holding the bag of food on her head with one hand, but
when she reached the shore, she recognized the place as being directly
opposite our camp. She had to set out again in the other direction and
arrived during the evening meeting. Seeing the mosquito nets rolled up,
she understood that her escapade was still a secret.

Tôn Ny was soaked to the skin, but she couldn't change her clothes
because our bundles were hanging up in the kitchen. I heated some water,
tossed in a little papaya cut into slices, and mixed it all up with some *ptih*
and vine leaves. After adding our spoonful of corn, we ate in the dark.
The next morning, I was feverish and unable to go to the bridge, the only
dry spot in our area, where they distributed the corn rations. Tôn Ny
shared her corn with me and prepared the papayas when she returned
from work.

After three days of this, the Mekong took an interest in my continued
absence. "Met Peuw, tomorrow you're coming to work. If you die in your
hut, we'll just let you rot, but if you die in the rice field, we'll remove
you right away in a hammock." I didn't think much of her sense of humor,
but the next day, sure enough, I was out in the rice paddy. My legs held
up for part of the morning, but around ten o'clock I fell unconscious. Tôn
Ny told me later she had seen me fall; she had been keeping an eye on
me from a distance, and ran over and supported me while calling for help.
Without her, I would have been abandoned in the mud like my father.

When I woke up, I was lying stretched out on the bridge. Some girls
were rubbing me, pulling my ears and hair. They told me to stay on the
bridge, that I'd get my share of corn. When the Mekong arrived to dole
out the rations, I asked if I might work at Vat Thmey, because I wasn't
able to work in the water anymore. She refused, adding, "What are you

doing with long hair? You'd better cut it off right away, and that goes for the rest of you, too. I don't want to see any more long hair." My hair hadn't been cut since my stay at the hospital; it had grown back thickly, and when Tôn Ny cut my hair that evening she said to me, "You'll be able to hold your head up better. Your hair is too heavy for you."

Well, she did such a good job cutting my hair that the other girls collapsed with laughter. "Who gave you that haircut?" I couldn't see myself in a mirror, but it seems that I had no hair on one side, a bit more on the other side, and a few wild tufts in the middle. I just kept my head covered all the time. Tôn Ny apologized—what else could she have done with the dull scissors she had to work with? They had been my mother's, and I was the one who had cut all my companions' hair. There was no use crying about it, I simply had to wait for my hair to grow out again, but I never asked Tôn Ny for another haircut.

Our worksite was now farther away from the bridge, and we didn't go back there anymore for our noon break. Now we stayed in the rice paddies while the Mekong and the cook passed by on the embankment at noon. We held out our hands for our pittance, popped it in our mouths, and the meal was over: back to work. Now it was Tôn Ny's turn to ask to go work at Vat Thmey, but the Mekong told her that we wouldn't be staying here much longer, we'd be going somewhere else soon. In the meantime, we saw the Mekongs up on the embankment with full bowls, gorging themselves on special rice, fish, or meat. At night Tôn Ny would tell me, "I'd like to die right now!"

Rain, wind, mud—when would it all be over? Two days later, at the evening session, they told us that we'd be leaving for Kat Holet, the place where we had built a road. And how many of the girls who worked on that road were still alive? Every day they carried away one or two, or five; the toll varied from day to day. What mass grave had swallowed them up?

After barely a day's march, we arrived at the worksite, where our job— for the moment—was simply chasing birds out of the rice fields, where the rice was coming to a head. We slept in a big hut prepared for ten people. Reveille was at eight, and they gave us a ladleful of rice—a feast! After a tour through the rice fields, we could go back to our hut—at ten o'clock. At noon, they handed out a can of rice for every two people, which we were allowed to prepare ourselves. The rain limited itself to small showers, although there were still great gusts of wind.

We had lots of spare time. I was able to go snail-hunting and fishing for mussels in the river. Sometimes, while we were chasing the birds out of the rice fields, we could also catch fish or crabs. It was like heaven! We had almost no obligations, except the obnoxious educational sessions in the evenings.

9 TWO WEEKS flew by like a dream. They sent us to Vat Chas, and on the way we met several groups of girls going to the same place. We all had to be reassigned to new teams because too many girls had died, but no one talked about it. The Mekongs called it "regrouping forces."

Those who were strong enough went down into the rice fields to pull weeds, while the invalids husked or winnowed rice. I lined up with the able-bodied, as I preferred to work in the water, where there was always a chance of catching crabs, frogs, even snails. The fish were reserved for the Mekongs. The crabs lived in mud holes, and you had to be careful because snakes also liked these holes. The first thing you did was flood the hole with water; then the snake would come right out.

A few weeks later, I was transferred to winnowing rice. Food was in short supply again, and they weren't giving us anything besides ground rice and bran. The temptation to steal a bit of rice during work was very strong, but there was only one punishment for this crime: death. Confident that I wouldn't betray them, two of my companions each carried off two handfuls of rice in their sarongs. Since they couldn't hide it anywhere, they cooked it that night in a corner of our hut. They should have realized that the smell would tip off our Mekong—everyone had warned them about it. The Mekong arrived like a Fury. "Who stole some rice? Bring out your bowls!" She didn't have to look very long—the hearth was still hot. What she didn't know was that there were two offenders, and she directed all her rage at the first girl she found, kicking her, yanking her hair, beating her with a bamboo rod until she was bloody. A second Mekong arrived, Met Niop, a woman even more ferocious than our Mekong. She tied our unfortunate companion's hands behind her back and, after punching her a few times in the chest, showed her the cooking pot full of rice. "Eat! Go on, eat!" She shoved rice into the poor girl's mouth until she choked, and finally vomited. The two harpies led the girl away, still beating her with their bamboo rods. No one ever saw her again.

Work went on monotonously, and our constant hunger was wrenching: rice powder and bran, which I sometimes roasted in an attempt to give it some flavor, had torn my insides to shreds. One morning I didn't have the strength to get up, and no one came to see what had happened to me. Everyone was so used to having people just disappear.

That day, by chance, Tôn Ny came by my hut at noon and found me in a bad way, passing blood with my stool. She called the neighbors for help and ran to the Mekong, who brought in the nurse from the hospital, which was only half a kilometer away. The hospital had recovered its former function, along with its death-house atmosphere. They carried me there in a hammock. Tôn Ny stayed close to me. My throat was on fire, but I couldn't get a word out to ask for something to drink. My old acquaintance Met Sim arrived and gave me a perfusion of serum. I gestured to indicate that I was thirsty, but Sim told me, "If you swallow any water, you'll die immediately." She mashed up a bit of rice with sugar, but I vomited it up right away. Tôn Ny took off my ragged peasant's black trousers and blue shirt to wash them, but a Mekong arrived and sent her outside. "There are nurses for that, you get back to work!" Tôn Ny went off after having put my things out to dry under the trees. She came by every day at noon, and Sy Neang looked in from time to time. The people around me died one after the other; only I seemed unable to die.

Astonished by my will to live, the Mekong had me moved to a cleaner place, right by the main entrance, where the inspection tours usually wound up. When I realized where I was, though, I burst into tears: it was the place where Vannah and Sithân had died. I thought of my mother. "Why don't you come get me, Mâ? You were lying in this very spot . . . Why are you leaving me alone on this earth? Mâ, take me away with you!" I slept very fitfully, and in the morning the night nurse asked me why I kept calling for my parents; my cries were bothering the patients, who couldn't sleep. Met Sim, overhearing the nurse's reproaches, realized that I had once lain in the same spot with my dying sister and brother, so she had me moved to another place in the room. There were plenty of empty ones, every morning a good third of the room was carried out, which kept the gravediggers busy. I still remember with affection a kind woman in a bed close to mine. She was about thirty years old, not quite as sick as I was, and she took care of me as if I were her younger sister.

The days and weeks rolled by. I was being fed—not much, but regularly. My strength was returning, and I wanted to leave: too many terrible memories were attached to this hospital. At least the monotonous work in the fields dulled my imagination. Both Met Sim and Nâ Rin told me that I ought to stay there at least another month, but my requests finally wore them out and they wrote a note for the Mekong, where I read that I'd spent six weeks in the hospital.

Met Sim escorted me back to my hut, which was quite close by. The Mekong was already there. "Tomorrow you'll join the Sra Tro Pen team!" That was Tôn Ny's group. We worked in the water, cutting rushes. Each girl had to account for two bundles of rushes of about fifteen kilos each and carry them to a great pile, where they were loaded onto oxcarts.

The first day back at work I was able to cut only a few handfuls of rushes, barely enough to tie into a bundle. Tôn Ny scolded me: "You see, you ought to have stayed at the hospital. Now I have to do your work as well as mine." It was true, the two of us were responsible for four bundles, but after a few more days I was able to hold my own again and had no regrets about being back in the fields, where there were always crabs just waiting to be scooped up by our bowls. There were even a few moments when we could smile. For example, I could see Tôn Ny's black trousers getting shorter and shorter every day. They had started to unravel at the bottom, so she had cut the legs off at mid-calf, but since we didn't have any way of sewing a decent hem, she eventually had to cut the pants off at the knee, keeping a somewhat uneven fringe that created a very nice effect. As for me, I had long black trousers with a good hem at the bottom, but patched in various places, and the pieces sewn one over the other gave me a carapace weighing more than two kilos. One of Pou Mân's companions said to me one day, "Whatever you do, hang on to those pants, Met Peuw. When the Vietnamese arrive, you'll be able to sell them for their weight in gold." Most of the girls had cutoffs like Tôn Ny's. I'd managed to save a needle, and sewed my patches on with hempen thread obtained from old string or from the pieces thrown away by other girls when they were shortening their trousers.

Our work cutting rushes lasted a good month, after which the Mekong sent us back to our huts at Vat Thmey to work with the adults. There we were put under the jurisdiction of a new Mekong, Met Yai, and her husband, Met Lun, a couple in their early twenties. They were in charge of organizing the rice harvest around Vat Thmey and Vat Chas. They had us build new huts near the graveyard, closer to the rice fields. Mi Vi worked a few kilometers away from us. The new huts were bigger, to provide room enough for twenty-five people. Since we didn't want to leave Sreï Peu all alone, we asked for permission to bring her along with us. Other families did as we did, and the children played with each other during the day.

10 AFTER A FEW DAYS, the groups of harvesters joined together and Mi Vi turned up working abreast of us in the field, but Tôn Ny refused to speak to her because she had been so nasty to Sreï Peu. Our little sister hid to avoid seeing Mi Vi, spending her days alone in the big hut. She was still asleep when we left for work in the morning at five, but if she happened to wake up, she cried and begged us to take her along. One day, when Mi Vi wasn't working because of an injured foot, Sreï Peu screamed and refused to stay alone with her. The Mekong Yai was amazed, so Tôn Ny and I explained that Mi Vi had often abused the child. Yai and her husband, Lun, who already had three children, offered to adopt Sreï Peu, but Tôn Ny refused. "Before they died, my parents made me promise that I'd never abandon Sreï Peu, that I'd never give her to strangers, and that I'd help her until she grew up."

The Mekong didn't push things any more that day, but we learned that she had been questioning our companions about us. Sreï Peu had very light skin, while Tôn Ny had become as dark as a peasant from the North from working out in the fields, and the Mekong found it hard to believe that they were sisters. Even Mi Vi affirmed that Sreï Peu was really Tôn Ny's sister, but Met Yai still wasn't convinced and took me aside to ask me about the family. I told her that Sreï Peu was the youngest daughter of Met Vong and Nang, and Tôn Ny was their oldest daughter. The Mekong was still doubtful, asking me the same questions several times. She offered again to adopt Sreï Peu, and when Tôn Ny still refused, Met Yai suggested that the child stay with her own children during the day. Tôn Ny could pass by the Mekong's house in the evening on the way home from work and pick up Sreï Peu.

The trouble started on the first evening, when Tôn Ny wanted to bring the child back to the communal hut. Sreï Peu had a tantrum and thrashed around. "There's food here, they give me fish and meat, but you don't give me anything to eat." Tôn Ny tried to explain to her: "Remember Papa and Mama. Have you forgotten your sisters? We all have to stay together." There was nothing to do but carry her away by force, promising her that she could return the next day.

The adults in the group had advised us to let her live with the Mekong because she would be well fed, but we didn't give in, and the child returned to us every evening after her meal. Met Yai renewed her attack at the end of two weeks. "Met Tôn Ny, either hand Sreï Peu over to me for good or take her back. Make up your mind." Tôn Ny didn't give in, and Sreï Peu didn't return to the Mekong's house anymore, but Met Yai became our enemy, sending us to do all the difficult jobs. It was useless to protest, since they had only one way of dealing with recalcitrance—a pickax blow to the back of the head.

When the harvest was over, we returned to our huts at Vat Thmey, and Mi Vi came with us. We were still sharing the same hut, so we were obliged to make peace with one another, but Tôn Ny and I were determined to take care of Sreï Peu by ourselves.

It was a nice thought, but it didn't work out; the Mekong in charge of girls came to fetch us to dig up mud from the dried-up riverbeds. We couldn't possibly take Sreï Peu with us. Tôn Ny went to find Mekong Met Yai and ask her humbly for permission at least to come home every evening. "Why should I allow you to do that? You're assigned to your work group, you have to sleep with everyone else. You must conserve your strength and stay at your worksite." She refused to give Tôn Ny a note for the Mekong supervisor.

Mi Vi offered to take care of our sister at night. We weren't too confident about the arrangement, but there was no other solution. Sreï Peu would spend her days on her own, playing with the children her own age who remained in the village. She'd get her noon rice ration by herself.

We were working about a kilometer away from Vat Thmey. In the evening we would sleep in a hangar with the rest of the group of fifty girls, but at noon we dashed over to Vat Thmey to see how Sreï Peu was doing. One day we found Sy Neang there: he was still working as an oxherd, but from time to time he helped in the collection of palm milk. He always brought something to eat to the hut, and Mi Vi gave him a pleasant welcome if he brought some fish. On that day he told us that he now had permission to spend nights at Vat Thmey, so Tôn Ny and I returned to work somewhat reassured.

When our job was finished, we were allowed to return to stay at Vat Thmey, but then it was Sy Neang's turn to be gone for a while. The job rotation was bewildering. We were never sure of staying in the same place, but we knew we'd never run out of work.

11 THIS TIME we were back at work within twenty-four hours: they sent us to plant vegetables not far from a secret school, the Great Re-education School, Sala Som Niat. It was a quiet spot two kilometers from Vat Thmey. We had permission to return "home" each evening, which made Sreï Peu happy.

We prepared the vegetable beds and planted the seeds. The strongest girls, including Tôn Ny, went back and forth with buckets, fetching water from the river for the garden. One evening in our hut, Tôn Ny showed me her foot, which had become infected after she dropped an iron pail on her toes. The next day she couldn't walk anymore; her whole leg was on fire and the ganglions in her groin were swollen. We washed the wound with salt and boiled water, and I made her a poultice of plantain leaves. While I stayed with Tôn Ny, we sent Sreï Peu off to collect our rice ration. She set out courageously and returned in an hour, carrying the bowl on her head. We couldn't help laughing when we saw her sedately climbing the stairs, one hand steadying the bowl, which was bigger than her head, and the other hand at her hip, as if she were a dancer. The cook had told her, however, that we had to come for our rations ourselves. The next day I dragged myself off to get provisions with a raging fever. The Mekong saw me but didn't ask any questions that time. On the third day, however, she wanted to know where Tôn Ny was.

"She's still sick."

"She has been sick for a while. Come on, all of you, bring a hammock, we're going to get her!"

She herself directed the group of ten girls who went to get Tôn Ny. "Met Tôn Ny, it's not good to hide away like this. We've come to get you for work." Since Tôn Ny really couldn't walk, they put her in the hammock, and four girls took turns carrying her to the worksite. That evening I went home to Vat Thmey alone, since no one wanted to carry Tôn Ny back.

I met our Mekong, Met Yai, at our door; armed with a big notebook, she was counting and registering the chickens being raised by villagers near their huts. We happened to have a chicken, brought by Sy Neang one evening the previous week when he had come to stay overnight. Met Yai wrote down: "One chicken at the Mân-Vi house."

Two days later the chicken laid an egg. It's difficult to share one egg.

"Let's keep it," said Mi Vi, "we'll have chicks." And in fact, one month later, we had eight or nine chicks. Mi Vi announced at that point that we were going to kill the chicken. "Watch out, Mi Vi, the Mekong will cut your head off." She yielded to reason and abandoned the idea. The chicks grew bigger; Sreï Peu had tamed them, they came when she called. But no joy lasts for long: the Mekong came to requisition the chicks for the community, and since she couldn't manage to catch them, it was Sreï Peu who had to collect them and carry them to the Mekong in a basket.

A few days later Mi Vi couldn't withstand temptation any longer. "Bang Peuw," she told me, "if you don't kill that chicken I won't give you your share of rice." I was lying down in a corner of the hut and in no mood for an argument. "If we don't do it right away, Met Yai will come and requisition it." Mi Vi is afraid, I told myself, the Mekong will kill her, and I don't want to die because of a chicken. I started to cry. "In any case, it's our chicken, Bang Peuw! Why should we give it to the kitchen?" She began to explain to me how to kill a chicken. "You see, it's not hard, you wring its neck, like this."

I didn't want to hear any more, so I took Sreï Peu and we went off to bathe. When we returned, Mi Vi picked right up again where she had left off, threatening, scolding, showing me how it was done. "All right," she said, "for tonight I'll just tie the chicken's feet together and put her in a sack. Perhaps tomorrow you'll be willing to kill her." She didn't give me anything to eat that night.

The next day, at first light, I still didn't feel very well, but I didn't stay in the hut, and if Mi Vi was going to kill the chicken, it would be better if I wasn't there. I took Sreï Peu, intending to go far away from the hut . . . but where? No matter where I went I ran the risk of meeting a Mekong who'd requisition me for work. And then it started to rain. We took shelter under the house. With a handful of leaves I wiped away the filth so that we could sit down.

After a few moments I thought I heard the chicken squawking, so I asked Sreï Peu to sing, trying to distract her attention. I could hear Mi Vi calling me to come help. I didn't budge, but I saw a drop of blood, and then another, drip down between the bamboo slats. I wiped them away with a handful of dirt.

It was still raining outside, the wind had come up, and we were cold. I decided to go inside, where Mi Vi was busy plucking the chicken. We watched her work, following her every move. Before the morning was over, the chicken was cooked, and Mi Vi settled down to eat it by herself. I'd have liked at least to have drunk the bouillon, but she didn't offer us anything. Finally, satisfied, she couldn't finish the whole bird and offered us what was left. Holding back Sreï Peu, I told Mi Vi to keep the rest for her husband. "No, Pou Mân mustn't find out about this."

Hunger proved stronger than good sense. We devoured the two little pieces left over, Sreï Peu licking her fingers over her share.

Mi Vi went out to bury the bones and feathers, then hurriedly planted some manioc over the spot. And it was a good thing she did, because Met Yai soon came to get the chicken registered in her list for the communal kitchen (which probably meant just for the Mekongs). "Where's your chicken?" I saw Mi Vi press her white lips together to keep them from quivering. "I don't know," she whispered. The Mekong went around the hut looking for telltale traces. She dug here and there in the ground— there must be feathers someplace. In the grass? Nothing. Over here, perhaps? It was the place where Mi Vi had buried the incriminating remains. Met Yai leaned over and noticed tiny manioc shoots. She wouldn't disturb this area, which promised food as much for herself as for those who lived in the hut. We were relieved when she went away, muttering to herself. It had been a close call.

This adventure brought us a bit closer to Mi Vi, who no longer kept all to herself the rats that Pou Mân sometimes brought her from the pagoda. She hunted the mice in the corners of the hut, and to keep as much of the meat as possible, she didn't skin them but shaved off the delicate fur with a sharp knife. One day, she found a whole litter of newborn mice, six or seven babies no bigger than beans. Feeling generous that day, she offered some to Sreï Peu and me. I felt a little squeamish, but hunger won out: I ate two tiny mice roasted in the bottom of a pot with a few leftover grains of rice.

A day or two later, Tôn Ny was still working in the vegetable garden but was now able to come home in the evenings, whereas I had been recruited to replant rice where it hadn't been growing properly in the fields. "You're strong," the Mekong told me. "We're leaving tomorrow at dawn for Phum Po." I knew the place—there wasn't too much water there, but the soil was hard and the water had stood in the fields too long, so the transplanted rice seedlings had all rotted. We changed fields every day, which meant there were no provisions, because the Angkar couldn't keep track of us when we moved around like that. My legs just couldn't hold me up. I asked to return to Vat Thmey, but that was out of the question. At the evening session the Mekong asked my companions, "Do you think that Met Peuw is really sick?" Everyone told her, "Oh yes, we have to help her all the time," and one voice added, "It would be better if she didn't die here. Let her die at Vat Thmey!" The Mekong seemed impressed by this, but she didn't say anything. Unable even to stand up, I was quite ready to die.

At noon, an empty cart was leaving after unloading its delivery of rice plants. "Bang Mekong, let me leave with the cart, I'd rather die at Vat Thmey!" She didn't answer, but signaled to two of my companions to hoist me up onto the cart. And that's how I found myself at the foot of the ladder to our hut at the end of the afternoon. My head was spinning; crawling up the steps on all fours, I collapsed onto a mat in the darkest corner of the hut. When I woke up, Mi Vi was leaning over me, with Sreï Peu at her side. She treated me very kindly—was it because I hadn't betrayed her to the Mekong after that business with the chicken? She helped me to drink something, and I lost consciousness again.

When I came to, it was pitch-black out, and I saw a candle flame wavering before my eyes. Only Mekongs used candles, so I wasn't surprised to see Met Yai holding the candle in one hand and three smoking sticks of incense in the other. I was astonished when the Mekong bent over me. "Met Peuw, do you recognize me?" She put the hand holding the incense sticks on my chest.

"What are you doing, Aunt Yai?"

"Your chest is very congested. Mi Vi came to get me."

I was more and more confused: this haughty, cold Mekong bending over me with incense to help me feel better!

The air was oppressive and I wanted to sit up. I was suffocating. Met Yai slipped two pillows under my shoulders . . . I hadn't seen a pillow in three years. She took off my faded blouse and rolled me up in a piece of white cloth.

Hours went by; at times I saw Tôn Ny, who came to touch my hand. They fed me sugared rice, and Met Yai brought some coconut milk. "I want you to get well," she told me. And I, trained for months in passive obedience, did begin to feel better. For once the Angkar's representative was giving me a pleasant order, and I had to obey. When I asked for fish, she brought some right away, and I was happy to share it with Mi Vi and Sreï Peu.

I'd been there for a week. Perhaps I could get up today? No need to worry about that: along came the Mekong in charge of girls.

"Come on, get up! All sick girls are to gather under the hangar."

"What hangar?"

"You'll see."

"But why?"

"All the workers must be assembled together. We'll find out who can and who cannot keep on their feet."

What was to be done with Sreï Peu? Mi Vi had left that morning for a worksite somewhere or other, and Tôn Ny wasn't there either. I took Sreï Peu's hand and we joined a group of disabled people heading toward the secret school, Sala Som Niat. Our Mekong, a girl of seventeen, seemed worried. It was as if she was afraid of something. It took us more than an hour to cover the two kilometers to the school, where we were met by a new Mekong, who came from Prey Veng and wasn't more than fifteen years old. Her assistant, in charge of everything concerning fruit trees, as we later learned, was a girl of eleven. These two had complete authority over all our Mekongs, at least over those in charge of girls, because Met Yai remained the Mekong for adults.

Five

WOLVES
AMONG THEMSELVES

1 THERE WAS SOMETHING of a change in the air. Arriving exhausted at the hangar of the secret school, we were allowed to rest. "You'll work tomorrow." They gave us something to eat and told us there was going to be a special meeting that night. A new leader was expected, one Pou Sok. I was surprised that they didn't call him Met Sok. It seemed that he had arrived by train from Moung Russeï with a band of Khmer Rouge and their families. They had come from the south, from Prey Veng and Takeo, and they'd taken over all the abandoned huts in the villages of the Battambang region. We'd never seen Yotears on horseback before: these arrived with horses and rode them out in the fields. Our Mekongs didn't understand what was going on.

That evening we seated ourselves in a circle, while behind us two fifteen-year-old girls marched up and down on guard duty, rifles at the slope. The new leader strode into the center of the circle, drew himself up, and began to speak.

"My name is Sok. I've come to help you. You don't have enough to eat, I know. Entire families have starved to death, I know. I have a whole list of them. Who's in charge of the population register here?"

"Prel is," said the new fifteen-year-old Mekong.

"Where is he?"

"I don't know."

"We'll find him. Who forced you to call everyone 'comrade'? That's an ugly way to talk. Go back to your old ways: I'm 'Pou' Sok, not 'Met'! We're going to get rid of that garbage. Who ordered you to be so sparing of rice? Our country has the richest harvests in the world. Who forbade you to wear jewelry? Jewels are beautiful. Don't be afraid to wear your necklaces, earrings, and bracelets again."

He went on like this for a long time, but I wasn't able to keep up with him.

What was certain was that from that night on everyone was given their ladleful of rice and two little fish. The boys were assigned to catch them for everyone. Several girls, even Mi Vi, started wearing their necklaces and earrings once more.

Pou Sok went off on his horse, as proud "as a Frenchman," people said. The new Mekong made the rounds of the huts right away, list in hand. She questioned each girl individually, and asked me the same questions she put to everyone else.

"Where is your family?"

"There's no one left."

"How many of you were there?"

"Seven."

"What was the name of your Mekong when your family died?"

"I don't remember anymore." (I had to be careful.)

"With whom do you live?"

"I'm alone."

"Who are your nearest relatives?"

"Tôn Ny and Sreï Peu."

"Tell me about Sreï Peu's family. How did her parents die?"

"Tôn Ny will tell you that better than I could."

"The two of you didn't have the same Mekong?"

"No."

"All right. You don't have the strength necessary to work digging and moving earth. You'll take care of vegetables. If you want to pick some fruit, just ask."

She went to interrogate Tôn Ny next, who was then assigned to work in the kitchen with three other girls. That evening we learned that Yai's husband had been executed in the woods, along with other Mekong men.

Our new Mekong didn't live with us, she slept at the quarters of Pou Sok's people, but Lin, who was twenty years old, always stayed with us. She was from Phnom Penh, the first city girl I had seen become a Mekong, and she was in charge of all the girls in our group.

Something was really changing, but we stayed on our guard. The older Mekong had said that she was going to take a census of the entire population in the nearest villages, and she added, in an offhand fashion, "If the Vietnamese arrive, you'll be at the rear, but I'll fight in the front lines." So it was possible that the Vietnamese might come. We didn't like them at all, and were afraid of them, but we wondered if their arrival wouldn't bring more changes that would be to our advantage.

I was thinking about all this, crouched down among my vegetables weeding and hunting caterpillars, when Lin, accompanied by four or five Yotears, came and told me to go with her to Sala Som Niat. She must have seen a glint of terror in my eyes, because she started to laugh. "I know, you're not used to being there, but don't be afraid. We're going to bring back supplies for the kitchen."

I had never been closer than a hundred meters to the school. We knew it was a dangerous place. Several horses were wandering around on the outskirts of the school, which surprised me. Inside, there was a group of more than twenty very important Yotears, most of them from twenty to thirty years old, and a few younger than that. Two boys invited me inside. "Come and have dessert with us." They offered me cakes, and on the table I could see dishes like the ones we used to use at home in Phnom Penh. How could the Yotears have such good food when we didn't even have the bare essentials? And who knew how to prepare dishes like these, which one never found out in the countryside?

We went back to the kitchen carrying full baskets on our heads. It turned out that this was special food for the Yotears who would be arriving that evening.

It puzzled me that the Mekong dragged me off to the school when I still had a lot of trouble walking. Every morning I massaged my legs with dew, and I walked with a cane. And yet Lin said to me, "When Tôn Ny goes to get special food at the school, you may go with her now and then to have some cake." Why us? I'd have liked to ask a million questions. "Don't let that keep you from working in the vegetable beds, though, or your companions will be jealous." I was well aware of that, and I worked every day until dark, when I rejoined Sreï Peu in the communal hangar. Tôn Ny spent her nights in the kitchen.

2 ONE DAY we could hear in the distance what sounded like the echo of artillery fire, or perhaps bombs. The Mekongs made us interrupt our work transplanting rice seedlings. "Everyone go to Moung Russeï, we're going to store the harvest in a safe place." So people shuttled back and forth between Moung Russeï and Vat Thmey, with bags or baskets of rice on their heads. Lin came to see me apart from the others. "You still can't walk too well," she told me. "Stay here and pick glowworms off your vegetables." So I never did see the former pagoda, the temple complex at Vat Thmey, transformed into a warehouse for rice. Since most of the people had gone, Lin invited me to pick oranges with her. "Bang Peuw, you're as thin as a ghost. Have you been sick like this for a long time?" What could I tell her? I couldn't remember being in really good health since we had left Phnom Penh. Lin told me that she was a Yotear's daughter. We squeezed a few oranges and drank the juice— it was so good.

In the evening the workers returned to the hangar where I stayed with Sreï Peu. This was our routine for several days. Some of the workers, particularly the women, preferred to stay at Vat Thmey, to be right on hand at dawn when work resumed storing the rice. That was how we learned that one night a boy had tried to steal some rice from the pagoda. One of the women who were sleeping in little groups at the various entrances to the building managed to wound the thief on the forehead. The thief escaped, but everyone knew it was Lin's brother. The next day, though, when the authorities demanded to know the thief's name, no one dared denounce the Mekong's brother. The forty women assigned to guard the rice in the pagoda were taken to the little grove behind the school and murdered. The faces were different, but the methods of repression hadn't changed.

Another evening two Yotears came to get a girl who had been sleeping near me in the hangar for the last few days. I didn't know her; she was around eighteen years old and very beautiful.

"What do you want with me?" she asked.

"Come with us."

"But what for?"

Then the older of the Yotear girls told her, "I have to go to Pou Sok's house, but it's dark out and I'm afraid of ghosts. Come with me!"

"You can take Bang Peuw along, too."

"Leave her alone, you're the one who must come with me. You'll sleep with me."

"Bang Peuw, please come with me . . ."

"That's enough!" said the Yotear. "You're coming with us and you're to leave the others alone."

I couldn't go back to sleep after she left. In the middle of the night, I thought I saw her go by in front of the hangar, but when I called her, there was no reply.

The next morning I asked the other girls if my neighbor had come back: after all, I saw her return to the camp! They acted as if I were crazy. I went to ask the Yotear girl, "Where is the girl who was sleeping near me?"

"There are some questions that shouldn't be asked," she replied. "You can all share her things. She disappeared last night."

"But where did she go?"

The Yotear didn't answer me, tapping her forehead to indicate that I should put my brain to work. That didn't satisfy me, so I went to see Lin in the kitchen. Even before I had a chance to open my mouth, she started in: "Don't ask too many questions, you know very well that she's dead. The old pickax again! I'll tell you what happened, but don't go repeating it to the others or you'll take the same trip yourself." She related the usual scenario: the girl dug her own grave, and then they split her skull open with a pickax. But why? It seemed she was wearing too many necklaces. We shouldn't be fooled by Pou Sok's honeyed speeches. And it was a bad idea to show off something someone else might want.

3 I DIDN'T NEED any more warnings and returned to my work in the kitchen garden. People on their way to the school went by within a few steps of me, but lost in the greenery, I passed unnoticed. Several times during the morning I heard screams coming from the school; one by one, Mekongs whom I knew by sight were taken there, and I heard them shouting repeatedly, "Why don't you just kill me, finish me off!" Then, silence, even heavier than before.

Shortly before noon a group of about fifty people, herded along by two or three Yotears, passed by within twenty meters of me. Their wrists were tied in front or behind their backs with cords of red nylon. Mothers were carrying their babies while older children clung to their sarongs; elderly people shuffled along. I recognized my two kind nurses, Rin and Sim, walking in the middle of the group with their heads held high. Behind them I saw our first Mekong, Met Rôn, her husband, and their three children. These people weren't led into the building, and when they had gone around behind the house they began screaming and wailing: they understood that they wouldn't receive even the pretense of a trial. I ran clumsily to the hangar to keep Srëi Peu, intrigued by the screams, from going to see what was happening, but she tore herself away from me and outran me. Suddenly I saw her stop in her tracks, petrified: one of the Yotear men had seized a baby by the feet and cracked its head open on a tree trunk. I caught up to Srëi Peu and started to take her back to the hangar, but a Yotear had seen me.

"Get me a machete from the kitchen!"

"What for?"

"We're going to cut some palm branches."

I took Sreï Peu back to the hangar, where she hid her head under a blanket, and then I carried a machete to the waiting Yotear. "If you tell anyone— You remember the guy who used to bring us palm milk every morning? He saw a bit too much, and we stuck him in with the rest of them."

I ran back to the hangar. Behind it, less than ten meters away, was a grove of orange trees. I could hear noises and went to look out through a partition, opening a little space between two bamboo slats: three Yotears were each dragging a man with them. The victims' clothes were torn and stained with blood. The Yotears tied their arms up over their heads to the lower branches of some orange trees and tore off the scraps of shirt that still covered their chests. One Yotear took a knife out of his pocket, but another one told him, "No, not yet—first the palm branches." These branches were studded with very long, hard prickles. The second Yotear gave a branch to each of his accomplices, and they began to whip their victims. "How's this, do you like this?" One of them laughed, and they kept beating, while the tortured men shrieked dementedly.

Overcome by curiosity, Sreï Peu stuck her head out from under her blanket to ask me, "What're they doing?"

"Promise me you won't tell anyone, not even the girls who are nice to you—promise me."

"I promise, but I want to see."

She sneaked up close to me, glanced outside, and pressed hard against my side. "Let's go someplace else," she whispered. But where? We hid under the covers. I could hear the blows raining down. The Yotears broke off their beating when the prisoners lost consciousness, but they woke them up again with kicks. I heard one of them say, "Be careful not to finish them off, they still have things to tell us."

When I heard the footsteps of new arrivals, I couldn't resist the desire to see what was going on. It was a changing of the guard: three new Yotears came to laugh in the faces of the tortured men. "So, you don't feel too well? You'll make it. Just wait, you'll feel better in a little while." Those sugary words, that irony—I recognized all that, it was the way the Yotears talked. A new arrival began to slash at the legs of one of the victims.

"So, your wife is gone?"

"She ran away," groaned the poor man.

"Where is she? In which direction did she go? Talk!"

"I don't know . . ."

"He doesn't know where his wife is, oh dear!"

They untied him, he collapsed, and they dragged him off toward the school. I recognized the man tied to the tree nearest me, a Mekong from Vat Chas. They asked him the names of his partners, tore off his clothes and beat him, cut strips of skin from his back. He gave them some names. "That's all?" Salt was rubbed into his wounds. "Talk!"

Prisoners and their torturers followed one another out under the orange trees until nightfall. I couldn't get up the next day, my body was all sore and shaking with fever. The Yotear girl with the gun came by to take a look at me. "So, you're not feeling well today? The others have already gone off to work. What're you going to do today?" Before I had time to answer her, she ordered me to get up and come with her to the school. "But what for?" I was scared and had absolutely no desire to get up. "Let's go, on your feet! We're going to pick up bundles of clothes."

I followed her, keeping my head well down. We weren't allowed to look at what went on inside the school, but I couldn't help seeing what was all around me. Dozens of people, their heads lolling on their chests, were hanging by the arms from the branches of the mango trees in the large front courtyard. My heart started to pound, I couldn't take another step. "Come on, let's go," the Yotear told me. "All these people disobeyed the Angkar." We reached the front steps, where she left me. "Wait for me here, I'm going to collect the dead people's clothes and belongings."

Keeping my eyes lowered, at first I didn't dare look at all the horrors on display in the courtyard around me, but after a moment I felt someone staring at me and I looked up. A woman was on her knees, her arms tied behind her back, while in front of her a baby held out his hands to her breast: he wasn't strong enough to sit up, and she couldn't bend over far enough to let him suckle. I felt that she was imploring me to help her, but my feet were nailed to the ground. Not far from her were other women sitting against the wall or stretched out, their bellies swollen as if they were about to give birth. I couldn't do anything for these women, many of whom had been very cruel to us. Now they were crushed.

In a corner of the courtyard a man was being beaten to death. His screams flew up to the sky, shattered, and rained down on me like hail battering my skull. Farther away, a column of people was beginning to move toward the grove concealing the gaping mass grave. Children followed, weeping; there was no need to tie them up, they went along with their mother or father, sharing their fate. Crows were wheeling overhead.

Long minutes went by, it was excruciating. Finally the Yotear returned, and I lowered my eyes again. She called to a Yotear boy, who answered, "Over here!" She took me with her, following the voice over to the area where they decapitated people: each condemned person was kneeling at the feet of his or her executioner.

"I won't be eating with you today," the Yotear girl shouted to the boy. "Pou Sok has invited me."

"Okay, fine," he answered.

And he brought his pickax down on the shaved skull of a woman. Blood spurted onto him; laughing, he kicked the body into the half-filled ditch. I buried my face in the bundle of clothes in my arms. "Let's go back," said the Yotear girl. Battered bodies floated on the surface of the pond just outside the school enclosure, and as we walked alongside it, I saw other mutilated corpses lying at its edge in pools of blood. Three Yotears were burning a heap of clothing doubtless too ragged to be of any further use. I clutched my bundle of clean clothes, carefully selected by the Yotear girl.

Underneath the hangar, she put her parcel of clothes down on the one I'd brought. "Here's enough to give you all new clothes. Make sure you tell your friends."

When the other girls returned from work, I showed them the pile of things.

"These are to be shared by everybody."

"Well, so now you're a Mekong!"

"Just wait a minute, Mekong yourself. I'm only telling you what I was told to say."

"But where do these things come from?"

"I don't know."

"What about you, why aren't you taking any?"

"I've got what I need." (That wasn't true at all.)

After we'd gone to bed, the girl to my left started asking me questions again. "Where do these clothes come from?"

"Ask the Yotear, she's the one who brought them."

4 WHILE THE TORTURES and executions went on close by, I continued working in the kitchen garden. After a few days my companions told me they'd been given a day off, since they'd finished repairing the dikes in the nearby rice fields. The next day the Yotear girl with the gun arrived at dawn. "You have a free day, but no one is to return to the village, I need to see all of you."

She began to interrogate one of the girls. "Do you know So-and-so?"

"No, I don't know her."

"You're lying, she's your aunt. Get your things and sit over there."

She turned to another girl. "Do you recognize this name?"

"Yes, of course. I lived in that man's house when my parents died. He's not a relative. I didn't have anyplace else to go."

"You talk too much. Get your things."

I was worried: if they ever arrested Pou Mân or Mi Vi, I was headed for Sala Som Niat, along with Sreï Peu and Tôn Ny. I had to warn Tôn Ny, but she worked in the kitchen and we weren't allowed to go there.

Right after our meal, I went down to bathe in the river, where Tôn Ny always went at this time to draw water for the kitchen. She arrived at around 2 p.m., but gestured to me not to talk: we could be seen, and Yotears hidden in the grass could overhear us. I passed near her carrying some water up from the river and whispered, "Ten girls have been taken away to Sala. Be careful of everything you say!"

The next day a new contingent of girls went off to Sala, and more the following day. There were only a few of us left, so the Yotear sent us to sleep in a hut near the kitchen. The hangar had been completely cleared out.

It began to rain rather hard and the ground in our shack became sodden, so they sent us back to the big hangar, which was raised off the ground and had a bamboo floor. Young girls were not to sleep on the ground, by order of Pou Sok. How considerate! They filled up the hangar with little girls who had been taken from their parents.

More girls arrived to plant vegetables or water the pumpkins. As for me, I was assigned to weed the gardens—that was my specialty—and Tôn Ny still worked in the kitchen.

5 ONE EVENING, out of nowhere, Sy Neang turned up, bringing some palm milk in a big bamboo container for me and Sreï Peu. Tôn Ny didn't suffer from hunger as much as we did, because she worked in the kitchen. Our rations were shrinking, they weren't giving us more than a ladleful of water with a few grains of rice, just like before. I asked Sy Neang to bring us some fish, and he said he would do his best. Two days later he came back with a few little fish. This time I warned him that it was risky—the executions at the secret school were still going on, and boys weren't supposed to see girls, even their own sisters. Sy Neang was rather small for his fourteen years, however, and could slip in and out everywhere without being noticed.

"Which way did you come?"

"Behind Sala, it's the shortest way."

"You'd better use the road. It's longer, but you don't risk being taken for a relative of someone being executed. They might arrest you."

He returned the following night. I'd shown him where I slept, so he sneaked under the hangar and slipped me five little fish, one by one, through the gaps between the bamboo slats. He kept coming back for a week, but then I told him that the Yotears were getting more and more bloodthirsty, it was too dangerous for him.

"But I need to see Sreï Peu, I haven't seen her for a year."

"No, Sy Neang."

He returned the next night with a huge fish. He wanted to see Tôn Ny, too, and watched for her over by the kitchen. She was happy to see her brother, but didn't hide her terror from him. "What are you doing! Do you want to die?"

He promised her to stay away for the moment, and in fact we didn't see him again for a long time. This was inconvenient for our food supply. I always gave part of my portion to Sreï Peu, who was constantly hungry; since she didn't work, she was only allowed a half-ladle portion. Our rations were cut even further: one week, they gave us nothing but a pinch of salt and a bit of hot water.

I was the last one to leave the hangar one morning, and I stumbled over a hen scratching on a blanket. How had she climbed up to the hangar? I woke Sreï Peu and showed her the hen. "You follow her, I have to go to work. Watch where she goes. Maybe she'll lay an egg, and you can pick it up."

After roll call at work, I asked to be excused for a moment and ran to the hangar. "She's over there, in the back," Sreï Peu told me. When I went to look, I found the hen had made herself a little tunnel out of some rolled-up mats. She had just laid an egg at the far end and was starting to cackle. With very slow movements, so as not to frighten her, I collected the warm and still moist egg. Hiding it in my sarong, I told Sreï Peu, "Perhaps tomorrow she'll lay a second one, and we'll each have an egg."

The next day, as I left for work, I put a few grains of rice on the path taken by the hen. When I returned at around ten o'clock, my hope that the hen would let herself be tamed was disappointed—she wouldn't allow anyone near her—but she had left a new egg. That night I boiled some water to cook the two eggs, which we devoured under our blankets. The Mekong had come over to see what was cooking on the fire, but I hadn't yet put in the eggs. "I'm just heating a bit of water for my little sister, she has a stomachache." I didn't let the eggs cook very long.

I tried again to make friends with the hen the next day. She recognized me and came over, allowing me to pet her.

A girl from the hangar arrived unexpectedly. "Since when have you been trying to attract that hen?"

"I'm not doing anything, she came up to me on her own. And besides, I like animals."

After the girl went away, I rolled up my blanket to make a nest for "our hen." When I returned, the hen was gone, but she had left an egg, and she came back to lay eggs on following days. One morning, however, my neighbor didn't go to work. I made up the nest a bit farther away and set Sreï Peu to watch it. The hen went straight to my blanket, leaving an egg that Sreï Peu, very discreetly, hid among my belongings.

This stratagem lasted for about ten days, but finally the other girls noticed that the hen kept coming back to my corner. "You haven't the right to tame that hen, it should be given to the kitchen for everyone." After one of the girls made this remark, the hen disappeared, probably ending up in a pot other than that of the communal kitchen, because we certainly never tasted any of it. And, in fact, a few days later, while digging a hole to relieve myself, I found first one feather, then a few others, floating around in the vicinity.

ONCE AGAIN Sreï Peu and I were reduced to the meager communal cooking pot. We weren't allowed to collect *ptib* or any other plant whatsoever. "It's bad for your health," the Yotear explained to us. But why didn't they give us something that was good for our health, a good serving of rice, for example?

The kitchen workers weren't any better off than we were. One day Tôn Ny was ordered to go outside to cook a fish behind the kitchen, near the shack where we had slept the month before. "Don't let the others see the fish," the Mekong told her. It was impossible to refuse an order without ending up being led away the next night under any pretext whatsoever. The Yotears were alerted by neighbors, however, who were only too happy to cause trouble for the Mekong. We heard talk about this at work, and I saw a Yotear heading for the kitchen, toying with a broad-bladed knife. I was afraid for Tôn Ny. In the evening, when they distributed the rice, I didn't see my cousin anywhere, so I asked Mekong Lin about her. She told me that it was another Yotear girl, with a gun, who had ordered her to make Tôn Ny cook the fish, and when the Yotear with the knife appeared in the kitchen, Tôn Ny had run crying into Lin's arms. Since the matter was between the two Yotears, Tôn Ny wasn't held responsible. Lin had sent her off to bed. I was relieved, but I dared less than ever to look a Yotear straight in the face. I could see them, every day, washing bloodstained clothes in the river before handing them over to a Yotear girl for sorting. They never kept anything for themselves, content with their black jacket and pants, set off by a *krâmar* with little red-and-white checks.

There were only seven left in our group, including the Mekong Lin. One evening, at the educational session, they announced that we were going to be doing some special work here. It would be impossible to take care of a little girl like Sreï Peu, so we'd have to send her back to Vat Thmey and find a family willing to take care of her. Tôn Ny and I were allowed to go with the child to find her a temporary home. We didn't know anyone else besides Mi Vi, so reluctantly, we asked her if she would keep Sreï Peu for a while. She accepted halfheartedly, and only because Pou Mân rushed home upon learning that "his" three girls were there.

We asked if there was news of Sy Neang, but no, Pou Mân didn't even know where he was working at that time. We hadn't seen the Mekong

Met Yai. We knew that her husband, Lun, had been executed and that she had given birth to a baby girl. It seems that she had become quite a pleasant person after Pou Sok arrived on the scene. But why had the Yotears spared her? Pou Mân told us that the people of Vat Thmey had interceded with the Yotears on her behalf because she was pregnant. "Fine, let her have her baby. We'll execute her afterward." She had given birth one month after the death of her husband. Three days later the Yotears came to get her, her new baby, and her three other children. If we had given her Sreï Peu when she had asked for her so insistently, our little sister would be dead now.

So we left Sreï Peu with Mi Vi. Pou Mân promised us he'd watch out for her, and that if he or his wife were sent to another area, they would hand the child over to another family in Vat Thmey, so that we would know where to find her. And that's exactly what happened a week later. We had neither the time nor permission to go see her, but a cowherd from Vat Thmey who was convoying cartloads of rice told me as he was passing through that Sreï Peu was with another family, one unknown to us. She was the only child left in the village, too small to work. She wandered around in a pair of white shorts with blue stripes that got bigger and bigger on her as she wasted away. The man told me that she was coughing a lot, without even a short-sleeved shirt to wear in the wind and rain. She really seemed to have been abandoned.

7 BACK AT Sala Som Niat, we busied ourselves with the kitchen garden for about ten days. One evening, the Yotear ordered us to go sleep at Vat Thmey, telling us that we'd surely find empty huts there. It was only two kilometers to Vat Thmey, but it was dark when we arrived, and we had to leave again at dawn, so it was impossible to find out where Sreï Peu was living. As soon as we finished our work for the day, shortly after five in the afternoon, we rushed back to Vat Thmey. We hadn't thought about why the Yotears didn't want us around during the night, but we did notice that "our" hangar had been closed in on all sides and that they were garnering tons of rice being delivered by the cartload.

We looked all through the village for Sreï Peu. The Mekong had given us only fifteen minutes on our own—we were supposed to stay together in a group. When I found Sreï Peu bathing at the river's edge, she pretended not to hear me. Tôn Ny arrived, and Sreï Peu moved a little way out from the shore and shouted at us, "You're bad sisters!" She was coughing. "Where are you living, Sreï Peu?" She didn't know what to say, but in any case she wasn't with Mi Vi. We called to her not to go too far away from the riverbank, the current could carry her off; then we had to rejoin our group. In the village, we learned that she'd been telling everyone that we had abandoned her because we hadn't wanted to have to feed her anymore.

We found out where she was living, but the Mekong wouldn't allow us to see these people because it was too late in the evening; we all had to stay together and go to sleep.

Neither Tôn Ny nor I got a wink of sleep that night. At first light the Mekong allowed us to go to see the people taking care of Sreï Peu. "But come back quickly, I'll give you five minutes."

A woman came out of the hut to speak to us at the top of her stairs.

"Who are you?"

"We're Sreï Peu's sisters."

"Have you come to get her? She's sleeping."

"Oh, we'd love to take her, but they won't let us, she can't work with us. We left her with Pou Mân—what happened to him?"

"He's coming back tomorrow. I promised to take care of the little girl in the meantime."

We returned to our group somewhat reassured. That evening, arriving at Vat Thmey to sleep, we met Pou Mân. He was working as a carter, delivering loads of rice to various places. He told us that the entire village of Vat Thmey would be evacuated the following day.

"But don't worry about Sreï Peu. As long as I'm alive, she'll be taken care of."

"I want to go with you," Tôn Ny told him.

"You're crazy—now is not the time to antagonize the Yotears, they've got their own problems. You two should stay together, we'll find each other again. Don't let yourselves be separated, if at all possible."

8 SO, VAT THMEY was over and done with. The Yotears told us this themselves that day when we returned to Sala Som Niat. "From now on, you'll be sleeping here, but you'll have a new job. You see this hangar? It's full of rice, and you're the guards. If someone comes, you're to cut off his head and slice open his belly. We'll show you how to do it."

Two Yotears came forward and handed each of us a long, sharp knife. We didn't know what to do with these unfamiliar tools. The leader asked, "Which one of you is brave?" His answer was an embarrassed silence. The Mekong woman standing close by gave me a swift kick in the ankle, and I immediately kicked the girl next to me. So it went down the line, until we all raised our hands and announced, smiling, "Me, me, me!"

"You're not afraid? Good. You know that you're alone here, because all the people have gone to work elsewhere. If you need to see me, I'll be at the school."

A shiver rippled down my spine, but I raised my hand with a question. "May we pick some oranges?"

The orange trees were laden with fruit going unpicked.

"Yes, but not too many. As for the rice, if one of you touches it or helps anyone to take some, all seven of you will die."

With these encouraging words, the Yotear left us. Lin organized our shifts of guard duty: three girls until midnight, then two girls until 2 a.m., and two until dawn. Lin stood guard sometimes with me, sometimes with Tôn Ny. From time to time, to keep myself awake, I picked an orange. There wasn't a sound around us, it was as if all life had ceased. I was frightened. "This silence gets on my nerves," Lin said to me. "There could be danger out there—they should have given us guns. With these knives, we have to let a thief get quite close to us. Well, if we have to die, we can only die once."

Tôn Ny and I had never prayed so fervently. The weather wasn't hot; it must have been February of 1977. For weeks people had been speaking of the Vietnamese as a permanent danger, but it was only later that we learned the Vietnamese had been inside our country for more than a month. Sometimes a fine drizzle fell, forcing us to take shelter under the trees. We'd been given a piece of canvas to hold over our heads, but we had to stay alert: a thief could sneak up in the rain like a fish gliding through the water.

I was often afraid during those nightmarish years, but I was really convinced at that point that we were all going to die. Not one of us was in any state to fight off an attacker. Those nights on guard duty were a long anticipation of death, which would surely come for us—either from thieves or as punishment from the Yotears. The only solution was to run away. But where, and how?

One evening a Yotear came to warn us that carts would be arriving to carry away some of the stored rice. He informed us that we were to help load the wagons. Fifty oxcarts lined up one after the other all night long at the entrance to the hangar. We were happy to get rid of this miserable rice but, unfortunately, in the morning the hangar was still more than half full. We'd have liked to have gotten rid of all of it.

One of the wagon drivers had asked, "Are there many of you guarding the rice?"

"Oh, yes!" Lin answered quickly. "There are fifty of us, and then there are lots of Yotears." (There were just three in the school.)

I thought that Lin was boasting, but she was being smart: if the carters had known that the rice wasn't well guarded, they might have come back in two or three days leading a band of thieves.

Two days after the carts had gone, there was a special evening meeting. The Yotears needed solemnity for the most banal affairs, but as for sentences and executions, there they didn't stand on ceremony. That night we were all assembled for the announcement that from then on we could sleep in the hangar. That wasn't very reassuring to us: there was no other exit from the hangar apart from the door, so we were caught like rats in a trap. Outside, we could still try to run away in an emergency. No one wanted to sleep near the door, so Lin took the place closest to it, saying, "I'll be the first to die."

Another two weeks went by, until one morning, at five o'clock, the Yotears arrived.

"We're leaving this place."

"But why? We're not going to abandon all this rice!"

"That's our business. You go and get whatever's left in the kitchen, kill all the chickens, and take the supplies of salt and palm sugar."

Seeing us hesitate, they went off themselves toward the kitchen, returning shortly afterward carrying strings of chickens slung across their backs.

"Look, here are your provisions for the trip. All you have to do is pluck them."

"But where are we going?"

"You'll see when you get there. Just start out in that direction," said a Yotear, pointing to the west. "You'll find some people from a village that has been evacuated; everyone is headed that way. You'll join up with them."

We set out with our bundles, each girl carrying a hen and a sack of rice. The sun came up, and the morning flew by. We followed the little paths between the rice fields or cut directly across the abandoned paddies, where the water was shallow. Lin called a halt for mealtime around noon.

While she ate, Lin admitted to us that she'd rather not find the people from the evacuated village: they were Yotears. It would be better to dawdle a bit in the rice fields without traveling on the road where the Yotears would be waiting for us. If we lagged behind, perhaps we'd be lucky enough to be caught by the Vietnamese. She spoke frankly to us, knowing that she could trust all the girls in the group because we'd all shared the same dangers for a month. Tôn Ny, however, wanted to rush on ahead, since Sreï Peu was probably with the Yotears.

9 WHEN NIGHT FELL, we stretched out under the trees bordering the rice fields. There were more and more trees as we got closer to the mountains. At four in the morning we set out again on our somewhat zigzag course. Whenever the sun became a bit too hot, we stopped for a rest. During the afternoon we met a group going toward the north.

"Aren't you the seven girls who guarded the rice supplies?"

"Yes, we are."

"The Yotears are waiting for you, and they're not very pleased that you haven't arrived yet."

"We're doing the best we can."

"Be careful! If you run away they'll catch you. You're headed for the plastic bag, all seven of you."

This slant on things sped our progress up considerably; since we'd been spotted, it was better not to try to give our brave patriots the slip. At the end of the morning of the fifth day, we arrived at the provincial highway to Phum Samraong at the outskirts of the mountain. One lone Yotear was waiting for us, lying in a hammock slung between two trees.

"Why are you late?"

"We got lost in the rice fields. You told us not to use the roads."

"You'd have walked faster with a pickax at your back! Now you'll have to hurry up. You can eat now, if you still have any food, and then you'll continue toward Prey Klod; that's at the entrance to the forest. I'll go ahead of you on horseback. You're to go straight ahead to the bridge. Cross that, and then leave the road: there's only one path on the left. Follow it through the forest until you meet our comrades, they're expecting you. Tell them that you belong to the village of Vat Thmey."

The Yotear rode off on his horse without waiting for us. After resting a bit, we followed the road to the bridge. He had spoken of it as if it had been a question of a few minutes' walk, but it took us until nightfall to get there. We found magnificent trees with great spreading branches but no place to settle down for the night. There were trucks parked by the side of the road, and near them were camped entire families of Yotears, neatly dressed in their black outfits. We asked them where they were from.

"Phnom Penh."

"From . . . ?"

"Yes."

"Why did you leave? Wasn't everything all right there?"

The little girl to whom I was speaking looked at me as if I'd fallen from the moon. "Well, the Vietnamese . . ."—and she ran away as fast as she could. I was overjoyed! They were here! We couldn't be worse off with them than we were with our own patriots.

We looked for a place to set up camp, preferably away from these hundreds of people, but all around us the earth and grass were filthy with excrement. Finally, a bit farther off, we found a spot. Lin asked me to start a fire; it was cold by the water's edge and we didn't have any blankets. Tôn Ny went off to get wood and another girl went to draw water, while I stayed where I was, shaking with fever. Lin gave me some quinine. Tôn Ny whispered in my ear that she'd found a boy who knew Sy Neang, but he didn't know where he was at the moment.

We left the next morning at four and found the path to the left on the other side of the bridge. It was hard going, over spongy earth into which we sank up to our ankles. After the trees came more abandoned rice fields, which we crossed by walking on the little dikes. At one point we met some people bathing on both sides of our slippery little path. Our Yotear was waiting for us beyond the rice fields. "You've been dragging your feet again! Hurry up! From here on I'm going to let you get there by yourselves. Go into the forest and you'll meet the people from Vat Thmey, they're in there somewhere."

It was a splendid forest of full-grown trees, and we soon began to encounter camps scattered here and there. Lin asked about the Vat Thmey villagers, but they were always a bit farther on. Finally, moving from group to group, we arrived at the one from Vat Thmey, where we were taken to the chief Mekong. Would he allow us to join his group? No. He had no food for us.

"Anyway, the Mekong in charge of girls should have taken care of you."

"But she has nothing to do with it, the Yotears of Sala Som Niat sent us here."

Glancing at us, he seemed to change his attitude. "We're here to work, everyone already has his or her job—I don't know what to do with you. You've come here so late." Tôn Ny told Lin that the group with Pou Mân and Mi Vi was even farther on in the forest, so we all left to look for Sreï Peu, who should have been with the others. Finally, we found her: she was with Mi Vi, but they didn't have a hut to themselves and were sleeping instead in a hut for five or six people made of two crossed branches covered with greenery.

10 IT DIDN'T take us long to build a similar hut for the seven of us. The tree leaves smelled good, so we strewed some over the ground. Lin went to see about getting some food for us, but the Mekong of the group didn't want to be bothered with her: there was no work for us, and therefore no food. Lin then went to find the Yotear woman in charge of us to explain to her how we had ended up here. The Yotear agreed to give us all work, except for me, because Lin had told her I was sick. They registered me with the adults of the Vat Thmey group.

The next day, along with another group, my six companions were assigned to help transport rice from the supplies at Vat Thmey, two days' march via the most direct route. The girls had to build a hut one day's march from Vat Thmey, where they would drop off the rice. From there others would relay it to Prey Klod, where it was being stored under a small hangar. Every two or three days men came to empty the hangar, carrying the rice to a safe place farther up the mountain.

I would have liked to work with Tôn Ny. People were saying that the Vietnamese weren't far from Vat Thmey. Here, we were five days' march away via the usual route. How had Sreï Peu gotten this far on her little

feet, on legs hardly bigger than matchsticks? If she lapped up a bit of
brackish water from a puddle, the Yotears would hit her with their rifle
butts; if she asked Mi Vi for some water from her gourd, that woman
just yelled at her. She slept clinging to me, fearful now that Mi Vi had
come to join me in the hut left by my companions. The Mekong woman
told me to be ready for work the next morning.

"What kind of work?" I asked Mi Vi.

"You'll see tomorrow. If I tell you now, you'll be frightened."

Pou Mân wasn't around. They were keeping him busy picking up the
rice delivered by the girls, who had to carry it on their heads; Mân then
took it on to Prey Klod by oxcart, returning immediately for another load.
He wasn't allowed to see Mi Vi for fear that he might be tempted to steal
some rice from the supplies.

We left for work at 5 a.m. Sreï Peu stayed by herself, guarding a little
bag of gold-leaf fragments that Pou Mân had salvaged from the ruins of
my parents' hut. Mi Vi showed the bag to me. As soon as she could, she
planned to exchange the gold for rice, because here we were getting only
a ladleful of liquid with a few kernels of red corn.

Armed with pickaxes, we were supposed to dig big holes "to plant
coconut palms, because we may be here for ten years." Plant coconut
palms in the forest? There were wild coconut palms not too far away,
but I'd already seen so many absurdities that this business was fine with
me. So I dug up the surface of the ground over an area between fifteen
to twenty meters long and five or six meters wide. Other teams came after
me to dig deeper. The whole thing seemed strange to me. Finally, that
evening it dawned on me: moving somewhat away from my companions,
I caught sight of a ditch twenty meters long, five wide, and at least a
meter and a half deep. Ten paces farther on was another ditch just like
it. It wasn't trees that were going to be planted there. We were digging
mass graves.

Returning to camp, I met our neighbor.

"You're in for a treat," she told me. "Vi bought some fish."

"Bought?"

"Yes. You can, too; you can buy what you want. You've got some gold
hidden away, haven't you?"

I continued thoughtfully on my way. Mi Vi was buying things with
the gold entrusted to her by Pou Mân, gold that had once belonged to
my parents. I asked her if she had saved me a bit of fish.

"Fish for you? No. It was mine, and I ate all of it."

"And Sreï Peu?"

"You have your rations from the kitchen. Listen, why don't you get my portion; the two of you can share it."

Three portions, that was three ladlefuls of lukewarm water with a few kernels of corn swimming in it. I shared with Srei Peu, who told me how mean Mi Vi was to her. The day before Mi Vi had caught a rat in a trap and had roasted it before Srei Peu's very eyes, devouring every bit of it herself. The child's eyes had gotten bigger and bigger in her poor shrunken little face.

11 I DUG IN THE FOREST with my pickax for five whole days without really accomplishing very much. The Mekong woman sent me someplace else to plant corn, but the ground there was just as hard, unfortunately, and the roots on the surface of the soil didn't make it any easier. I still wasn't getting much done. At the evening meeting the Mekong gave me another job, one reserved for children from eight to sixteen years old: fetching the rice brought in by oxcart and carrying it on foot to the mountain, where the Yotears took charge of it. We would leave at four in the morning, run to the carts, load the sacks on our heads—each sack as heavy as fifty or sixty cans of rice—and arrive exhausted at the foot of the mountain. We were then free to go back to Prey Klod, where we'd arrive only at nightfall to claim our meal. There was a check-up meeting each evening. "How long did it take you to transport the sacks? Did you all stay together? Who lagged behind? Ah! You arrived at the mountain after twelve o'clock? From now on you'll leave here at 3 a.m. so you'll arrive on time where they're waiting for you."

It was hard work, but not as difficult and depressing as digging graves. One morning at dawn, after we had been walking for three hours, we came across a group of people lying under the trees. They had just arrived and hadn't yet had time to build their huts. They asked us where they could find some water. "You have to walk a long way," I told them, "farther than Prey Klod." These people were so skeletal they could hardly stand up.

"Why are you here?"

"The Yotears keep pushing us farther and farther toward the mountain."

They saw our sacks and begged us to give them a bit of rice; if they hadn't been so weak, they could have stolen the rice from us. We had no armed guards with us, and they would have been risking only a quick death instead of a slow one. Instead, they were begging from children. I turned my head away: I didn't want to die for a handful of rice missing from my bag.

We began to run to escape from these living skeletons, arriving at our destination before noon to find the Yotears waiting for us. First they verified the fastening and weight of the bags while we rested under the trees. They usually told us that we were free to go at this point, but today they were watching us, and I had the feeling they were going to pick a few of us to go along with them. I had absolutely no desire to be the lucky winner of a one-way trip. One of the convoy workers had spoken kindly to me when I had asked him for news of Pou Mân, whom he saw occasionally, and I gathered up my courage to ask him what was going to happen to all this rice we were bringing to the mountain.

"The mountain has its own secret, little girl."

"What secret?"

"The mountain is covered with impenetrable vines."

"That's not a secret, everyone knows that. But why are they carrying rice up there? Surely it's just going to rot under the vines."

"Not if there's someone to eat it. But don't talk about it, it's not healthy."

I understood from this that the Yotears were hiding their families in the virgin forest of the mountain. But how were they managing to get water?

"You see this rubber tube?"

"Yes. Why are you carrying that with the rice?"

"Every other day I carry water bottles, and after you children have left, I drive my cart through the forest to the mountain, not an easy job. When I get there, a Yotear on guard comes to meet me. We attach the tube to a water bottle, and he unrolls it for twenty meters until it disappears behind the bushes. He discharges the water back there, I don't know where, exactly, but he signals me when it's time to attach the tube to another bottle. I've never seen anyone return after going into the heart of the mountain."

Back at Prey Klod, I decided that the work I was doing was too exposed. That day I escaped selection by the porters by slipping behind the trunk of a big tree. The next day it would definitely be my turn. I preferred to become ill, so I stayed in bed with Sreï Peu in our hut of branches. At noon I went innocently to ask for my soup.

"You didn't go to work," the Mekong woman said, "and you won't get your soup."

"But I'm sick."

"We've got too many people with your particular illness. Wait here, the nurse will come and decide whether you're sick or not."

The nurse declared that I wasn't sick, so I didn't have the right to claim my ladleful of tepid water with floating corn kernels.

Mi Vi had in fact told me that this Mekong didn't like girls, and that she got rid of them at the first opportunity by sending them to work far away, so I wasn't surprised when she came to see me that afternoon. "Tomorrow you must come to the assembly at the rice hangar at four o'clock. Don't bring any baggage with you, just your mosquito net."

That didn't tell me anything one way or the other. All night long I thought about escaping—but where could I go? I decided to try to rejoin Tôn Ny, and together we'd set out for Phnom Penh. If we didn't find the Vietnamese on the way, we risked being killed by artillery, but I preferred that to having my head split open by a pickax.

At 4 a.m. I kissed Sreï Peu goodbye. Mi Vi was still asleep. When I arrived at the hangar, the Mekong was already there, along with a carter and four other women. We were all supposed to follow the cart; we weren't allowed to ride on the bags of rice because it would have tired the oxen. Off we went in the direction of the bridge, crossing it after two hours. The man was driving his animals hard. No one spoke. We didn't know where we were going. On the other side of the bridge, we left the road and entered the forest. Unable to keep up with the cart, I prayed with all my might. After an hour they stopped for a rest. When I caught up to the others, the women had gone off a little ways under the trees, and the man told me, "You, little girl, go back to Prey Klod. I made my oxen sweat so that you'd lose us, but you're a tough one. So I'd rather just tell you: Return to Prey Klod. Whatever you do, don't say that you're sick. Find another Mekong and tell her you lost track of the cart wandering around in the forest. If you're sick, they'll make you take another journey like this one. There's no return trip."

The cart moved off into the forest, leading the four women unwittingly to their deaths. I rested for a while under the trees and waited for evening to arrive before recrossing the bridge. There also I stopped for a rest, arriving at Prey Klod at sunrise. I went up to the first group getting ready for work and told the Mekong man in charge that I had gotten lost in the forest accompanying an oxcart but that I was ready to work in his group. Fine, I could join the group leaving to relay the girl porters from Vat Thmey. The Mekong would accompany us himself because there were people to be replaced. I learned on the way that the place where we were

going had come under artillery fire. What was uppermost in my mind
was that I'd see Tôn Ny again. Pou Mân had told us particularly that we
shouldn't become separated. And besides, I'd be a day's march away from
Prey Klod, far from my former Mekong, who "didn't like young girls."

12

WHEN we got to the relay station, though, I couldn't find Tôn
Ny. We heard a few shells go whistling above the trees. The
Mekong told us to build a shelter of branches for the entire
group, about fifty people, mostly adults. Since I didn't know
anyone, I didn't dare settle down in the shelter, and I slept on the ground
under the trees instead. One man in the group seemed to recognize my
face and came over to me.

"Didn't you live in Mân's house?"

"Yes, I did."

"You shouldn't stay here—there are groups reserved for young girls."

"Yes, of course, but I'd like to see Pou Mân."

"Then listen: you see this big tree about a hundred meters from here?
Keep an eye on it, because that's where Mân spends the night when he
comes back with his oxen."

I checked the tree each time I woke during the night. Early in the
morning it was time to get going, but people were looking at me with
hostility. I didn't belong to the group, I was an extra mouth to feed, and
that diminished their own rations. I didn't have the courage to insist on
joining them, so I hid under the trees to wait for Pou Mân.

I spent the day nibbling on what I could find in the forest, keeping a
constant watch on Pou Mân's tree, and at the end of the afternoon I saw
him making up his bed. I ran toward him, weeping, but he seemed terrified
to see me. "Don't come over here, go back to your shelter, I'll come over
to you."

When he joined me after a moment, I asked him why I couldn't go over
to where he slept. "It's reserved for men and oxen, nobody else can go
there."

The people who had left in the morning now arrived with sacks of rice
on their heads to be loaded onto waiting oxcarts. When his cart was full,
Pou Mân came back to tell me that he had spoken to the Mekong, who
was an acquaintance of his, and they had found me a little corner of the
shelter to sleep in. Then he began to scold me: "You mustn't cry, they'll
say you're crazy. And you know what they do with crazy girls. There's

only one thing for you to do, rejoin Tôn Ny. Her camp isn't far from here. You two should stay together: things are going badly for the Yotears." He had brought me a small piece of waterproof cloth to lie on. "And now I have to go. Tomorrow you'll find Tôn Ny again, her camp is over that way. I don't think we'll see each other again for a few days. We'll meet again at Battambang or . . . at Phnom Penh."

As soon as 4 a.m. rolled around, I hurried to Tôn Ny's camp. She was still with Lin, who told me that I could come back and sleep with her girls in the evening, but that during the day I had to work with my new group, because she couldn't give me anything to eat. All the provisions were controlled by the Yotears. It was easier for a group of fifty to provide a small extra portion than it was for her little group of seven girls. I promised Lin that I'd manage to find a way to help out with supplies, and that I'd do everything she wanted, if only she'd let me belong to her group. Then I dashed back to my Mekong and asked him to let me rejoin my old group, which I'd found once more. He scolded me for having lost track of my group in the first place, telling me that I couldn't keep changing around all the time, but finally he allowed me to go. "Just don't try coming back to me if things don't work out with Met Lin!"

I trotted back again to Lin. The whole group was ready to leave. Lin told me to stay and guard their belongings; at noon I was to cook the rice for all seven of us. In the evening I slept near Lin. The next day I wanted to work with the other girls, to see Vat Thmey again, so Lin stayed at the camp. The rest of us left on the double; everything was done at a run because the Yotears were very strict about schedules; we couldn't keep the oxcarts waiting. During the morning we arrived in sight of Vat Thmey, but were halted by an artillery barrage at the Moung Russeï bridge. We took cover in the grass for a few moments, and when things quieted down, we set out again. The rice hangar was in a hamlet called Phum Trâ. We each picked up our thirty kilos of rice and returned that afternoon to the place where the wagons were being loaded.

We made the same trip three days running. I had found Tôn Ny, but we hadn't met up with the Vietnamese as I had hoped. They weren't where they should have been, at Moung Russeï, when we crossed over the road beyond the bridge before entering the forest.

When we got back in mid-afternoon on the third day, however, something unusual was going on. Instead of going up to the oxcarts one by one to deliver their bags of rice, the fifty workers in the other group were running around in all directions, calling out to each other, regrouping and setting off at a run in the direction of Prey Klod.

Lin, who had stayed at the camp, ran to meet us. "Don't follow the

people from Prey Klod! We're going to join the people from Phnom Pet."
That group had come from the region near Battambang; they had already
seen the Vietnamese, and they weren't running away. Lin said goodbye
to us and went off to hide. Tôn Ny began to cry: she would have liked
to run toward Sreï Peu at Prey Klod. I clung to her, we were both in
tears. "We can't go there, there's nothing we could do."

At the entrance to a hut, a young couple saw us and called out to us,
so we told them why we were crying. "No, now isn't the time to go to
Prey Klod. Come in here quickly!" The woman took us by the hand and
literally threw us to the ground in a corner of the hut. The man covered
us with a blanket and the two of them sat in front of us to hide us from
the searching eyes of the Yotears. Their three children, playing in front
of the hut, kept watch to warn us of the Yotears' arrival.

A few moments later, two Yotears, guns slung over their shoulders and
rush whips in their hands, passed by shouting, "Prey Klod, Prey Klod,
get ready to leave!"

13 ONCE THE WORKERS had left for Prey Klod, we came out of hiding.
"I'm going to fix you a nice plate of rice," the woman told us.
Her husband had recovered the two bags of rice we hadn't been
able to carry to the oxcart in time. They hadn't had anything
to eat for several days. Tôn Ny and I were also hungry for rice; we'd
been fed nothing but badly cooked red corn for weeks. All four of us sat
down to husk the rice, and even their little four-year-old helped out. After
an hour, we were left with the equivalent of half our load, about thirty
kilos. We spent a peaceful night after an ample meal.

The next day the husband asked Tôn Ny to help him dig up some
manioc in a nearby field, and I decided to go with them. I pulled up three
manioc roots, but while I was straining to pull up the fourth, bigger than
the others, I heard a cracking sound in my back, and ended up sprawled
on the ground, my legs in the air. Since it was impossible to get me back
on my feet again, the man dragged me to the hut. He didn't have much
strength left, either. It turned out that his wife was a nurse: she massaged
my back with Tiger Balm and loosened my jammed vertebrae. "And now
I want you to lie down and rest," she told me. She gave me and Tôn Ny
each a clean sarong.

A group of armed Yotears came by the next day, with orders to break
up the camp. "Everyone to Prey Klod. We're going into the mountains!"

I warned our hosts that I was familiar with that area, where there wasn't a drop of water. The woman discussed our departure with the Yotears. She was a nurse, her sister had wrenched her back and needed to stay off her feet for one more day; we'd leave as soon as I could walk. The Yotear was all smiles. "Don't say I didn't warn you. It could get very hot around here tonight."

A few families in neighboring huts also decided to stay. Night fell, a clear evening, sweet-smelling and crisp.

Suddenly, around eight o'clock, when we had just finished eating our rice after the Yotears had left, a bomb exploded over by the highway about ten kilometers away. We saw the sky go up in flames, blotting out the soft moonlight, and then slowly fade into darkness. This display lasted for about fifteen minutes, and when it was over, we all looked at each other: this time, the Vietnamese had won!

Then oxcarts appeared from the direction of the deep forest.

"Where are you people coming from?"

"Prey Klod. There's blood everywhere, they're cutting off heads, bodies are piling up. You'd better get out of here."

"Where can we go? You heard the bombs."

"Exactly. We can go between the bombs, but we won't escape having our heads cut off if the Yotears catch us."

All of a sudden my back didn't hurt anymore. Everyone agreed we should head toward the south, toward Okrirt on the road to Phnom Penh. They all hung their bundles on bamboo poles, while I carried mine on my head. As we made our way under the trees, I realized that it wasn't as light out as I had imagined. That light had been mostly within my heart.

We tripped over tree roots, the children were crying, we were all bumping into one another . . . Someone stumbled into me, shouting, "Hurry up! Three kilometers from here they're cutting off arms and heads!" I didn't need any such encouragement to keep going. Within an hour the forest was swarming with people coming from all directions, heading for the highway where the Vietnamese were supposed to be.

We became exhausted very quickly. The nurse's husband told his children to rest with Tôn Ny and me under a big tree. "Wait for us here, we're going to carry the baggage on ahead. I'll come back for you." He returned for us in fifteen minutes, and we all rejoined his wife, who was guarding the baggage. An hour later I stayed behind with the little three-year-old girl while Tôn Ny followed the parents, holding the other two children by the hand. This time it was the woman who came back for me, and we were all reunited at the foot of a bridge. No one dared set foot on it. "There must be mines! Of course there are mines, look, you can see the fuses!"

It was impossible to continue on toward the south if we couldn't cross the bridge, but in any case, we were closer to Battambang than to Phnom Penh, and the Vietnamese were in both cities. No one even thought about stopping to sleep. We'd go back up toward the north. We followed little roads, avoiding going down into the muddy rice fields.

The sun came up, and we felt better in daylight. While we were resting under the trees, we suddenly heard the sound of a truck: friend or foe? Standing in the back of the truck were Vietnamese soldiers, beckoning to us. People were waving to them—they were our liberators, after all—but there was little warmth or joy in our greetings to them. A man shouted, "*Di! Di!*" meaning we had to keep going. The truck had stopped in the road, and the nurse asked them in Vietnamese where they were coming from, but they answered, "You mustn't stay here. We haven't taken this ground yet."

The truck set out again, going south. A column of armored half-tracks arrived. "Where are the Khmer Rouge?" asked the soldiers. "At Prey Klod," everyone shouted, "at Pursat. But they have lots of people like us with them as hostages, don't shoot at them!"

We arrived at Moung Russeï at nightfall. The nurse's husband went on ahead to look for a place to stay, but he returned an hour later without having found anything, so we spent the night by the side of the road. Early the next morning he went looking for wood to build a rudimentary hut, a bit farther along, because the road was constantly filled with people and the noise and dust were disturbing the children.

Tôn Ny and I went to fetch water. We had to walk for a while, but we were always hopeful of hearing Pou Mân calling to us, or of finding Sy Neang or Sreï Peu among the throngs.

14 THE NEXT MORNING Tôn Ny asked the couple, "Do you mean to leave here right away?"

"Yes, the children are rested. We're going to leave for Battambang."

"The two of us want to stay here. We're hoping to find our sister and brother among the refugees, along with another couple."

"All right," said the woman, who was named Min Ry. "We'll wait three days with you."

While we continued to help Min Ry with the fire, the cooking, and fetching water, we still kept watch on the road. On the third day Min Ry told us that her family would be leaving for Battambang sometime the next morning. Tôn Ny wished her a safe journey, but I persuaded Pou Mêth, the husband, that they should wait another night: Tôn Ny and I had enough rice for one more day, whereas they had to buy theirs with gold. Min Ry allowed herself to be won over.

We kept an eye on the busy road, and toward evening we caught sight of Pou Mân, heavily laden with two big bags at the ends of his bamboo pole. Turning his head from side to side, he was studying the groups of people camped at the edges of the road. "Pou Mân, Pou Mân!" We were so happy to see him! This young man had been like a father to us, and there he was. He lowered his burden to the ground. There was no news of Sreï Peu, or of Sy Neang. He didn't mention Mi Vi.

Pou Mân introduced himself to our friends, who were happy to welcome him when they saw his bags of rice. Pou Mân made it clear immediately that the rice was for Tôn Ny and me, and that we didn't have to rely on Mêth's charity. The couple invited him to spend the night with us, but he could see that there wasn't enough room under our roof, so he declined and went off to find a place somewhere else.

At dawn the next day, Pou Mân was back on the road. He wanted to go toward Pursat, which was in the south, on the road to Phnom Penh; perhaps Sy Neang was in that area, with the Vietnamese, or perhaps he would find his wife, Vi, there, and little Sreï Peu. Not wanting to touch our rice supply, Pou Mêth decided to go alone to Okrirt; the Vietnamese were there, too, and there must be stores of rice abandoned by the Khmer Rouge. Ry wanted us to go with him, because he wasn't very strong and the three of us could bring back more rice. After all, Tôn Ny and I had been sponging off them for a week. We preferred to stay where we were in case Pou Mân came back, though, so that we could travel on with him. Ry was grumpy, and kept after us to make sure that we didn't sit around with nothing to do. We gave her some of our rice for our meal together, but still she complained constantly about Tôn Ny. "She doesn't work much, she's always sitting down." Well, Tôn Ny was fetching water, husking rice, watching over the children, and besides all this, she couldn't walk very well: she had scraped the sole of her foot on a sharp shell and the wound was becoming infected. This irritated Min Ry, who would have liked us to be always in good shape and capable of carrying out her slightest wish. "We have to find some vegetables and gather some fruit. Tôn Ny, will you get some water?"

After Tôn Ny had gone off for the water, an errand that would take at least half an hour, Min Ry began to question me, "Do you have any gold left from your mother's jewelry?"

"No, I gave everything to a man who gave me palm milk when I was dying."

"Maybe you have some papers that say you own some houses or some land?"

"Our two houses burned. The land has certainly been taken over by strangers, and I haven't any papers to help recover it."

"And Tôn Ny? She must have something left from her parents. She may very well be your cousin, but that doesn't mean she's telling you the truth. Do you trust her?"

When I didn't say anything, she added, "Tôn Ny eats a lot. You do, too, by the way. We have to think about economizing, you never know what the future will bring."

We waited, but neither of the two men returned that evening. Pou Mêth showed up at dawn, carrying two sacks tied with vines. He was feverish and very tired, but his wife took care of him, giving him an injection, and in the evening he felt better. "I heard people say there were lots of vegetables abandoned at Vat Thmey," he told us. "We should go there." That sounded fine to me. "Tôn Ny should go, too," said Min Ry, but I wanted Tôn Ny to stay where she was in case Pou Mân should return with her brother and sister. Min Ry insisted so much, though, that we gave in. Besides, it was safer that way. The Vietnamese controlled the area, but there might be Khmer Rouge hiding there, too, and with three of us going, we had a better chance of getting back alive. Tôn Ny took along the little bit of gold she had, hidden in the belt of her shorts—one never knew.

We went directly to the village. All the houses were destroyed, and many people were sifting through the ruins, hoping to find something valuable hidden, abandoned, or forgotten. Gold was now the only medium of exchange.

I knew about the hangar that had been used as a warehouse near the secret school; it was only two kilometers away, but people weren't anxious to go in that direction. It took us only a few minutes to get there. When I talked about Sala Som Niat, Pou Mêth said his hair stood on end just to think he was on the soil where so many crimes had been committed. The place gave me the shivers, too; crows wheeled in the sky or perched on tree branches, while headless bodies lay scattered around the hangar, and the earth was polluted with pools of blood. A rotten stench hung over everything.

Should we go inside the hangar? What if Yotears were hiding in there? Suddenly three men in black burst out at us from behind the hangar! Pou Mêth dashed toward the river and jumped in, while Tôn Ny and I ran to the bridge leading toward Vat Thmey. Pou Mêth joined up with us again on our way back. We would not be returning there. But we were going home empty-handed, and what would Min Ry say? Walking along the river, we came across a hut off to our right, near a tree, and we could hear someone moaning and calling out. Pou Mêth went to investigate. When we followed him, we discovered an old man lying on the ground. "Oh, please, give me something to drink!" Pou Mêth went down to the river to fetch some water in his bowl. The poor old man wouldn't last much longer.

Continuing on our way, we were suddenly confronted by a Vietnamese soldier who sprang out from behind a tree, machine gun at the ready. *"Di dê, di dê?"* (Where are you going?) We pointed in the direction of Vat Thmey and indicated that we were looking for food. He bent down over a bulging bag at his feet, pulling out a coconut, which he tossed toward us without coming any closer. After we'd picked it up, he motioned to us to go on to Vat Thmey. We soon reached the village, and I showed Pou Mêth where our hut had been. He salvaged a few bits of iron and some bamboo, they were always useful. Then we showed him the grove of orange trees that had belonged to Met Yai, where we picked a few oranges. On the way back to Moung Russeï, Pou Mêth found a zinc plate that must have fallen off a Vietnamese truck. So we weren't returning empty-handed after all.

Pou Mêth related our adventures to his wife, and the two of them went off "to the city" to find some fish. I knew they had some gold, because one day Min Ry had had me weigh a bag of gold that must have been at least three kilos. I don't know how she saved up or got her hands on all of it.

While they were gone, Tôn Ny checked her belongings; someone had gone through them. We lived very close to each other without knowing one another. Everyone distrusted his neighbor, and people spied on one another. A neighbor woman told us, "If you have anything, hide it carefully, and don't leave it with your things when you go somewhere."

"Thank you very much," Tôn Ny replied, "but in any case we don't have anything valuable."

"I can hear a Phnom Penh accent in your voice, my girl." The woman told us that she used to teach dancing in the school at the royal palace, and that she herself lived in the king's house—not as a servant, no, her father was related to the royal family.

"And your parents, what did they do at Phnom Penh?"

Tôn Ny told her the name of her father, and it turned out that the woman knew him. "Then we're relatives!" The conversation stopped there, because Mêth and his wife were returning, their arms full of provisions.

Just as we were about to eat, Pou Mân arrived; he hadn't been able to find Sreï Peu or Sy Neang. Min Ry invited him to share our meal. He rested nearby and set out again at dawn the next day, because he wanted to explore all the surrounding territory. Min Ry reproached me for having served him too much food, forgetting that she had eaten his rice for several days.

Tôn Ny and I decided to return alone to Vat Thmey, where we could certainly find more vegetables. We returned to the site of our hut, where the corn was growing thickly but was still far from ripe. At the place where Tôn Ny's father had built their hut we were almost overcome by emotion, and the memories flooded into our hearts, but we had to get on with it—we had to go on living. The corn was growing beautifully there, too, but wasn't ripe yet either.

On we went to Pou Mân's hut, which was still standing, but the roof had been torn off by the wind. The papayas there hadn't been touched, and we took an ample supply. Then we went to check on the manioc we had planted, digging up a few roots. The other day, when we'd been there with Pou Mêth, we hadn't mentioned the manioc, not knowing whether we could take any of it without Pou Mân's permission, but the evening before he had encouraged us to take some. "We won't be going back there, and it's better that you should get some right away."

We found eggplants near the ruins of an unknown hut; no one said anything to us, everyone helped himself. We headed back to Moung Russeï carrying an impressive load of fruits and vegetables on our heads. Min Ry greeted us with a smile, invited us to eat, and even served us some fish.

That night, down by the river, Tôn Ny and I talked things over.

"We can't trust Min Ry," said my cousin. "She's nice to us today, but what about tomorrow, when we won't be bringing any more provisions? Believe me, it would be better to join up with Pou Mân as soon as he comes back."

"In the meantime, they still haven't left for Battambang."

"Naturally—they're hoping that Pou Mân will help them with provisions. That's the main problem at this point."

"With the Yotears, we were hungry, but once in a while it felt as if we were doing something useful. Now there's nothing. We're just trying to survive!"

Now and then I would venture out on the road going toward Pursat, hoping to find Sy Neang and Srë Peu. I happened to ask a passerby carrying what looked like vegetables on a bamboo pole where he had found all that food.

"These are mangoes. I put them into bags so they couldn't be seen, but you're just one person, you couldn't eat up all there are in the forest. Take the first path you find on the other side of the road. Don't be afraid to go rather far, and you'll find the mango trees."

"I'm afraid of getting lost all by myself."

"No, no—just take your bearings from that great big tree you see over there. You can see it even in the middle of the forest."

I ran to get Tôn Ny, since it would be easier with two of us. We had to walk more than twenty minutes; in many places the grass was completely trampled, and the trees had been stripped, but we finally found some that still had mangoes in their upper branches. We knocked down the fruit with a long bamboo pole, and Tôn Ny went back to our camp to fetch some sacks, carrying part of our harvest in her *krâmar*. When she returned, she told me that some people had warned her not to go too far into the forest because she might get her head cut off. I suspected that they wanted to discourage us in order to keep the fruit for themselves.

Min Ry was all smiles: she set the mangoes to ripen near the hut. Our laborious and empty life continued: wood detail, water detail, Min Ry's grouchiness. We went off on our own for whole days to escape her reproaches and bad temper.

15 AFTER Pou Mân's departure, I had dreamed that Mi Vi was sitting on a bridge, shaking with fever, her body swollen from starvation. Srë Peu, also bloated from hunger, was sitting next to her, crying bitterly because Mi Vi was dead.

My dream did not come true. Ten days after he had left us, Pou Mân came back with Mi Vi and Srë Peu. He had in fact found them on a bridge in Pursat: they had just arrived and were staring at the water flowing under the bridge, red with blood.

Behind the trio came Sy Neang, leading a young bull at the end of a rope.

Pou Mân had met him on the road shortly before arriving at the bridge.

What a reunion, after so much misery and fear! We were all crying, overwhelmed by our emotions. Sreï Peu was unbelievably thin, it was frightening to look at her. Still, I'd certainly seen some thin people in my time; we'd have to take special care of her. Tôn Ny quickly explained to Pou Mân that she couldn't stay with Min Ry anymore. "Wait for just a little while longer," he said. "Let me have enough time to find a place for all of us."

That night the six of us ate with the Mêth family: Mân, Vi, and we four children. Pou Mân and Sy Neang went someplace else to sleep, but when they returned the next morning, Min Ry looked at them reproachfully. "So, you're going to eat with us again?" Pou Mân gave her a little bag of rice. "Be good enough to take care of the girls for the moment; Sy Neang and I are going to try to come up with something."

Min Ry was obviously not pleased. After the men left, Min Ry took me along with her while Tôn Ny stayed with the children. Mi Vi was resting; she hadn't said a word about her experiences on her own with Sreï Peu.

We went over by the pagoda, where there was a beautiful ornamental lake covered with water lilies; the water was cleaner there than it was anywhere else. Min Ry wanted to wash her children's clothes, but it was forbidden to dirty the water, so she needed me to draw water for her laundry. While she washed the clothes by the edge of the lake, she started in on me: "Why didn't Mân take his wife with him, along with Sreï Peu and Tôn Ny? You, you could stay with us. If you go off with Tôn Ny, you'll never have enough to eat. You'll die with them—Pou Mân hasn't any gold or silver, and neither does Tôn Ny. They'll all die of hunger. I wouldn't advise you to go repeating all this to them, though."

I didn't understand at the time that she wanted to keep me as a servant. "My husband will be a father to you, I'll be like a mother to you, and you'll have a brother and two sisters. I'll feed you and take care of you."

My heart didn't want any part of her proposition, but my famished belly listened. I was shaken and confused. I didn't say anything to Tôn Ny. On the way back from the pagoda, Min Ry added that we would have to start being more careful with her gold, which was running out very quickly. In the distance, I could see Tôn Ny busy husking rice with Mi Vi. Sitting silently in front of the hut in a state of extreme weakness, Sreï Peu mechanically brushed flies from her face, over and over. Min Ry's children were playing a few steps away; from time to time they would glance over at the intruder unkindly, even contemptuously. Our little sister was truly a pathetic sight.

Six

STRANGERS IN OUR OWN LAND

1   AFTER SPENDING more than three weeks camped at the entrance to Moung Russeï, Min Ry decided to set out for Battambang. It was a much more important city, the capital of the North, and we'd find opportunities there to do some trading.

Pou Mân agreed to rent an ox to draw the baggage cart. We hadn't much baggage, but Min Ry, with everyone's help, had enough to fill the cart.

We set out one morning and reached Phum Krokoah in the early afternoon. We were eleven kilometers from Battambang. The ox was shambling along—he was just as tired as we were and needed a few days' rest. I had stayed with Tôn Ny and Sreï Peu the whole time, and Min Ry was angry that I hadn't looked after her children. She took me aside after our meal. "You have to make up your mind. Either you go with Pou Mân or you stay with me, but you know that Pou Mân hasn't got anything to feed you." I didn't know what to say. My heart was with Sreï Peu and Tôn Ny. "This evening we're going to meet to decide what to do. Don't choose Pou Mân—say right away that you're staying with me." I felt hypnotized and frightened, and I just kept quiet.

After our meal and the evening washing up, we sat down in a circle under a tree. Pou Mêth and Pou Mân asked Tôn Ny with whom she wanted to stay, and she chose Pou Mân without hesitation. Min Ry stared at me fixedly. I was going to answer "Pou Mân" when my turn came, but Min Ry's eyes cut right through me and I couldn't make a sound. With tears in my eyes, I pointed to Pou Mêth.

I didn't sleep very much that night. Min Ry woke me up at dawn. "Come on, get up, we're leaving for Battambang right now!" She had rented a cart and a pair of oxen. Pou Mêth would have liked to stay and rest for a few more days, but Min Ry was very tense. She couldn't stand the presence of Sreï Peu and Tôn Ny any longer. Her husband was too tired to help her load the cart, so he stayed in bed while Min Ry and I did the work. Taking advantage of a moment when she was busy elsewhere, I kissed Sreï Peu goodbye, but my little sister ignored me completely. Tôn Ny gave me a kiss: she understood my decision. Sy Neang didn't say anything. Pou Mân told me, with tears in his eyes, "Go on, we'll see each other again. I'm sorry I'm not able to feed you."

The nurse and her husband were somewhat irritated with each other, but they set out together, Pou Mêth leading the oxen, Min Ry watching over the baggage piled up in the cart. I was in charge of keeping the children moving along.

I was already sorry about my choice. What had possessed me to leave the people I loved? Min Ry scolded me constantly: "Come on, keep moving. What are you moping about? Don't you dare start missing Tôn Ny, that witch!"

We stopped the cart to let the oxen rest about every hour or so. The tarred surface of the road was beginning to heat up and my feet hurt. Noticing this, Min Ry gave me a pair of sandals cut from a truck tire when we stopped for a rest at noon. Her gift didn't lift my spirits, though; my heart had stayed behind in Phum Krokoah.

Battambang came into sight at the end of the afternoon. We'd come as far as the railroad tracks, but they were set on a rise several meters higher than the road and the oxen would never be able to climb the stony embankment. While I unloaded the cart, Mêth and his wife crossed the tracks to look for a place where we could spend the night. The children were fidgety, and I couldn't manage to keep them in one place.

After what seemed like a very long time, Mêth and Min Ry found a spot for us near a textile factory at the entrance to the city. We carried the baggage across the railroad tracks and loaded it onto a hand cart Min Ry had rented with some of her gold, while Pou Mêth led the oxen back to Phum Krokoah.

It took us several trips, but finally we were all settled with our baggage near the factory wall, where Pou Mêth would build a hut the next day. In the meantime, we had to find some water for cooking and for the children's baths. Min Ry was making plans: she'd buy fruit in the central market with some of her gold, then resell the fruit for a profit and buy some rice.

2   AT NIGHT I would wonder how Tôn Ny and Sreï Peu were getting along; later on, they told me how they had managed to survive where I had left them. Pou Mân knew the region around Moung Russeï very well, and he preferred to stay there. He and Sy Neang scoured the countryside looking for rice. Having convoyed many wagons of rice stocked by the Khmer Rouge, Pou Mân knew where their hiding places were, and although most of them had already been emptied, he and Sy Neang were still able to glean a bit here and there. When they did bring back some rice, Tôn Ny would make rice cakes and peddle them at Phum Krokoah or along the roads. Pou Mân didn't have a reserve of gold that would have allowed them to try their luck in Battambang.

All day long Mi Vi did nothing but stay with Sreï Peu, who continued to wait, as she had always done. From time to time Mi Vi would collect a bit of wood, when Tôn Ny asked her to; if she took it into her head to cook some rice, it was inedible.

Since the region was still dangerous, Pou Mân would go along with his neighbors on his expeditions. One day, when he had located an almost untouched storehouse of rice, he obtained a cart and hitched up the young bull Sy Neang had brought back with him. As long as they were on the highway they didn't have too many problems, but they had to leave the road at a certain point to enter the forest. Pou Mân stopped the cart and cautiously went on alone to check out the path; he had proceeded about a hundred meters when a shot rang out on his right, answered immediately by a burst of machine-gun fire on his left. Lying flat on the ground, Pou Mân crept back to the edge of the forest, where his companions were hiding. The bull had run off across the muddy fields in the direction of Moung Russeï, and Sy Neang chased after him.

Pou Mân immediately went after the two of them, while his companions returned to camp. From time to time he saw a few traces of their passage, and he found a field of cucumbers, where he picked a small supply so he wouldn't go home empty-handed. After that he lost all trace of Sy Neang and the bull; they must have returned to the road somehow.

As for Sy Neang, he had also lost track of the bull and went back to where Pou Mân had gone into the forest. He went farther than Pou Mân had, and came to a bridge, but just as he was about to set foot on it, a burst of rifle fire sent him diving for the ground. He was at the edge of a bomb or shell crater, already overgrown with thorn bushes, and without thinking he let himself roll down into the hole, praying with all his might that no one would come to see if he was still alive. Scratched bloody by the thorns, he waited for half an hour, then risked crawling out of his shelter and crossing a hundred meters to the riverbank under the cover of the trees. The water was low enough for him to ford the river. He walked a kilometer or two without really knowing where he was going, and then followed a path into the forest. He did want to get back to his family, but how wonderful it would be if he was able to find the warehouse of rice on his own!

At a turn in the path, he was suddenly face to face with a man dressed all in black like the Khmer Rouge. The man wasn't armed, though, and said to Sy Neang, "What are you doing here all alone? It's dangerous, get out!" Sy Neang dashed off without even asking for directions. After an hour or two, he met some people gathering wood and learned that he was five kilometers from Moung Russeï. He arrived at nightfall, but when he didn't find Pou Mân there, he decided to go home to Phum Krokoah: eleven kilometers, which he traveled hitchhiking on a wagon. Pou Mân got home shortly before Sy Neang did. He had found the bull grazing by the roadside and the cart smashed to pieces.

The next day Tôn Ny wanted to try her luck at the market in Moung Russeï. Accompanied by a neighbor, a little girl of nine years old, she left at 5 a.m., carrying a load of small green lemons wrapped in a *krâmar* on her head. All day long she tried to sell them, but no one stopped to buy. The girls earned nothing, not even one can of rice. It was already eight o'clock, it had been dark out for a long time, and they hadn't eaten a thing. What could they do? Abandoning their supply of lemons, about thirty kilos' worth, by the side of the road, they started walking back to Phum Krokoah. Tôn Ny was soon dragging the exhausted little girl along after her; they covered about ten kilometers this way, stopping often in the hope that a late-returning cart would catch up with them . When they had just one more kilometer to go, and were slumped at the foot of a tree, the little girl jumped up screaming: a centipede had bitten her on the heel. Tôn Ny took her limping back to her hut, where she had to be taken care of immediately. Luckily, a neighbor who heard about the accident brought over a remedy, a seed about as big as a hazelnut. He rubbed the child's lips with this seed, and then the bite. This seemed to ease her pain somewhat, but her entire leg was soon very swollen, and it took her several days to recover.

Finally, since the area around Moung Russeï hadn't provided the resources he'd been counting on, Pou Mân decided to leave for Battambang with his wife and the children. He rented an ox and harnessed it with the young bull to carry a load of straw intended to cover the hut he was going to build. Sreï Peu was installed on the straw, while the others followed on foot.

A column of Vietnamese vehicles passed them on the road about ten kilometers from Phum Krokoah, and the bull, which wasn't easy to handle in the first place, lurched across the road and started going back the other way, dragging the ox along with him. Pou Mân had a lot of trouble keeping the load balanced and getting the animals turned around in the right direction. After a few halts, they arrived at Battambang in the evening, having tipped over into the ditch only once—Sreï Peu got off with a fright.

They stopped in the neighborhood of Phum Tien, a neighborhood familiar to Pou Mân. Everyone collapsed on the ground, without even the strength to eat. Pou Mân had to return the ox he had rented in Phum Krokoah, so he went off again into the night, munching on a mango. The others tried to get some sleep, but the ground was hard and they were worried that thieves might steal the cart. Sy Neang and Sreï Peu solved that problem by settling down in the cart, wrapped up in the mosquito net, and were soon joined there by Mi Vi and Tôn Ny.

They had stopped on the near side of the river, because the Vietnamese didn't permit any animals to cross the bridge. When Pou Mân returned in the morning, the rest of the group went into the city while Sy Neang forded the river with his bull, but he was still sent back by the Vietnamese, so Pou Mân decided to build his hut on the near side of the bridge.

3   I WAS STAYING at the Mêth family's hut during all this time. While the parents were busy trading in the city, I was taking care of the children, fixing the meals, and guarding their little bag of gold. Afternoons, I had to draw water for Min Ry's bath and husk the rice.

It didn't take long for my legs to swell up again, then my arms, and finally my whole body. It was hard for me to walk, and I couldn't urinate anymore. Min Ry steeped some roots in rice alcohol and told me to rub my arms and legs with it. This didn't help very much, and the running back and forth bringing water from the river tired me out. The two water buckets hanging from a bamboo pole were really very heavy. Pou Mêth tried to help me out, but then his wife would scold him.

Since I wasn't able to carry heavy loads, Min Ry tried me out at a different game. She took me to the market, where I was supposed to buy fruit at a stand as a cover for stealing whatever fruits and vegetables I could and slipping them into a basket kept behind my back. Then I was to sell off the merchandise. I wasn't at all gifted at this kind of thing, however, and Min Ry, quite displeased, sent me back to my work at the hut.

Returning from fetching water one morning, I was delighted to run into Pou Mân, and asked him about Sreï Peu and Tôn Ny. He said that he had left them and wasn't living with Mi Vi anymore, because he was ashamed of not being able to support them. I didn't dare stay too long with him or tell him all my troubles, but I asked him to wait for me. I ran to tell Min Ry that I'd met Pou Mân and that he was very close by but didn't want to disturb her. "Let him come in!" She was always generous with visitors. She invited him to eat and asked him what brought him to the neighborhood. Pou Mân told her that he had wanted to see me and that he was looking for food. He described the location of the hut he had built for Mi Vi and the children in the Phum Tien district.

The next day Min Ry's husband went to the hut to explain where he lived to Tôn Ny, and I think he took her a bit of rice. Tôn Ny promised Pou Mêth that she would come to see me with Sreï Peu. Mi Vi wasn't home very much, she was running around the city earning her living as best she could. They missed Pou Mân. If Mêth should see him again, would he please tell him to come home?

Tôn Ny began to visit me from time to time. Pou Mêth said to her one day, "If it's too hard to feed Sreï Peu, bring her along, we'll give her something to eat." I was touched by his generosity, but I saw what he had to put up with from his wife because of this invitation. One day, though, Tôn Ny did leave Sreï Peu with me, with Pou Mêth's approval.

My little sister slept with me. Min Ry had given me strict instructions that at mealtimes her children were to eat first, and they were to be spoon-fed. Sreï Peu would watch all this, her eyes wide with desire, while I told her that we were going to eat together afterward. When the other children were full, we'd have what was left in the pot, and since it was Min Ry who decided how much was to be cooked each time, the size of our leftover portions depended on the little gluttons' appetites. We went hungry more than once, and Min Ry would say to me, "You shouldn't let your stomach get used to eating too much." I'd already had more than enough of that kind of advice.

One day Sy Neang came by to see his little sister. He was hungry: it had been a long time since he'd tasted a spoonful of rice. I didn't dare take any rice from Min Ry's stock, so I went to ask a neighbor for a handful, explaining the situation to him. He gave me some rice, along with a few scraps of meat; enough to make a nice plateful.

When Min Ry's five-year-old son saw Sy Neang eating his meal, he ran off as fast as he could to look for his mother. Luckily, Sy Neang had enough time to finish his meal and disappear. As soon as Min Ry returned around noon, I told her what I'd done, and she began to scold me: "You never ask anyone's permission!"

The neighbor had been keeping his ears open, and he came running over to defend me. He was the one who had given me the handful of rice, and she, Min Ry, could at least make an effort to get it through her head that we weren't living under Pol Pot anymore. Of course this irritated Min Ry even more. "Everybody in Tôn Ny's house just wants to eat other people's food; they're all starvelings who don't want to fend for themselves."

Sreï Peu felt miserable at Min Ry's. After a month had passed, when Tôn Ny had come by one day to see me and Sreï Peu, I asked her to take our little sister back with her. Tôn Ny explained to me exactly how to get to their hut, and I promised to drop by there.

A few days later, while doing an errand, Tôn Ny stopped by to tell me how Sreï Peu was doing. The child was becoming more and more dispirited, and now that she was alone once again, she didn't even have the hostile company of Min Ry's children. Tôn Ny had sold the young bull to a peasant; the animal didn't cost anything to feed, but it served no purpose. The peasant had given them a little gold chain in exchange for the bull, and Tôn Ny bought some rice with part of the gold. Then she had made cakes from a mixture of rice, bananas, and crushed coconut, and it was selling these cakes from hut to hut that had brought her to Min Ry's door. That day she had collected ten cans of rice in all, after having been on her feet since four in the morning. Passing through the market, she had sold a few cakes to a grocer, who had proposed that she marry his son. Tôn Ny had refused: this wasn't the Pol Pot regime anymore and a girl no longer had to bow to the wishes of a boy. The Khmer Rouge were very touchy on the subject of young people's virtue, but if a Khmer Rouge wanted to get married, the girl was forced to go along with it. Tôn Ny wanted to keep her freedom. After all, she had her little sister to bring up.

4   LIFE WAS BECOMING more and more difficult for me. One morning, while everyone else was still asleep, I took my things and left to look for Tôn Ny's hut. Pou Mân had explained to me how to get there: it was about three or four kilometers from the Mêth family's hut. Along the way I met some Vietnamese soldiers on patrol. I think they asked me where I was going, and without understanding their questions, I pointed in the direction of Psa Dam Dong, Tôn Ny's neighborhood.

When I arrived at first light, Tôn Ny was in front of the hut boiling some water. I went to hide under a bamboo mat. Mi Vi hadn't been there when I arrived, but she returned shortly afterward and she must have heard me, because she called out, "Where are you, Peuw? There's no use hiding." I came out from under the mat and went to sit near Tôn Ny. Almost immediately I caught sight of Min Ry's husband approaching on a bicycle.

After saying hello to Tôn Ny, he turned to me. "I can understand why you ran away, but did you have to take my wife's gold?"

"What! You know very well I wouldn't steal anything."

"If she hadn't told me that, I wouldn't have come to get you."

"But I didn't steal anything. You can tell her so and ask her where she hid her gold. I can even tell you where it is, you can see for yourself."

"Okay, I believe you, but you chose to live with us. You have to come back. Or else bring back the sarong and the rubber sandals my wife gave you."

"Fine, I'll return them."

"No, come back right now with me."

He settled me on the bicycle's luggage rack, and I returned to my prison. His wife made a big speech that wound up something like this: "Who feeds you? Would you rather die with Tôn Ny or be fed at my house?"

"I'd rather die. And I'm giving you back your sandals."

"You'll stay right here."

Tôn Ny came to get me the next day, as I had asked her to do. Min Ry hadn't expected this; she stood there looking her up and down.

Tôn Ny said quietly, "I've come to get my sister."

"I'm not holding her back," said Min Ry. "Let her get out, that witch.

I don't want anything to do with a thief. She eats my rice and does nothing all day long."

Attracted by all the shouting, the neighbors gathered around. The nurse pointed at me and told them all how ungrateful I was. The people shook their heads. They knew what to believe. Tôn Ny went off without another word, and I ran after her barefoot. Min Ry shouted after us, "Thieves and fools!"

I had lived three months with Min Ry, and I bitterly regretted having left my real family. Now we were all together again, except for Pou Mân, and we were all hungry. After a few weeks Mi Vi, who was spending most of her time in the city, brought home a young man to live with us, but they soon saw that we weren't going to support them and they both left.

We used to pick edible plants along the riverside and the fruit still left on the trees. One day Sy Neang brought home a young hen, which Sreï Peu tamed, and we let her hatch a dozen eggs in order to be able to buy some rice. Sy Neang built a little cart out of salvaged wood, into which we put Sreï Peu with the hen and her chicks. I took the cart to market with a heavy heart. The first would-be buyer offered us a tiny amount of rice, which we refused. Another showed us a bit of thin gold chain half a finger long, and after talking it over with Tôn Ny, we accepted his offer. We sold the cart, too, in exchange for a little rice.

Sy Neang decided to make more small wagons. He scavenged wood from abandoned houses while I gathered little pieces of wood here and there. With the help of other boys, he tried to salvage whole doors without breaking them. Unfortunately, one day a very heavy door they had removed from its hinges toppled from the first story of a house, landing on a child passing by in the street. We only just managed to run away before a mob gathered, and I never dared go into another ruined house.

Tôn Ny and I would collect wood in the nearby thickets. Sometimes we'd steal papayas when we went through orchards and hide them in our bundles of wood.

Sy Neang fell ill: his old leg injury from Phnom Penh was hurting again and had to be taken care of. Luckily, there was always someone around who provided treatment for all sorts of ailments. As soon as he felt better, Sy Neang decided to try his luck near the frontier, where trading was more active; it was easier to find rice there than it was in the city. Tôn Ny gave him a gold ring set with diamonds for his stake.

We hadn't been able to use the few diamonds Tôn Ny kept in her waistband because people wanted gold. One day when Tôn Ny wasn't there, Mi Vi had found the little bag of diamonds in her things and called Tôn Ny a liar because she had told Mi Vi that she didn't have any valuables. That's how we learned that some people would trade gold for precious stones. The question was, how could we find them?

After Mi Vi had gone off with her boyfriend, not without encouraging us to follow her example (she was ready to open a few doors for us), Tôn Ny started looking for someone who might be interested in her diamonds. She found, of all people, Min Ry's sister, who gave us three little gold chains in exchange for a diamond pendant and a bracelet with rubies.

Tôn Ny began to sell pieces of the first little chain to buy rice while we waited for Sy Neang to return. He'd been gone a long time, and we were getting worried. He reappeared, finally, after having been gone a month. Had he brought back enough for us to live on for a while? We were quite upset to learn that he had traded the diamond ring for a big bag of candy and a T-shirt for Sreï Peu. I think he let himself get swindled by gamblers who promised him heaven and earth, and he had wanted to bring back as much as he could to his sisters. Tôn Ny was very angry and sold the T-shirt immediately to buy a bit of rice.

Disappointed by her attitude, Sy Neang gave the candy away to all the children in the neighborhood, keeping only a handful for Sreï Peu. To appease his sister, he told her, "We have to know how to give to others, it's good for us. We'll get it back one day."

5 WE DREAMED of going back to Phnom Penh, but Sy Neang advised against it: it was a journey of more than two hundred kilometers and Sreï Peu would never have survived the trip. Besides, we'd have had to cross regions where fighting was still going on and could be caught in an artillery barrage or a bombardment. And soldiers can be cruel to girls they find on the roads.

After talking it over, Tôn Ny agreed that Sy Neang should return to the frontier; she gave him one of the two remaining gold chains, and he set out immediately. We decided to leave the next day, intending to go at least as far as Sisophon, sixty kilometers to the north. This would bring us closer to the Thai border, which was fifty kilometers farther west. We agreed, however, to wait for Sy Neang's return at the marketplace in Sisophon.

We left at dawn the next morning, carrying our bundles on our heads.

Tôn Ny went first, while I followed, holding Sreï Peu's hand. It was the end of August or early September, not a good season for traveling; it rained every night. Sreï Peu was almost six years old, but she didn't even look four, while Tôn Ny and I were as thin as skeletons. We had to be careful when we arrived at the outskirts of villages, because no one was allowed to leave the place where they had settled, now that the Vietnamese had arrived.

Toward the end of the afternoon, after covering about fifteen kilometers, we reached Mongkol Boreï. An isolated outlying house opened its doors to us, and the owner, a woman living there alone, allowed us to hide behind the house, where there was a hut to protect us from the rain.

About an hour later the woman ran out. "Children, you have to leave; some men have come to check my house. The village chief sends out regular patrols—he's answerable to the Vietnamese for everyone traveling without permission. You can't stay here, because they might come back."

"But where can we go?"

"Find someone in the center of the village, it's safer."

Another half kilometer to travel. We mingled with the crowds of people going about their daily business in the open air. Behind the town square, two or three houses farther on, there was an isolated house . . . we decided to try it. The woman said we might spend the night. Hardly had she closed the door behind us when the inspection patrol arrived.

"Who went into your house?"

"My nieces—they're from the neighboring village and they'll be going home again tomorrow, after they've taken care of a few things here."

She sent us out into the garden behind the house. "You must leave tomorrow morning, very early." We begged a bit of rice from the neighbors and settled down under a little roof, rolled up in our mosquito nets. Sreï Peu was exhausted, dropping with fatigue, but Tôn Ny and I couldn't sleep. What would we do in the morning? How would we manage to live? We set out again at 4 a.m. Sreï Peu stumbled along; she was so tired that Tôn Ny and I took turns carrying her, but the sun was barely up before our backs ached terribly. We had to drag the poor little girl along all day.

We spent our second night of the journey on the ground in front of a house. The people inside had given us three little planks, enough to sit on—and then they shut their door again. There was a sudden downpour that left us soaked and shivering when we hit the road the next morning. Our feet hurt from walking for two days on burning asphalt. Sreï Peu's sandals seemed to have melted away; she had nothing on her feet and complained of burns. Tôn Ny admitted to me later on that her feet had also been hurting badly, but if she had said so, we wouldn't have wanted to go on.

Tôn Ny allowed us twenty minutes' rest at noon to bathe our feet in a pond, but then moved us relentlessly back out onto the road. We learned from a passing traveler that Sisophon was about ten kilometers farther on, so there was no question of arriving that evening. The sun had set, and we were surrounded by forest on either side of the road. We had to make it to the nearest village. The first houses loomed up at us suddenly out of the darkness, and we lay down in a courtyard paved with concrete without having seen a living soul. At least the floor wasn't water-logged. We straggled along the road at dawn with empty stomachs, walking beside the railroad tracks to avoid patrols. Once in the city, we started looking for the marketplace in front of the town hall, where we were to meet Sy Neang when he got back from the frontier.

It was already late in the afternoon when we found the market. I asked a woman at an empty stand if we might spend the night near her.

"Is that your family with you?"

"Yes, they're my sisters."

"You can't sleep here at the market—soldiers patrol at night to check for vagabonds."

"But we just got here, and it's so late that we can't register at the town hall this evening. Couldn't you let us stay until the morning?"

"All right, get under the stand."

We slipped under the bamboo screen, which the vendor covered with a blanket. At around midnight a patrol of Vietnamese soldiers went by, lamps in hand, checking the stands. They passed ours without stopping, though, and after they left we slept until dawn.

The next morning we went to the edge of town, where we found huts set up by unfortunate people like ourselves. We stopped near one of them, inhabited by a couple and a child of three or four. All around us the grass was trampled and foul with excrement. We asked permission to stay there for one night, and the man agreed, being so kind as to lend us a bamboo screen to protect us from the rain. We were overwhelmed by swarms of flies, so we tore out the filthy grass and cleaned up our little spot.

Sreï Peu slept between the two of us. Her cough was getting worse and worse, and her little body was burning with fever. I hadn't anything to give her to ease her distress. In the morning a thick fog blanketed us, then distilled into dew; it was cold, and everything was wet.

We had enough food for three or four days, if we were careful. On the third night the woman took Sreï Peu into her hut, but the husband re-

claimed his bamboo screen to keep the child off the bare ground, so Tôn
Ny and I slept on our rubberized cloth. My fever had returned.

After our last handful of rice was gone, we were reduced to begging.
"Ma'am, I haven't anything to eat," Sreï Peu would say, but people turned
their heads away from this walking cadaver, tricked out in nothing but a
pair of tattered shorts. I hardly dared show myself in my filthy, patched,
old peasant's trousers. I went down to the river to do a bit of laundry,
and whom did I see on the bank? Pou Mân.

"Oh, Pou Mân! Why didn't you come back at Battambang?"

"You know very well why. I couldn't find anything to eat. Where's
Sreï Peu?"

"She went back to the hut, she's coughing a lot."

"I'll come see her tonight."

"And what are you doing now?"

"I play basketball with the soldiers, they give me a little food." Sadly
he added, "If only I could help you! But I haven't anything." Now that
he was without resources and unable to set himself up in any kind of
business, this man, who had been our foster-father, was too ashamed to
let himself be supported by children. He went away, his head hanging.
We never saw him again.

After my bath I tried my luck at begging once more, but people would
look at me and say, "You've got a head and two hands, why don't you
work?" I wasn't about to tell them the story of my life, so I just went
back to the hut. Min Pôn, the woman we were staying with, gave a rice
ball to Sreï Peu, but Tôn Ny hadn't had any more luck begging than I
had. We went for two days without food.

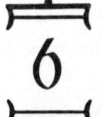 ON THE THIRD DAY Tôn Ny came back from the market with her
hands full of little bags—she had met Sy Neang! He had been
crossing the market to take the road to Battambang, and he was
furious that we hadn't waited for him where he'd left us.

"But we want to go the frontier."

"So you want to die, is that it?"

"We couldn't stay in Battambang anymore—people were laughing at
us, we couldn't beg anything."

His anger died away all of a sudden. "Sister Peuw, you have to take

care of me, I've got a fever." His leg was very painful, and his old scar
was an ugly purple.

We put everything he had brought us on the ground: rice, powdered
sugar, cakes, toilet soap. We had to help him right away. Tôn Ny and I
gathered up all our strength to give him a good *koktchaï*. While we massaged
him his whole body turned red, he twisted every which way, and tears
streamed from his eyes, but Sy Neang didn't make a sound. He knew we
couldn't leave that place until he got well again.

"Now just rest, Sy Neang."

He fell asleep. Tôn Ny and I went off to try to sell the soap. No one
wanted to give us any gold, but we managed to trade twelve little cakes
of soap for ten cans of rice. Our sugar proved difficult to dispose of, but
someone suggested that we try the pastry shop on the square, where the
proprietress gave us a small piece of gold for the sugar.

We went home happy to have sold everything: three little children's
shirts and twelve packets of candy in addition to the other things. Now
we had more rice and a bit of gold.

We found Sy Neang awake when we got back; his fever had gone down,
and he was feeling better, but he wasn't pleased when we showed him
our loot. "That's all you got? But you don't realize—all that stuff was
heavy, I walked a long way to bring it back, and the road was really
dangerous!" Tôn Ny didn't say anything at first.

"Listen, Sy Neang," I told him, "we're not fancy businesswomen, we
don't know how to talk up our goods for the customers. Mister, madam,
come and see something you've never seen before, American shirts, cakes
of Turkish soap with all the perfumes of Araby, and all that yakety-yak!"

Tôn Ny broke in: "You can't make wheeler-dealers out of us!"

"Okay," said Sy Neang, laughing, "we shouldn't get all upset about it.
It doesn't matter, Bang Peuw."

"It doesn't matter, Sy Neang."

"It doesn't matter, Tôn Ny."

And we all had a good laugh, which was something we hadn't had in
a long, long time. Sold at a loss, our merchandise had still bought us a
little rice for our journey.

Sy Neang was definitely feeling better, hungry for meat. Tôn Ny ran
to the market to buy a chicken leg, paying two cans of rice for it. We
divided it among the four of us, licking our fingers.

Feeling energetic, we hit the road, after having thanked the people who
had taken in Sreï Peu for several nights. We bought three pairs of sandals
for our journey, but my feet were so swollen that I couldn't keep up with

Sy Neang. He urged us on, taking Sreï Peu upon his back so that we could move faster. She was ecstatic.

The road had no tarred surface: it was made of thick red dirt, mixed to the consistency of mortar by the nightly rains, then back to dry red dust by noon. We stopped at the edge of the road to eat. There were many isolated houses with cement cisterns or tubs full of water, where a half a coconut was set out for thirsty travelers—a good old custom from before the Khmer Rouge nightmare. We also found bamboo benches to rest on under the trees in front of the houses.

It was getting toward the end of the afternoon, and even Sy Neang was wearing out. He put his little sister down. "Walk a bit on your own." I was dragging my feet. We caught up with a carter and asked him if he'd give us a ride.

"You can see that I've got a full load, and I can't overwork my animals."

"Just the little girl and our bundles?"

"No."

"Just for a kilometer."

"I'm sorry, I can't."

Was he afraid for the sacks of rice he was carrying? We were turned down by a second and a third wagon. Finally, one of the men agreed to take on Sreï Peu and our bundles, but only for half a kilometer, "just to that tree over there."

Sy Neang was already far ahead; he didn't have the same problems we had with our aching feet. "Come on, sisters, keep going," he said when we caught up to him. "I know some people not far from here who'll take us in. I'm going on ahead."

The sun had set. People were camping by the side of the road, and we could see dim lights glimmering in the shadows and hear people arguing, clustered around a cardsharp.

There was a village not too far away, and Sy Neang led us to a house where two closely related families lived. They welcomed us and gave us water to wash our feet. Then we settled down to eat some rice and grilled fish wrapped in banana leaves.

"Go get our children," the woman said to her husband, "so that they can see how poor these children are."

The husband lighted a candle and went to get their three children from the neighboring house. Then they brought us blankets and a mosquito net, and showed us where the toilets were inside the house. There was no need to go outside in the rain!

After having rested for a few hours, Sy Neang and Tôn Ny set out during the night with a group of travelers to get some rice at the frontier. It would take them six or seven hours to arrive the next morning at a military camp for Prince Sihanouk's soldiers, where they'd be able to get some food. Some of the areas they had to go through were dangerous. There were mines and bombs, and dozens of travelers disappeared every day under the bombardments.

The woman who had taken us in didn't want me to share the little bit of rice we'd brought—she was quite ready to feed us—but I didn't want to be a burden, so I offered to fetch water or wood. The water was two kilometers away, in a deep pool at the bottom of some rather steep and slippery dirt steps. My legs and stomach started to swell up again, and I had attacks of fever. I didn't say anything to our hostess, but she could see that I was depressed. I took some aspirin tablets Sy Neang had brought us, and I gave some to Sreï Peu, who still had her cough.

7

FOUR DAYS went by like this. I wasn't sleeping well at night. Half awake, I heard Sy Neang's voice one night . . . he was back, standing in the doorway, completely covered with mud and carrying two muddy bags on a bamboo pole. Tôn Ny arrived a half hour later, just as muddy as her brother. She told me how she had had to step over corpses in the road—the Vietnamese were murdering travelers and spreading the rumor that it was the work of the Khmer Rouge hiding in the forest. The road was really a dangerous place to be.

The two of them had brought rice, sugar, soybeans, three or four packs of cigarettes, candies, and cakes. Sy Neang told me that a woman had lent him some gold so that he could buy things, and he was to pay her back after we'd sold this lot.

Our hosts explained to us how best to dispose of these goods. We had to go to Sisophon, where the demand was greater than it was here on the road. Sy Neang offered them cigarettes, but they declined his gift. "Sell all that at Sisophon."

Leaving Sreï Peu with Sy Neang, Tôn Ny and I set out while it was still dark. There was mud everywhere, thick and sticky, constantly churned up by travelers' feet. My sandals were lost in the mud, so I had to go barefoot. We walked along for several hours without stopping. At one point we overtook a carter returning to Sisophon with an empty wagon; he had been supplying provisions to the Khmer army of liberation, which was billeted at the border. He was willing to load up our bundles, but his animals—two rather thin cows—were very tired, so we had to walk by the cart. He stopped at a house to water his cows, but the cistern was empty: so many people were traveling by. When I went into the house to beg a little water, they gave me some for myself and Tôn Ny, and we lay down on some bamboo pallets under the lemon trees. There were little pieces of gravel hidden in the mud that had pierced the soles of my feet. I needed a pair of sandals. I spotted someone sleeping near us who had taken off his thong sandals. "My God, please forgive me. Look at how cut up my feet are." I slipped them on and we hurried away from the scene of my crime. The sandals were too narrow, unfortunately, and after a few steps I asked Tôn Ny to trade with me, because she had old sandals that had stretched. "Mine" fit her quite well, while hers were rather large but a bit short for me. I had to walk with my toes curled under.

We arrived at Sisophon before sunset. Stopping to say hello to Min Pôn, we found her quite sad: she was waiting for her husband to return from the frontier; he had been gone for eight days now. On top of that, her child was sick and she hadn't any more rice. We gave her a can of our rice and went on to the market. When the merchandise was interesting, things moved quickly. We sold our sugar at the pastry shop, where they also bought our cigarettes. We'd earned almost half a finger's length of gold.

Since we hadn't anywhere to sleep, it was best to start back that night. It had begun to rain, and we ran the entire way home, arriving at Tuah Psiem at midnight. Although Sy Neang was ready to leave immediately for the frontier, Tôn Ny asked him to let her rest until cockcrow; the two of them were back on the road before dawn. Sy Neang left me a bit of gold and some rice. This time our hostess accepted the rice I offered her, and she also allowed me to cook separately for Sreï Peu and myself, because I hadn't anything to give her in exchange for the fish or meat she put into her rice. I went back to my duties carrying wood and water, but my stomach hurt and I had diarrhea again. Was I going to die there, two steps from the border?

Our hostess took care of me, giving me a warm blanket and putting hot-water bottles on my stomach and at the soles of my feet. This continued for several days. Sy Neang and Tôn Ny still weren't back yet, and I was worried. I knew that their expedition was dangerous because of the Vietnamese as well as the Thais themselves. These last were divided into two camps: the merchants who furnished provisions for our compatriots and the army that pursued both them and their clients, then turned around and resold whatever it confiscated.

8 SY NEANG and Tôn Ny returned after a week, bringing back rice and dried fish. I told Tôn Ny about my illness and insisted that I didn't want to stay behind anymore. "Let's all go to the frontier together, we'll see what we can do. I can't stay here without working, and I haven't the strength for it." My plan was fine with Tôn Ny, but she wanted to rest up a bit first.

As for Sy Neang, he set out again the next day, saying he would wait for us at the frontier. He wasn't in very good shape, either: he had an open wound that was beginning to suppurate running the length of his bruised calf. He put on a bit of a show anyway: "Okay, kiddo, chin up. This boy's still good for something!"

When we told the couple sheltering us that we wanted to leave for the frontier, they tried to dissuade us. Seeing that we were determined, the father decided to go with us. "I have to find provisions for my family, too." His wife brought up the danger, the mines, the Vietnamese, and the Thais, but he stuck to his plan. He advised me to cook some rice to carry along, and I also prepared a potful of sweetened soybeans.

We left at cockcrow. The first few kilometers were fairly easy going, but soon we had to walk in water, at first up to our knees, and then up to our waists. I held my pot of soybeans straight out in front of me and carried my bundle of belongings on my head. Our former host carried Srei Peu on his shoulders, and Tôn Ny held my hand to keep me from slipping on the muddy ground. Once we got through the deep water in the rice paddies we had some cover on drier ground. The man warned us not to pull on any vines or pick up any strings lying around, because anything could be hiding a mine trap. In a fairly open clearing we had to follow a tiny little path winding among needle-sharp young bamboo shoots that we couldn't avoid brushing against, and it was in just such new fields as these that the mines were hidden.

Then we came to several kilometers of thorn-bush forest that had to be crossed quickly: the Vietnamese patrolled through there, and they killed without mercy. It was hard for me to run, and Tôn Ny scolded me. Srei Peu cried the entire way. Luckily the rain made it very difficult for any Vietnamese sentries to spot us. We ran as fast as we could, but other travelers kept passing us, and we ended up being the last ones. "O God in Heaven, help me! Mother and Father, come help me!" The bamboo shoots had cut my feet. I would rather have died where I was than take another step, and yet I kept going. "Another thirty meters," Tôn Ny told me. "If you stop they'll cut you to pieces! The roadside was littered with disemboweled women, decapitated bodies, and severed heads.

Another few steps and all was calm: we heard the voices of dozens of people sitting around, chatting and arguing. We collapsed under a tree. Our former host had disappeared somewhere up ahead. We found ourselves seated near a man off by himself who seemed about thirty years old. He had left his wife and children in Battambang, he hadn't any gold, and he had no idea how he was going to manage. He reminded me of Pou Mân, so unhappy over not being able to help us.

We told him our story, too: we were going to rejoin our husbands at the frontier. Sreï Peu was Tôn Ny's daughter, and I was Tôn Ny's sister. We had drilled this into Sreï Peu. "You call Tôn Ny 'Mama' and me 'Auntie.' " Girls alone on the road ran more risks than women provided with husbands. Sreï Peu found it very amusing to call Tôn Ny "Mama."

I offered the man our pot of sweetened soybeans, but he forgot to ask if it was to be shared and ate the whole thing. When he brought the pot back after washing it, it was full of sweet water, which was very refreshing. When I went to get another potful, however, so many people had come to the pond that they had stirred it all up, so the water was now turbid and stank of cow urine. I tried to drink some, but my stomach heaved and I lost almost all of my meal.

We decided to keep going. The man was quite willing to help us, and offered to take Sreï Peu on his bike. That was fine with her—anything, as long as she didn't have to walk! She got up behind him and held on to his waist as tightly as she could. "I'm going on ahead," he told us. "Don't worry, you'll find me again at the border." We trusted him and set out reassured, without having to drag our little sister along. The road was easy to follow, as thousands of people were using it every day. This time we didn't let ourselves fall behind.

9

IN TWO HOURS we were within a kilometer of the border. Suddenly we heard someone calling us: "Hey, girls!" The voice was familiar, but we didn't recognize the man. He had taken a bath and put on a clean T-shirt . . . it was the man with the bicycle! Sreï Peu was asleep under a tree. "Rest here a little while," he told us. "I'm going on ahead. You've got one kilometer to go until you reach Site 7: it's a camp of soldiers from the regular army who keep an eye on the border." Sreï Peu wanted to keep traveling by bicycle with her protector, who was quite willing to let her off at the entrance to the camp, but Tôn Ny was afraid of losing her. "Let's all walk together instead, if it isn't that far."

Sreï Peu climbed onto the bicycle and the man walked along with us, holding his bike upright. In a quarter of an hour we were within sight of the camp—and just in time. Our food and gold were all gone, and we hadn't had any news of Sy Neang.

We were met by soldiers in camouflaged combat clothing, and we had to say goodbye to the man who had helped us; he was directed over to the commandant's hut. Since we were a family, we each received fifty cans of rice, and we settled down at the foot of a tree to prepare some food. There'd be time enough to think about building a hut later on.

There was no problem getting wood, but it turned out that there was no water within the perimeter of the camp. We didn't have time to join a group leaving to fetch more water a half kilometer away, so we bought a half bucketful of water in the camp for three cans of rice.

We hurried to cook our first military rice, because the wind was rising and it was going to rain. Some salt fish we found completed the menu.

Having eaten our fill, we looked around to see how other people had built their shelters. First you drove four stakes into the ground, connecting them at the top with four other pieces of wood, and then you stabilized them with two crosspieces from corner to corner. With the knife that my father had made for me I managed to cut the tree branches we needed: ten rather straight poles between two and three meters long. Before night-fall we'd set up the posts and the roof pieces, which we secured with vines. Then, since we didn't have any banana leaves or long grass, we threw a blanket on top to serve as a roof.

We slept under this precarious shelter, battered by the rain. The next day the search for Sy Neang began. He had to be somewhere in the camp, but a crowd of several thousand people was milling about. That evening we found a man waiting for us near our hut.

"You have to remove your hut," he said. "This place is reserved for soldiers."

"But we've just arrived, and we've come a long way."

"If you don't take it down, I'll do it myself."

"At least let us spend the night here."

"All right, tomorrow morning, then, at dawn."

"But we're waiting for our brother. Let us stay here just another day or two."

"No—if you're not gone by noon tomorrow, I'm taking down your hut."

Sy Neang arrived the next morning: he had been looking for us on his own. We had thought he would earn a bit of gold to help us out with our food problems, but he came back to us completely broke, robbed by cardsharps who had dazzled him with the hope of winning a fortune. When we told him that a soldier had ordered us to dismantle our hut, he said it wasn't serious, he'd find us another place.

We asked advice from a soldier in uniform, who helped us find a site not far from the officers' big hut. "No one will chase you away from here." He made sure that we were issued enough rice for three days. Sreï Peu stayed on the site to guard our rice while the three of us went back to dismantle the hut. The man from the day before was already there. Hardly had we torn out our support poles than he installed his own. It was just as I'd suspected—the man wanted our spot for himself; he wasn't any more a soldier than I was.

Our new hut was quickly set up, but now we had to solve the water problem. Sy Neang had a bright idea: "It's certainly going to rain tonight, so let's collect the water that falls off our roof."

"You're not the first one to think of that."

"No, but we've got only one pot. I know what we can use to collect more water."

We really should have thought of it before: collecting the orange-juice bottles the officers threw away behind their hut. The bottles weren't very big, but by lining up a dozen under the edge of our roof, we collected enough water to cook our rice. And since the rain kept falling for several days running, we bathed in the downpour, washed our clothes, and laid in a supply of water.

When the rain stopped, the ponds around the camp were replenished, but not for long, unfortunately; too many people needed water. Soon there was nothing within the radius of a kilometer but turbid, useless mudholes. After a few days, we felt as dirty as pigs, and Sy Neang and another man went off to look for a well. Sy Neang returned in the evening with a bucket of water. Out of the five bucketfuls they had collected, the man had given one to him. They continued their expeditions, going farther and farther away from camp. Meanwhile, we girls were buying water four kilometers away: two buckets for ten cans of rice.

One day our water diviners discovered a source providing up to twenty buckets a day, and we took advantage of it, bathing in water cleaner than any we'd seen in a long time. It was very far away, however, on Thai territory, and we lost a lot of water along the way from bumping and jostling the buckets, when we had to hide.

Some Thais came to complain to those in charge of the camp that people were digging anywhere and everywhere, taking water needed for the Thais' crops. The Thai population was very hostile to us, filling in the wells we dug and hacking to death any "water thieves" they found; occasionally the army even lobbed a shell onto groups they'd spotted several days straight in the same place. People had been wounded, and supposedly some had been killed. From now on, when a group went out looking for water, there was always a Khmer soldier with us. If we met any Thais, the soldier tried to frighten them off while we hid.

Once again we went without water for three days because someone had spotted Thai soldiers hidden under the trees. Then the situation eased somewhat, so we went back to our distant well, only to find it fetid and filled with rotting leaves.

The Khmer soldiers decided to send a message to the Thai commanding officer, who agreed not to bother people escorted by a soldier responsible for certain wells approved for our use. A few girls who had gone with me to get water in the outskirts of a small city decided to give our soldier the slip, running to the city to ask for shelter from Thai families. This happened a few times, and most of the time their desperate efforts succeeded, but occasionally some of the girls came back in tears and didn't want to have anything more to do with the Thais.

10

THIS STATE of affairs continued for a long time. Our rice rations started shrinking, and water was ever more difficult to find. The nearby hospital was full of wounded and crippled people, back from Thai territory where they had gone looking for water. The situation was so bad that the camp commandant forbade anyone to cross over into Thai territory and Thai merchants were no longer allowed into camp.

So we went looking for water along the border toward the north, in the direction of the city of Siem Reap, being careful to remain on Khmer territory. At first people were generous: six buckets of water for ten cans of rice. Prices went up quickly, though, and then the road was put off limits because of the advancing Vietnamese troops. I saw a Vietnamese arrested by our soldiers; he allegedly admitted that he had been sent to blow up the camp ammunition dump. He was beaten, tortured, and finally killed.

We saved our rice to buy water from those who were willing to sell some. One day the lack of water was cruelly felt: a family cooking near the hospital forgot to put out their fire, which spread to a hut and then to the hospital. Everything was in flames within seconds, fanned by the wind. Dozens of patients were trapped in the blaze. I had only enough time to carry off a blanket with our rice supply. Tôn Ny wasn't there at the time. Loudspeakers began broadcasting orders to move away from the fire and soldiers piled up bags of rice around the ammunition dump, but luckily the wind died down and rain began to fall in torrents. When I went back to our hut, I found Sy Neang there, too. There wasn't anything left to save. We decided to build a new hut a bit farther away.

In the face of this disaster, the soldiers sent a message to some Americans stationed about twenty kilometers away in Thailand, and a tank truck arrived daily in the camp from then on. In principle, everyone was allowed two buckets of water, but the soldiers gave extra rations to their own families, so most of the refugees didn't get any.

Sy Neang recognized one of the young guards in charge of the water, a boy with whom he used to play under the Pol Pot regime, and he went to talk to him.

"How did you manage to get this job?"

"I told them I was the son of a dead soldier."

Sy Neang wanted to become a water guard, too. "Impossible," his friend explained. "It's too late; you should've spoken up right away. But don't worry, I'll give you some as if you were part of my family." So I would go every day to collect our water ration of two buckets.

The days went by, monotonous and hopeless: we were surviving, but for what? And then one day a tall American arrived in the camp, wearing a *dhoti* wrapped around his hips Gandhi-fashion. He spoke Khmer, and he gathered all the children together and told us, "My name is Steve, I'm a reporter, and I'm looking for children who have lost their parents."

Tôn Ny and I invited him to stay in our hut. He spent two nights with us, and since he was very tall, his feet stuck out over our threshold.

Steve returned to Thailand, promising that he was going to take care of us and the others. A few days later the camp loudspeaker called all the orphans together; they took our names and told us not to leave the camp. Adults were chosen as "fathers" and "mothers" responsible for us. They regrouped us, so that when the Americans arrived we could assemble quickly.

11 ONE MORNING they told us to go with our belongings to a big central hut. There were about sixty of us, boys and girls. We were given a good meal, with meat and vegetables. And we waited.

A canvas-backed truck arrived around noon, ready to take us away. The adults stood around watching all this, shaking their heads. "They're going to be sold or killed for sure." Some of the children, especially the girls, disappeared into the crowd of onlookers, but there was no time to look for them, so we ended up with about thirty in the truck, mostly boys. The driver was a Thai, and there was someone else sitting up front with him. The truck drove off.

We very quickly felt far away from Site 7. After some roads in fairly terrible condition, we came to a highway, where we saw red, green, and white houses covered with sheet metal gleaming in the sun. Houses being built! They were beautiful.

Soon after we reached the highway we were stopped by a patrol of Thai soldiers. The driver showed them some papers, argued for a moment, and then drove on. A kilometer farther along, another checkpoint: the soldiers looked to make sure there were no adults hidden among the children.

We drove on and on. The boys had rolled back the tarp, and we could now see toward the horizon; the atmosphere was different from what it had been in the forest. After an hour the truck stopped at a roadblock manned by soldiers. We were beginning to get used to these halts, but this time it seemed more serious. "You can't go any farther. You're from Site 7? You have to go back there!" The driver tried to bargain, waved his papers around, invoked the Americans, but it was no use: we had to go back. Some of the children began crying; off in our little corner we began to pray.

The truck turned around, all right, but after a few kilometers it left the highway and we were tossed about by the holes and bumps of a country road. Then we entered a forest, where the truck rolled along in deep ruts. The driver turned left, right, then left again, and we came out onto a tarred road. The dust was blinding, so we lowered the tarp. After traveling a long time along a completely straight road, the truck stopped. Peeking out, we saw a big gate opening in front of us. The truck rolled through the gate very slowly: we were in Kao I Dang camp. It was four in the afternoon, December 27, 1979.

Epilogue

ORPHANS
IN SEARCH OF
A FAMILY

STIFF AND ACHING all over, we climbed down from the truck. They lined us up in a small open area. Two men arrived, one of them carrying a notebook, and asked us to step forward one at a time to give our names and those of our parents. "Do you still have any family? Brothers and sisters?" A red minibus stopped in front of us and a woman got out; her name was Katy, she was from Switzerland, and she was going to take us to the section of the camp reserved for orphans. "Climb in." I didn't have the strength to haul myself up into the minibus, so Katy lifted me up herself.

We drove through the camp, which was full of straw huts. People were clustered around cisterns in small open spaces waiting for their turn to draw water. In a few minutes we arrived at section 7, the orphans' section, where we were greeted by the couple in charge. Roll was called, and for the first time in a long, long while we heard once more the names our parents had given us, and our nicknames: Sreï Peu had become Chet again, Tôn Ny was Vann, Sy Neang was Rîth, and I was Dâ.

We were too tired to stay up for a formal meal. The "mother" responsible for us gave us slices of cake, a glass of milk, and some chocolate. Then we all quickly got ready for bed. Each one of us was given two towels, two blankets, a pair of sandals, a toothbrush, and some toothpaste. We went to bed in four little dormitories, brothers and sisters grouped together. The next day, however, they decided to separate the girls from the boys because there was too much uproar and mayhem when everyone woke up.

On our first day in the new camp we explored our surroundings. Our hut was somewhat isolated, but all around us Khmer families were living in their huts. People called out to us, "Why are you in rags? You should be ashamed! Why are you still wearing your black outfits from Pol Pot?"

We explained to them that we'd only just arrived, but they turned away in disdain, forgetting that they themselves were probably just like us only a few weeks ago. Actually, some of them had been there for eight or ten months. The other orphans were all properly dressed. Anyhow, that very day Katy turned up again with her minibus full of clothes: American T-shirts and blouses, white shorts. We were transformed in a flash.

The first weeks went by like a dream, but our "mother" warned us, "Don't go to the edge of the camp. The Thais on guard might kidnap you." Our "father" patrolled at night, gun in hand.

Katy visited us quite often. One day, after talking something over among themselves, Katy and our "parents" called us all together in the main office to tell us that the King of Thailand was offering ten orphans from each center places in a big orphanage he had had constructed at the seaside. It was a trap, though, because the children sent to this so-called orphanage were in fact put to work in the fields or building roads. At night they were shut up in bamboo cages and spoon-fed through the bars.

Katy cried when she told us all this. "If someone from the King comes to recruit children, you must say that you want to stay here. Do you understand?"

We were all gathered around her when the Thais arrived, dressed in yellow outfits and wearing blue hats clearly marked with a red cross. We all lined up, and the oldest of the men in yellow read the roll call. "Who wants to come with us?" No one answered. Then they had a boy of about twelve step forward. He explained that he was from section 3 and that he wanted to live in the King's orphanage. He invited the children of section 7 to come along with him, but no one answered. We were terrified, and no one moved. The Thais went away again, saying, "Think about it, we'll be back."

On the following nights our "father" distributed the orphans among Khmer families for fear the Thais would come back at night and take us away. During the day we had to stay in our hut. Certain families agreed to take care of children even during the day, and our "mother" took their food around to the various houses.

Sreï Peu chose this moment to catch measles. She had a high fever and had to be watched day and night. When were our troubles ever going to end?

After a few days we thought the crisis with the Thais was over; there were other refugee camps in Thailand, and the King's men were probably going around to each of them in turn. We went back to sleeping in the orphanage, but a boy ran over that night. "Quickly, go out the back way without letting anyone see you—the Thais are here!" I slipped outside, dragging along poor Sreï Peu, still sick. A woman opened her door to us and hid us under some blankets at the foot of her bed.

By noon the child hunt was over: the Thais had taken away four or five, but no one from our section. In the evening the little ones slept around their "mother," while we older girls slept in the next room.

The next day we learned that Katy had been expelled from the country, or perhaps put in prison. She never came back to the camp. Some children who had her address in Switzerland wrote to her, but the Thais tore up all the letters they sent.

Two "mothers" and "fathers" went to visit the boys of the neighboring sections who had agreed to live in the royal orphanage, but they could see them only at a distance, working in a rice paddy. They weren't allowed to talk to them or even go near them.

After our Khmer New Year's Day, in April of 1980, a twenty-three-year-old American woman, Suzy, came to visit the orphans in the camp. She started an English course at the adult center. Unfortunately for us, the teachers had to be paid, so it wasn't a free class. Sy Neang sneaked up against the outside wall of the hut and followed the courses through the gaps between the bamboo, taking notes on his lap; then he came and repeated everything to us. He was caught at his post and chased away several times, but he kept going back throughout the week, until he got to the point where he could make himself understood by the Americans and understand what they were saying.

Tôn Ny and I tried to follow Sy Neang's example, but our "mother" scolded us, saying it was unsuitable for girls to be hanging around outside a hut full of adults. Our "father" tried to console us by teaching us a few words of English, but in any case, we needed pencils, notebooks, and elementary-school texts. We used to sell our bread to get the money we needed, but when our "mother" realized what we were doing, she started giving us our bread in such small portions that no one would buy it. We had to beg her to give us the entire loaf. Half the time she'd give in, knowing exactly where the bread would end up. When we couldn't sell the bread, we peddled our soap, towels, sandals, and so on.

Unfortunately, fat Miss Suzy stuck her nose everywhere, checking to see if we were selling the things she was giving us. Since we big girls (whom the Thai soldiers pursued with extra zeal) were often unable to leave the orphanage, we conducted our business via a little seven-year-old girl, a real sharp item, who would slip underneath the camp gate and run to the market in the city. Tipped off by an anonymous letter from our adult neighbors, Suzy came to scold our "parents" publicly. This humiliation of those closest to us upset us very much and we promised to make sure that our private business dealings didn't get out of hand.

Months passed, and we girls went each day to section 11 for sewing lessons, by hand and on the machine. Some of the more talented girls even learned to cut out garments. The smaller children went to school, where they learned to read Khmer, with Khmer teachers. The boys had music and painting lessons. I would have liked to go with them, but everyone made fun of me. The boys also learned to do odd jobs, and how to draw up a floor plan for a little house.

Taking advantage of her outings to attend sewing class, Tôn Ny would go every day to check a bulletin board hanging on the wall of the main office in the camp. Posted there were the names of people looking for members of their families, with their addresses in America or Europe. One day she found the name of a Khmer living in Paris who was looking for his daughter and whose last name was the same as hers: Sisowath. (This was a rather common name among the Cambodian upper classes, stemming from one of the two branches of the royal family.) We talked it over, and Tôn Ny decided to write to him. December was drawing to a close, and soon we would have been in this camp for an entire year. The war didn't seem close to being over; we could still hear the big guns thundering on the far side of the hills. Should we wait for the end of the turmoil in Cambodia and go back to our country? And live with whom? Doing what? It was better to pin our hopes on Europe, if we couldn't make it to America.

Our four huts weren't full, and every day they brought in one or two children from other sections or other camps. Among the five newest girls to arrive was one who stayed off by herself. Her name was Ny Ren, and she came from the camp at Mayrut, far away on the coast. Her camp had been shut down, and she didn't know anyone here. Worst of all, though, she hadn't received any news from France, where she had found a couple who were sponsoring her. She had been getting letters and little packages—not through the mail, of course. A Frenchman in charge of an association to help orphans used to come every three months, bringing letters, packages, and a little money. They had even sent her a certificate of sponsorship, but now her address had changed and the authorities weren't the same ones anymore. What was going to happen to her?

Ny Ren had been assigned to our group, and our "mother" put her in the room with us. After a month she received another letter and two little packages from the people she called her father and mother in France. She even showed us their photograph. We started dreaming about going to France one day, going anywhere at all, as long as it was out of this camp.

Ny Ren became ill at the end of March. She had been coughing for several days, and then her fever went up suddenly, so she was taken to the hospital. Then it was my turn to join her in the sick ward.

Three days later Tôn Ny ran to the hospital. "The four of us are leaving!" The man to whom she had written, a former diplomat who had fled to France in 1975, had agreed to sponsor us. Our travel document listed all four of us under the same last name, since our sponsor believed me to be Tôn Ny's sister. Ny Ren was in despair, but before I'd gotten all my things together, Sy Neang came dashing in. "Ny Ren, you're leaving, too!" We were delirious with joy.

By nine o'clock the next morning we were all ready. We didn't take along anything besides strictly personal belongings, since we were told, "You'll have everything you need at the transit camp." A little truck dropped us off in front of the main office, where a big van came to pick us up around noon. The children staying behind waved goodbye to us sadly.

That evening we arrived in Bangkok, all lit up in the night as the van drove down toward a blazing mass of stars. On the other side of the city was Soun Flou, where we were to wait for the plane to France. Ny Ren said goodbye to us tearfully in the van, because she was going on to another transit camp before leaving for Italy. She had given us the address of her French "parents," and we promised her that we'd give them news of her. France wouldn't accept Ny Ren because she had no family there, whereas the supposed "uncle" to whom Tôn Ny had written was vouching for us.

Climbing down from the van, we found ourselves in a big hangar where about a hundred people were waiting to leave for France. With our meager bundles, we felt somewhat at a loss. A few people came up to us.

"Where have you come from?"

"From the orphanage at Kao I Dang."

"Don't you have any baggage?"

"No, this is all we have. They told us we wouldn't have to bring anything."

A man offered us a blanket to spread over the cement floor so that we could lie down, and a woman brought us a mosquito net. In the stifling heat, and with empty stomachs, we slept rather poorly.

The next day I wrote to a French priest who had visited us at the camp a few times: "Please come and see us. We're waiting to take a plane to

France, but we haven't any money and we must pay for the photographs we were required to have taken." Someone from the emigration service had come by during the morning, and in order to save money, we had all had our picture taken together, in one photo—the first since Phnom Penh.

When a friend of the French priest arrived the next morning, a friend of Tôn Ny's served as our interpreter. The Frenchman returned the next day and slipped an envelope into Tôn Ny's hand. "Don't let the others see this." Inside were three hundred bahts, and he added another three hundred out of his own pocket. Our first money! There was enough to buy some food and two remnants of cloth, from which we made ourselves skirts. And we treated ourselves to our first ice cream!

On the ninth day, the last one before our departure, they called our names and gave us a few items of clothing: a woolen jacket, jeans, a pair of socks, some sneakers. It seemed that France was not a particularly hot country.

At nine that evening we boarded the plane at last, a superb Air France Boeing jet, full of European passengers. A stewardess led us to our seats in the rear of the plane and buckled our seat belts herself. Tôn Ny was seated on my left, Sreï Peu and Sy Neang on my right. They served us something to eat, but the plane was buffeted so strongly that our stomachs couldn't handle the sudden ups and downs and our meal came back up again. We didn't sleep a wink.

Much later the stewardess came by to refasten our seat belts. "Get dressed, put on your jackets—we're arriving in Paris." The plane landed at Orly-Sud, and we emerged into a chilly fog. We had to stay in the airport lounge, waiting, still waiting, without anything to eat. At noon a van arrived to take us to . . . a camp. Again!

It was almost three in the afternoon when we arrived at the shelter at Achères. The man in charge of the center was a Vietnamese, and his assistant was a Khmer woman. We set our baggage down in a large entrance hall. The "camp" wasn't at all what we had imagined: it was a big building, several stories high, in the middle of a vast plot of land. We saw adults and children of all the nations of Southeast Asia walking around— Khmers, Laotians, and lots of Vietnamese.

They took us to the dining hall, where a good meal was waiting for us, and then to our rooms. The next day we were registered at the center, where they gave us all a little pocket money. We made a beeline for the nearest supermarket, where we were astonished at the abundance of goodies. What we craved most were chocolate and sweet things, after so many years of going without.

The following days brought medical checkups, plus a trip to the Red Cross, not far from the Eiffel Tower. I had once dreamed of seeing the Eiffel Tower without knowing what it looked like. In my dream a lady sent me across the ocean and told me that I would stand one day at the foot of the Eiffel Tower—and here I was, but I couldn't go visit it yet. Tôn Ny and I were assigned to a home for young students, where we'd study French for three months and be given some introductory professional training. Sy Neang and Sreï Peu would be going to an orphanage. Were we going to be separated again?

In the week since our arrival we hadn't had time to contact Ny Ren's "parents." Tôn Ny had kept their address, though, and she decided to write to them now. That letter changed our lives.

.   .   .

This spring marks the fifth year of our new life in Paris. As it turned out, we were unable to live with the man who had sponsored our arrival in France because he had his own family to look after, and his own share of the usual material difficulties all refugees must face. In his place, after much time and effort, a French couple obtained custody of Tôn Ny, Sreï Peu, and me, while Sy Neang was adopted by another family. He is now studying in business school and dreams of living one day in the United States.

Vicky (Sreï Peu) is twelve years old now and has begun her secondary education. She is very pretty, very sophisticated—a real Khmer princess. She is considering a career in electronics.

Sodavann (Tôn Ny) has passed her accountant's exam. She has a job in an office and intends to continue her professional studies while she works.

As for myself, I'm studying for a degree as a professional photographer, after having tried for three years to complete my secondary education through correspondence courses.

The years of slavery, fear, and starvation have left their mark deep within us. We have been most fortunate in the love and understanding of our adoptive parents, Jan and Carmen Szymusiak. My name is on the cover of this book, but it would never have been written without their help, or without the contribution of my two sisters, who added their memories to mine.

MOLYDA SZYMUSIAK

HISTORICAL NOTE

The Mekong River Delta in Southeast Asia has long been inhabited, but the first major civilization to emerge there was Angkor, ruled by the Khmer people, which dominated the region from approximately A.D. 800. In 1431 the Khmer were driven out and Cambodia became a vassal of Siam (now Thailand), also paying tribute to the Vietnamese. Partly to defend the country from its hostile neighbors, the French established a protectorate in 1864, and for nearly a century they alternately supported two branches of the royal family, the Norodoms and the Sisowaths, crowning nineteen-year-old Norodom Sihanouk in 1941.

Sihanouk gradually broke away from the French, and in 1955 he abdictated the throne and was elected president. He was a popular leader, with strong support from the peasantry, despite the slow growth of the Khmer Rouge rebel movement in the 1960s. But Sihanouk's position was gradually undermined as the Vietnam War began seeping into neutral Cambodia, and in March of 1970 he was overthrown by a right-wing military faction headed by Lon Nol.

From 1970 to 1975 Cambodia was increasingly drawn into the Vietnam conflict. Half a million soldiers and civilians were killed as the Lon Nol government, aided by heavy American bombing, fought against both the Viet Cong and the Khmer Rouge insurgents, whose numbers had increased dramatically. Ostensibly the rebels were now led by Sihanouk, but in practice they still took orders from a small band of Communists that included Khieu Samphan, Ieng Sary, and Pol Pot.

On April 17, 1975, the victorious Khmer Rouge entered Phnom Penh, whose population had been swollen by refugees from 600,000 to over 2 million; within days, all of its inhabitants were evacuated to the countryside. A second major displacement was carried out at the end of the year, when hundreds of thousands of people southeast of Phnom Penh were forced into the northwest. Food was scarce under Pol Pot's inefficient system of collective farming, and administration was based on fear, torture, and genocide. In less than four years, as many as 2 million Cambodians were executed or starved to death.

On Christmas of 1978 Vietnam invaded with a force of 120,000, and soon installed its own government. In 1979 nearly half the population was in transit, either searching for their former homes or fleeing across the Thai border into refugee camps such as Kao I Dang. The situation is now more stable, with most people remaining grudgingly tolerant of the present leadership despite its being under Vietnamese influence. Both Sihanouk and Pol Pot continue to wage guerrilla war in some parts of the countryside, but their effectiveness is limited, as the bulk of the population is willing to accept virtually any alternative to a resurgence of the Khmer Rouge.

NEW HANOVER COUNTY PUBLIC LIBRARY

3 4200 00064 9299

959.6   649299
S   17.95
   Szymusiak, Molyda
   The stones cry out.

NEW HANOVER COUNTY PUBLIC LIBRARY
201 CHESTNUT ST.
WILMINGTON, NC 28401